Challenging Researches in Economic Sciences
Legal Informatics, Environmental Economics, Economics, OR and Mathematics

Challenging Researches in Economic Sciences
Legal Informatics, Environmental Economics, Economics, OR and Mathematics

Edited by
Munenori Kitahara
Hiroaki Teramoto
Hiroshima Shudo University

Volume 8 in a Series of Monographs of Contemporary Social Systems Solutions
Produced by the Faculty of Economic Sciences, Hiroshima Shudo University

Kyushu University Press

Volume 8 in a Series of Monographs of Contemporary Social Systems Solutions
Produced by Hiroshima Shudo University

All rights reserved. No part of this publication may be reproduced or transmitted in any form or by any means, electronic or mechanical, including photocopying and recording, or by any information storage and retrieval system,without the written permission from the publisher.

Copyright © 2017 by Munenori Kitahara and Hiroaki Teramoto
3-8-34-305, Momochihama, Sawara-ku, Fukuoka-shi, 814-0001, Japan

ISBN978-4-7985-0206-9

Printed in Japan

Preface

Hiroshima Shudo University established the Faculty of Economic Sciences in 1977 and the Graduate School of Economic Sciences in 2001. One goal of this faculty is to unify information sciences and economics and the faculty has endeavored to make progress in the research fields of operations research, computer sciences, mathematical economics and econometrics. While the definition of economic sciences has not been established yet, our specific understanding is that the economic sciences should unite system sciences and qualitative economic analysis and construct new fields relating to the management of the international economy, the financial system, and the national economy, or environmental issues, legal policies in communication.

The Faculty of Economic Sciences is a unique academic institution. There are no other faculties titled as "economic sciences" in Japan. Basically, we pursue analyzing various issues of contemporary economies and social systems, but its uniqueness can be observed in our efforts to balance the traditional economics and information sciences as means of analytical tools.

The Faculty consists of some 30 highly qualified members, whose research interests span a wide range of topics but more or less concern quantitative analytical frameworks. Since 2005 we have been publishing our research results in a form of monographs in English, one or two volumes a year, in order to present our academic contributions to possible readers in the world.

In the past several years, members of this faculty have made plans to expand these new frontiers as follows:
1. Macro-econometric models or micro-models which contain international economics or micro-models.
2. System analysis of financial institutions and international trade.
3. Information sciences, such as network systems or information systems or theory of reliance.
4. System sciences, such as operations research and production system analysis.
5. Research on information society and social systems.
6. Legal informatics, applying information technology to legal fields and solution of legal problems in digital society.
7. Environmental Economics, researching environmental issues from the economic viewpoints.

Faculty members have undertaken joint research with the aim of constructing these new fields and to publish our new research as a monograph as follows:

**Quantitative Economic Analysis, International Trade and Finance* (2005)
*_Applied Economic Informatics and Systems Sciences_ (2005)
*_Quantitative Analysis of Modern Economy_ (2007)

*System Sciences for Economics and Informatics (2007)
*Quantitative Analysis on Contemporary Economic Issues (2008)
*Research on Information Society and Social Systems (2008)
*Social Systems Solutions by Legal Informatics, Economic Sciences and Computer Sciences (2009)
*The New Viewpoints and New Solutions of Economic Sciences in the Information Society (2010)
*Social Systems Solutions Applied by Economic Sciences and Mathematical Solutions (2011)
*Social Systems Solutions through Economic Sciences (2012)
*Legal Informatics, Economic Science and Mathematical Research (2013)
*New Solutions in Legal Informatics, Economic Sciences and Mathematics (2014)
*Contemporary Works in Economic Sciences: Legal Informatics, Economics, OR and Mathematics (2015)

In these monographs our aim is to develop new methods and materials for constructing new fields of economics.

The authors of papers in these monographs have participate in building this new faculty and worked to develop new horizons of system sciences, information sciences, economics, economic sciences, environmental economics, computer sciences and legal informatics. We would welcome comments or suggestions in any forms.

The 2016 monograph is also entirely financed by the Faculty of Economic Sciences and is entitled under the title of "*Challenging Researches in Economic Sciences*: *Legal Informatics, Environmental Economics, Economics, OR and Mathematics*" edited by Munenori Kitahara and Hiroaki Teramoto.

This book contains contributions from wide variety of research in information society, information sciences, environmental economics, economic sciences, systems approach to the economic, managerial, mathematical, environmental, and legal subjects. The focus of most articles is on the recent developments in the relevant. The set of papers in this book reflect both each theory and wide range of applications to economic and managerial models. The economic sciences is based upon an interdisciplinary education and research area of sciences economics, econometrics, statistics, information sciences, system sciences, application information sciences, operations research and legal informatics.

This book consists of six chapters as follows:

Chapter 1, by *Munenori Kitahara*, refers to the ownership and propertyzation of personally identifiable information from a viewpoint of economics of personal information. The importance of personal information has been emphasized in various senses for the past few years. Industries are focusing on the economic value of personal information. The government intends to use personal information for tax policy. The business world stresses on that personal information is new oil for new industries. Therefore, there is a strong tendency to trade personal information as a public good. This is a movement towards publicization of personal information, ignoring the original owner's right of personal information. However, personal information would not become public goods attributing to public domain.

Even in the advanced information society, there presents the status quo that a property right can't be set in information and there is no ownership right to personal information. This is because the property theory unique to tangible thing might be applied to information. It is now required to challenge to establish the rights to information and personal information so that the information subjects and the owner could get economic benefit by exploiting them.

The author will propose that we should admit the property value or economic value of personal information, and set a property right or ownership over personal information. By respecting those rights, transactions of personal information are legitimized and transparent. As a result, we will respect individuals and contribute to the realization of personal information protection.

Chapter 2, by *Chris Czerkawski* and *Osamu Kurihara*, will deal with the new international lending structure. In this paper the growth of the newly formed Asian Infrastructure Investment Bank is discussed in view of the parallel, to the World Bank and the Asian Development Bank, new international lending structure initiated and managed largely by China. The deficiencies of the existing system are presented as well as the expected and prospective advantages for the new international investment group and its members.

Chapter 3, by *Hiroshi Hasegawa* will research on the forest conservation policies from the viewpoint of environmental economics. This chapter introduces Among various forest conservation policies, the current study has taken up the forest certification project and the clean development mechanism (CDM) project, to apply the environmental economic evaluation system. The forest certification system is expected not only to control illegal logging but also to contribute to maintain the ecosystem service, while the CDM projects have positive effects not only on air quality by absorbing CO_2 and producing O_2 but also on total ecosystem as well. In particular, the study has researched on potential monetary valuation methods to internalize environmental benefits and costs through cost-benefit analysis of these projects, as trying evaluations of natural ecosystem in Sabah including the Kinabalu National Park (UNESCO world natural heritage) as well as the Deramakot Forest Reserve Area. Finally, ecosystem service of the tropical forest (natural forest, production forest, and farmland) has been estimated for Sabah, with some political implication.

Chapter 4, by *Setsuko Sakai and Tetsuyuki Takahama* will research on the effect of JADE with group-based learning. The chapter is as follows: Differential Evolution (DE) has been successfully applied to various optimization problems. The performance of DE is affected by algorithm parameters such as a scaling factor and a crossover rate. Many studies have been done to control the parameters adaptively. One of the most successful studies on controlling the parameters is JADE. In JADE, the values of each parameter are generated according to one probability density function (PDF) which is learned by the values in success cases where the child is better than the parent. However, search performance might be improved by learning multiple PDFs for each parameter based on some characteristics of search points. In this study, search points are divided into plural groups according to some criteria and PDFs are learned by parameter values in success cases for each group. Objective values and distances from a reference point, which is the best search point or the centroid of search points, are adopted as the criteria. The effect of JADE with group-based learning is shown by solving thirteen benchmark problems.

Chapter 5, by *Ryoko Wada* and *Yoshio Agaoka* will deal with generators of irreducible components of harmonic polynomials. The abstract is follows: Classical harmonic polynomials on $\mathbf{C}_d$ are generalized to several vector spaces from the Lie algebraic viewpoint by Kostant-Rallis. In their formulation, the case $\mathbf{C}_d$ corresponds to the real rank 1 Lie algebra so(d, 1). In the series of papers we further investigate harmonic polynomials corresponding to the Lie algebras su(d, 1), sp(d, 1) and $f_{4(-20)}$, etc. that are also real rank 1. In this paper we consider harmonic polynomials for the real rank 2 case so(d, 2), and determine the generators of irreducible components of harmonic polynomials for the principal part. Further, we give an algorithm to obtain generators of lower irreducible components, give some examples, and state several conjectures for future studies. We also give reproducing kernels of the lower irreducible components of harmonic polynomials in some cases.

Chapter 6, by *Akira Kubo*, will examine the solvable models of noncompact real Grassmannians. The author says as follows: Any Riemannian symmetric space of noncompact type is isometric to the solvable part of the Iwasawa decomposition of its isometry groups with a left-invariant Rieman-nian metric. The solvable Lie group, or the corresponding metric solvable Lie algebra is called the solvable model of the symmetric space. In this paper, we construct the solvable models of noncompact real Grassmannians explicitly.

We hope that these articles provide a comprehensive yet lively and up-to-date discussion of the state-of-the-art in information society, social systems, and the relevant research fields. We believe that this book contains a coherent view of the important unifying ideas throughout the many faces of systems approach and a guide to the most significant current areas of approach. We also appreciate that this book should contribute to build the ubiquitous society in Japan. We would like to thank Hiroshima Shudo University and the Faculty of Economic Sciences for financial supports of publishing this monograph. Also we would like to take the opportunity to thank Kyushu University Press for publishing this book and for authors for their contributions.

Finally, a profound thanks goes to our families, in continuing appreciation of their support and many other contributions.

November, 2016
Munenori Kitahara
Hiroaki Teramoto

Contents

Preface i

Chapter 1   Economics of Personal Information:
               The Ownership and Propertyzation of PII .... *Munenori Kitahara*   1
   1. Introduction 2
   2. The Background and Resolved Issues 3
   3. Behavioral Information 7
   4. Generation of Personal Information 9
   5. Property of Personal Information 11
   6. Trade of Personal Information 14
   7. Conclusion 16

Chapter 2   The Asian Infrastructure Investment Bank
               and Building up a New Parallel International Financial System
                .... *Chris Czerkawski and Osamu Kurihara*   19
   1. Introduction 19
   2. The AIIB and the US Response 21
   3. Criticism of the Existing International Funding Infrastructure 22
   4. The Chinese Rationale for the AIIB 24
   5. The AIIB and the New Silk Road 26
   6. The Governance of the AIIB 29
   7. Potential for Growth of the AIIB 32

Chapter 3   Application of Environmental Economic Evaluation to Forest Conservation
               Policies in Sabah, Malaysia .... *Hiroshi Hasegawa*   37
   1. Introduction 37
   2. Necessity of Environmental Economic Evaluation for Forest Policies 38
   3. Cost-benefit Analysis 38
   4. Application of Environmental Economic Evaluation to Forest Certification Project 39
   5. Application of Environmental Economic Evaluation to CDM Project 40
   6. Monetary Evaluation Methods for Environmental Values 41
   7. Applicable Evaluation Framework 43
   8. Results of Economic Evaluation for Natural Ecosystem in Sabah 47
   9. Contribution to Forest Policy/Project by Environmental Economic Evaluation 48

Chapter 4   A Comparative Study on Grouping Methods for an Adaptive
  Differential Evolution .... *Setsuku Sakai and Tetsuyuki Takahama*   51
  1. Introduction 51
  2. Related Works 52
  3. Optimization by Differential Evolution 53
  4. Proposed Method 56
  5. Numerical Experiments 59
  6. Conclusion 63

Chapter 5   Generators of Irreducible Components of Harmonic Polynomials
  in the Case of $\mathfrak{so}(d, 2)$ .... *Ryoko Wada and Yoshio Agaoka*   93
  1. Introduction 93
  2. Preliminaries 94
  3. Irreducible Decomposition of S_n 95
  4. Generators of Principal Components 97
  5. Generators of Lower Harmonic Components 101
  6. Some Conjectures on Lower Harmonic Polynomials 107
  7. Reproducing Kernels of Irreducible Subspaces of $\mathcal{LH}_n$ for $n \leq 5$ 116

Chapter 6   The Solvable Models of Noncompact Real Grassmannians
  .... *Akira Kubo*   125
  1. Introduction 125
  2. Preliminaries 127
  3. The Structure of Noncompact Real Grassmannian Manifolds 128
  4. Proof of the Main Theorem 131

Contributors 135

Chapter 1

Economics of Personal Information:
The Ownership and Propertyzation of PII

Munenori Kitahara
Faculty of Economic Sciences, Hiroshima Shudo University
1-1 Ozuka-Higashi 1-chome, Asaminami-ku, Hiroshima, JAPAN 731-3195

Abstract

   The importance of personal information has been emphasized in various senses for the past few years. Industries are focusing on the economic value of personal information. The government intends to use personal information for tax policy. The business world stresses on that personal information is new oil for new industries. Therefore, there is a strong tendency to trade personal information as a public good. This is a movement towards publicization of personal information, ignoring the original owner's right of personal information. However, personal information would not become public goods attributing to public domain.

   Even in the advanced information society, there presents the status quo that a property right can't be set in information and there is no ownership right to personal information. This is because the property theory unique to tangible thing might be applied to information. It is now required to challenge to establish the rights to information and personal information so that the information subjects and the owner could get economic benefit by exploiting them.

   The author will propose that we should admit the property value or economic value of personal information, and set a property right or ownership over personal information. By respecting those rights, transactions of personal information are legitimized and transparent. As a result, we will respect individuals and contribute to the realization of personal information protection.

Key Words:

   Personal Information, Ownership, Property Right, Privacy, Data Protection, Economic Value

1. Introduction

The various data is being collected from the huge amount of devices placed in long distance by using the most advanced method of cloud computing, IoT,(internet of things), M2M (machine to machine), and AI (Artificial Intelligence). The system can monitor and control those devices through the Internet, based upon those analyzed data. In other words, the system could predict the operational failures and detect the abnormality of the devices themselves through visualization of the devices data. This is new invention and use in such data.

Such systems have been being addressed to human beings and individuals. As a result, various kinds of personal information have been collected to the organizations as life-logging data, behavior-trucking data, or, user-historical data. And those data will be combined with big data, personal data and open data, which will be used in order to create new industries. Therefore, personal information is called NEW *OIL*.

Now, as for the life-logging, or life-behavior records, the organizations would normally store those data in the server computers (including the Cloud). Of course, the same data might be recorded and stored on the IC cards, which individuals as players always bring. In these cases, whom those data will belong to? Who is the owner of the data? Who has the ownership of the data? This is the first question of this article.

Maybe, people generally think that the server owner also is the owner of the collected personal information. That is, the personal information would belong to the organization which has installed the servers. In addition, they also think that the organization has produced the personal information. The entity only did collect, record and store the information. She did not create the information. Then, this is the second question: Who produced the personal information?

The reason why personal information is very significant for marketing and creating new industries is that each information should originally include personal attributes, even if the data is statistically processed. The personal information should represent the personality of data subject. No meaningful information comes from fictitious data, using any analyzing method. That means, organizations must use the personal information which is living at present. It is very difficult for organizations to get living personal information. Then, for the purpose, it is important to create an environment for parties to legitimately trade personal information.

The author must consider what is necessary in order for personal information to be an object of trade. It is essential to prepare an environment, where anyone says, "My personal information is mine," and "The ownership of personal information would belong to the data subject." The environment would be inevitable to be apart from the traditional framework over the information in general and personal information.

As for the lifelogging data and users historical data, many issues have been left unresolved: Who produced the data, individual or organization? Who is the owner, individual or organization? Who possesses the data, individual or organization? What is the right-duty relationship? And so on. Will these problems be solved through a traditional framework?

2. The Background and Resolved Issues

2.1 General Understanding over Information and Personal Information

This is a short story, which motivated me to write this article:

"The resident card data is not mine. My resident address was also given by a local government. My name was not given by me myself, either. My personal information is not mine, in the sense of that law only recognizes a property right. An author is able to have a controlling right to the work produced by himself by copyright law. A producer who produces personal information is not the very person. A producer who produced customer information (a customer relational database), is not the customer him/herself, but a business entity. A bank or hospital has credit or medical information much more than a customer or patient him/herself. In short, almost my individual information is not mine." [1]

This may be a general understanding over personal information. This is also a common belief. It is now a turning point to change a framework to deal with personal information, people welcoming an era of big data, personal data, and open data. Otherwise, people couldn't response to the era, and serious problems should certainly occur in dealing with the information. As a result, we will become to live in an advanced information society, where individuals would not be respected and treated as human beings.

Then, the author has tried to examine those problems based upon the viewpoint completely apart from the story as quoted above. That is, the author will insist that:

(a) a person can hold the right of ownership to information, and personal information,

(b) a data subject has the ownership of personal data,

(c) a person property right to personal information,

(d) a person can exploit his/her personal information, and,

(e) business entities are neither a producer nor an owner, but only a collector, or possessor over personal information and data.

2.2 Revised laws: Promoting Using Personal Information

The personal information protection law was revised in 2015 September. The revised law aims to ensure due consideration that proper and effective use of personal information contributes to the creation of new industries and the realization of a vibrant economic society and an enriched quality of life for the people of Japan among other useful applications. The numbers use law was also revised at the same time. As for specific personal information, the law aims public organs to use the information among the organs in the fields of social welfare, tax and disaster prevention as well as in the other administrative services and in the collaborative fields between public organs and private business entities. The name of the law "Personal Information 'Protection' Law" would rather give people a kind of misunderstanding. The original purpose of the law would aim to promote using personal information. The law provides many articles ruling the information controller's obligation, unless the controllers should infringe the right and profit of individuals'.

2.3 Trawling Personal Information

It is now in the age of cloud computing, big data, personal data, open data, IoT (internet of things) and AI (Artificial Intelligence). The Internet of Things refers to the ability of everyday objects to connect to the Internet to send and receive data [2]. Many sensors have been embedded into the devices. Then, the sensors read and send the data of devices through the Internet. This system also applies to human beings. As for individuals, personal data or information has been being collected by any method the Web7/24. The status quo can be called 'trawling personal information.' The trawling net should be a fishing method, which could catch fish en masse.

New business industries have been produced by producing and using such new kinds of data as lifelog data, behavior tracking data, or life stream data. It is needless to say that these data should include personal data. Personal data could be call 'new oil' in the business world. In addition, this kind of data will be automatically recorded and stored in the servers possessed by the entities [3]. Then, the entities should be not producers but collectors. A person who produced the data is the very individual who took the behavior the same as the data showed. The data could not be produced without the person's behavior.

Companies that conduct behavioral targeting are able to predict Internet users' interests by using sophisticated technology that tracks and gathers information about users' online activity. Online content is free only in monetary terms; with respect to privacy, however, behavioral targeting exacts a hefty price [4].

2.4 Public Ownership

Personal information is exactly going to be publicly owned and belong to a public domain. That is, personal information is becoming to be treated as "public goods." If information is left copyrightable, the information will belong to public domain, after the protection terminates. As a result, anyone can freely access the information without any cost. It means that the exclusive dominion is beyond the author's power. As for goods, nobody has the ownership. Therefore, a public good is regarded as low in economic or property value [5].

However, it is hard for the author to think that personal information will belong to public domain and become public goods. Personal information would have value, because it might include a specific individual attribute. In that sense, personal information would represent a person's personality. It can be also said that it is personality information. The information would represent a person who now lives his own life. No meaningful information is produced from fictitious one by any analyzing method.

2.5 De-identified Information

The revised personal information protection law has introduced a new definition "de-identified information," which means information regarding an individual that is gained from processing personal information so as to prevent the identification of a specific individual taking measures prescribed by the items, and that do not allow restoring of said personal information.

The Government has a plan to produce a new industry dealing with the de-identified information and new enterprises to create new information from the de-identified one because the de-identified information is out of the category of personal information. This is so-called "data mining business."

By the way, the Japanese statistics law provides that administrative organs may provide "anonymized data" to the citizens for the academic research. The term "anonymized data" means questionnaire information that is processed so that no particular individuals or juridical persons, or other organizations shall be identified (including by way of collating it with other information), for the purpose of providing it for general use. The population census will be conducted only to produce a population census statistics. If it is right, nations need not to write such personal information as name, address, and telephone number. The administrative organs would require nations of true individual information as material information. The meaningful information couldn't be produced from fictitious or fabricated information.

The internet makes true anonymity more possible today than ever before. At the same time the internet makes anonymity in physical life much harder. A world where everything about a person can be found and achieved a world with no privacy [6]. That's why many smart people are eager to maintain the open of easy anonymity — as a refuge for the private. Today anonymity is far more commonly used as a way to escape responsibility.

2.6 Ownerless Personal Information

Personal information is being trading and disclosed in a mailing list broker, which the data subject could not recognize. Personal information has been buying and selling. Neither the buyer nor the seller would know the owner of personal information. A social environment where no one says, "My personal information would be mine." will forgive the improper trading personal information. But personal information itself would tell whose information is. Because each personal information would have always such an identifier as name, address, and phone number. Personal information belongs to the very person who has name.

Neither property nor torts theory recognizes individuals' rights in their information. At the heart of that nonrecognition is a view that personal information is no one until collected, a view similar to the 'wild animals' theory.' In that famous early American case, the court concluded that wild animals in the state of nature are not owned by anyone until captured, and that whoever captures the animal first has the prior claim to it [7]. Even though they often acknowledge that personal information has become a valuable commodity, they believe that it belongs to no one until collected. Accordingly, it can only be the property of a collector.

Then, the author will propose the ownership of personal information, so that anyone can insist, "My personal information is mine." and "I am the owner." Protective and secure awareness of personal information will dramatically increase, through establishing the ownership of personal information. The improper trading personal information dramatically decrease. A business entity has an obligation to pay some cost to the owner, if the entity has a plan to use the information and produce some profit. The personal information protection law would not prohibit selling personal information.

2.7 Ubiquitous Surveillance and No Privacy

Ubiquitous surveillance is inevitable [8]. In a small town, a coveillance worked because it was symmetrical. A person knew who was watching the person. A person knew what they did with the information. A person could hold them accountable for its accuracy and use. And a person got benefits for being watched. Finally, you watched your watchers under the same circumstances.

In a coveillance society a sense of entitlement can emerge: Every person has a human right to access, and a right to benefit from, the data about themselves [9]. But every right requires a duty, so every person has a human duty to respect the integrity of information, to share it responsibility, and to be watched by the watched. Big governments are tracking us, but with no chance for symmetry. If symmetry can be restored so we can track who is tracking, if we can hold the trackers accountable by law and responsible for accuracy, and if we can make the benefits obvious and relevant, then we suspect the expansion of tracking will be accepted.

To enable that kind of relationship we have to be open and transparent and share my life with our friends so they know enough about us to treat us personally. We want companies to treat us as an individual too, so we have to be open, transparent, and sharing with tem as well to enable them to be personal. We want our government to treat us as an individual, so we have to reveal personal information to it to be treated personally. There is a one-to-one correspondence between personalization and transparency. Greater personalization requires greater transparency. Absolute personalization (vanity) requires absolute transparency (no privacy) [10].

3. Behavioral Information

3.1 The Outline

Internet users are being increasingly tracked and profiled and their personal data are extensively used as currency in exchange for services. Behavioral targeting is the practice of tailoring online content, especially advertisements, to visitors based on their inferred interests, or 'profile'. The process of constructing this profile using data mining is known as *online behavioral profiling*. The underlying data is typically a log of the user's web activity, and the data collection process is called behavioral targeting [11].

Behavioral information is a set of data of people's everyday behavior over time to use the collected data for data mining. The collected data will be stored in the servers owned by organizations. This data group will include such behavioral data as behavioral targeting data, lifelog data, stream data, behavior tracking data, as well as life recorded data, medical data, and population census data. All kinds of data that include the data identifying individuals come to the category.

This kind of data is called "lifelog data," or "lifestream data." A lifestream is a time-ordered stream of documents that function as a diary of your electronic life [12]. This kind of data is composed of the records of people's everyday activities in the society—job, entertainment, shopping. Today, people always go around with such IC cards as a railway card, a bus card, a credit card, a highway card and a royalty card. When people use the IC card, all the activities will be recorded and stored on their own IC card and in the server owned by enterprise as personal data. In this way, all the steps of everyday behavior would be recorded in any electronic method. Then each analogical activity will be changed to digital data. The sum of the data must be much more detailed than their diaries.

3.2 Generation of Behavioral Information

When people use an IC card, on which such personal attributes as name, address and phone number are imprinted, each activity will be made into data and recorded on the card as data and the data will be transmitted to the server owned by the company via the Internet. This is the moment when action changed to data. There might be imprinted the data: yy/mm/dd; start (get on) time; end (get off) time; fee; amount, on the card.

The true data should have not been generated, if the person did take no real activity on that day. The information system owned by the business entity only read those actions as data and stored it on the server owned by the organization. The data would be electronically transmitted to the storage. The organization did only collect the data. The organization does not intervene in the generation of data at all. I would like to confirm this clearly.

3.3 Personal Information as Personality

A copyrighted work means a production in which thoughts or sentiments are creatively expressed, and an author means a person who creates a work. Then, it is considerable that person's thoughts or sentiments are creatively expressed in the work. That is, the author's personality is expressed in the work. It is the reason why the work might be parts of the author's personality.

Conceiving of personal information as property is justified by viewing it as an extension of personality. As the authors of our own lives, we generate information as we develop our personalities. The growth of individualism spawned the belief that one's actions and their history belonged to the self which generated them and were to be shared only with those with whom one wished to share them [13].

3.4 Personal Information as Property

John Locke asserted that individuals have property rights in their person and the fruits of their labor [14]. According to Locke, property flows naturally from selfhood: "[E]very man has a property in his own person." From this principle, Locke deduced that property extends to the products of one's labor: "Whatsoever then he removes out of the state that nature hath provided, and left it in, he hath mixed his labor with, and joined it to something that is his own, and thereby makes it his property." Conceiving of personal information as property is justified by viewing it as an extension of personality. As the authors of our own lives, we generate information as we develop our personalities [15].

3.5 Personal Information as the copyrightable

Human behavior might be something like the copyrightable. Dancing and silent plays are under the protection of copyright law as copyrighted works. For certain plays in sports, there are some plays that are called by the player's name. The play patterns could be created by the player. It is nothing else than that creativeness could be discovered in those play patterns. Then, there is room for considering human behavior as copyrighted work, apart from whether or not that action is protected by law. The author must be the person who actually takes behaviors. Of course, the person is also the author of the diary. Diaries will be recognized as copyrighted works. A diary is one that summarizes the behaviors conducted on a day. Then, the person who recorded the behaviors is also the author of the diary

4. Generation of Personal Information

4.1 Produce of Personal Information

Let's examine the case of generating boarding data in using public transportations, for example. For generating the boarding information of a railway transportation, it is necessary for a user (passenger) to actually get on and off the transportation facilities as stated before. Then, the person must pay the boarding fee. The set of data, which is composed of the name of getting on/off stations, boarding fee, and amount, will be recorded on the IC card, or credit card. The data also will be sent to the server owned by the transportation company at the same time. At this moment, the company does only collect the boarding data. It is impossible to say that the company herself did produce the data. It is essential to make clear whether the company should be a collector or a producer of boarding data.

The producer of the behavioral information in this context would be the person who executed the corresponding activity. The reason is that if the person him/herself actually does not carry out the real activity, the tracking data should have not been recorded.

These behaviors almost are conducted in a public domain. Each activity is conducted in such a public space as public transportations, store, highway, park and other public place. The behavior would be an analogue information, while it is in a public domain. Then, the analogue information will be digitalized into data, at the moment when the information is recorded and stored in the system. The content of the information will be fixed through recording. The digitalization also means personalization of information as public goods or commodity. That is, the recorded data will include individual attributes (name, address, phone number), and many activities.

As one of the characteristics of behavior record data, we must accept the fact that a person him/herself actually carried out exactly the same behavior as "the data," which the system recorded. That means that if the data subject did not actually take same activities, that data was not created. The server owned by the entity only records and saves the data. If it is boarding data of railway transportation system, it would include a boarding data (station, time) at the entrance gate, a getting-off data (station, time) at the getting-off station.

Then, the person who took the behavior, would be a producer of the data. It shall be not appropriate that a railway company produced the boarding data.

4.2 Generating Cost of Behavioral Information

No one has ever suggested that some cost is required to generate behavioral information. One of behaviors is movement of places by means of transportations. In order for the boarding information of a railway transportation to be generated, it is necessary for a person to actually use transportation facilities as stated before. Then, the person must pay a boarding fee.

The boarding fee also will mean the generating cost of the behavioral information. In other words, a person payed the boarding fee to create the person's behavioral information as the personal information. The boarding fee will change according to a kind of transportations. Therefore, generating cost of behavioral information also will change according to using transportation.

In this way, considerable expense is borne for the user to create the using information of the transportation facilities. In supermarket, convenience store, and other stores, people pay money for purchasing some goods, and the activity will be recorded as their behavioral information. In that case, the purchasing price of goods will become a cost of creating behavioral information. In the same way, we can calculate the cost of creating behavioral information in using hotels, entertainment facilities, etc. usage information is created by paying a usage fee corresponding to that service usage history information, so it is considered that the usage fee is applied as the creation cost.

4.3 Use and Disclosure of Personal Information

Various kinds of behavioral information which we have covered so far, are stored in the server owned by the relevant business operator. Business operators are in the position of collectors and retainers of the behavioral information. The operators are neither producers nor owners of the information.

A passenger railway company entered into a contract to offer (sell) the boarding data to an information processing company for 5 million yen. The transaction was not executed due to the customer's dispute. The contract was concluded between the organizations without the data subject's consent and compensation. After all, the contract was abandoned. In this case, I would like to make a matter that no compensation was paid to the information subject in the sale of personal behavioral information rather than the cancellation of the contract.

The railway company will earn 5 million yen in profit from selling the boarding information. The boarding information would be generated by payment of the usage fee of users'. In such a case, it is assumed that the business operator should be obliged to pay a compensation equivalent to the usage fee to the users.

If the business operator uses the user's personal information collected by the company owned system for the purpose of improving the service for the users (passengers or customers) and the personal data processing is performed within the organization, there will not occur the problem of data processing procedures (user's consent) and compensation. With regard to such use purpose of collected personal information, in particular, the business operator should take measures of noticing the purposes to the user in advance.

In the first place, does the business operator have the right to sell the collected personal information? Perhaps, it is able to be assumed for many operators to have the ownership of personal information collected in the enterprise. Regarding behavioral information, it is, rather, considered that the information subject should own its ownership.

5. Property of Personal Information

5.1 Ownership of Information in General

Japanese Supreme Court judged [16], "The object of a property right is a tangible thing, and the right to the art work as copyrightable means an exclusive control right limited to the aspect of the tangible thing rather than the authority to directly and exclusively control the art work as the intangible thing."

It is common that it is not able to set the property right to information. It means that a person cannot own information. The relationships of rights to information might be clearly represented in purchasing and using an application software. A person goes to a store to purchase a computer software on CD-ROM. Depending on the sales contract, the person can purchase the software from the store. The person will become to be an owner of the CD-ROM. After a while, the user has an obligation to return the CD-ROM with program installed on to the manufacturer after the use purpose has ended. The user is also obliged to return the copied program to the manufacturer, if it had made it. Because a user of software has no disposal right to the purchased program. As for the program, a license agreement has started to move between the user and the manufacturer, at the moment the user broke the plastic packaging. It is said to be "a shrink wrap contract." The license agreement would only permit users not to dispose but to use the program for the copyright holder is the manufacturer itself. After all, the user could not be the owner, who has an exclusive controlling right to the software, as the user could not be a producer of the information. The software maker only has the exclusive right prior to the users. This is the status quo of the rights relationship over information.

A property right is a right to a tangible thing. It means that the right holder also has the absolute control over the thing and the exclusive possession of things. In trading goods, the thing would physically move to the buyer from the seller. The property right does, too. The purchased good has not presented at the hands of the seller. That is, things can't exist at the two places at the same time. In that sense, tangible goods are rivalrous [17]. Creative works were nonrivalrous, meaning that the fruits of the labour of the mind could be shared between many [18]. The mere use of a copyright work without permission does not interfere with the copyright holder's ability to enjoy his work. There is no concept in copyright which is akin to trespass in physical property [19].

It is impossible to apply the property structure to information in general. Especially, such concept as transferability and rivalrousness should not be applied to information. Traditionally property law does not define information as a good unless it is of a particular character. This is not to say that ownership in information is impossible. The most obvious examples are the statutory intellectual property rights created over certain categories of information, perhaps the best-known example of which is to be found in the law of patents [20]. The owner of a patent has the right to prevent others from developing competing products or services based upon the idea or process outlined in the patent.

This, so to speak, "patent information theory" proves that persons can own information. According to this theory, information such as trade secret information and confidential information should also be an object to ownership. Then, "personal information" will definitely fall within this category as well. This type- of information might have an inalienable nature of the creator.

Incidentally, in these days, there appears such the expression as "ownership of data," or "ownership of contents" on the Cloud. Dropbox declares [21], "We create products that are easy to use and are built on trust. When people put their files in Dropbox, they can trust they're secure and *their data is their own*. Our users' privacy has always been our first priority, and it always will be." Amazon AWS says [22], "We know customers care deeply about privacy and data security. That's why AWS gives *customers ownership and control over their customer content* by design through simple, but powerful tools that allow customers to determine where their customer content will be stored, secure their customer content in transit or at rest, and manage access to AWS services and resources for their users."

5.2 Ownership of Personal information

"My personal information is something of my own." Why don't we say so? As "personal information" should be regarded as a kind of "information," the framework of information might be also applied to personal information as stated before. Is it right? "Name," "address," or "phone number," which is legally defined as an example of personal information, also is placed in the category of information in general.

This kind of personal information was not produced by the possessor itself. The ownership should be attributed to the possessor, as long as the use of personal information is permitted to the possessor. The sense of belonging to the person is of considerable strong. No one does oppose the sense. Or, it would be wrong that we call the sense the ownership consciousness. Not only that, people think that a person must have the absolute control over his/her own name, address, and phone number. The person who was disclosed his personal information on the Internet by others without consent, will try to regain the information in the court. Such feeling would incite the person to the trial.

Personal information might consist personality information. Personality image is formed by joining personality information like a mosaic. The right of forming the image attribute only to the person him/herself. That means the person only has the authority to draw the person's personality. Then, the ownership of personality image would attribute to the person him/herself. Nevertheless, TV commentators are discussing a personality image from various viewpoints. The commentators are committing serious constitutional violations by building up the personality image of others.

Personal information would be unique and rare information. Moreover, personal information is not intended to mimic the other information. From these points, personal information is provided with the copyrightable on the copyright law. Then, personal information should be given the same authority as copyrightable information in general. Personal information should be given economic value for it is unique and rare.

A property right of personal information may be based upon the ownership right. Therefore, a person cannot exploit his/her own personal information for benefit, if the person might be not permitted to have the ownership of personal information.

Rodwin calls for public ownership of patients' anonymized data. And, he argues that treating patient data as private property precludes forming comprehensive databases required for many of its most important public health and safety uses and proposes that federal law require providers, medical facilities and insurers to report key patient data in anonymized and de-identified form to public authorities, which will create aggregate databases to promote public health, patient safety, and research [23].

5.3 Economic Value of Personal Information

Many commentators and several organizations have argued that individuals should receive fair compensation for the use of their personal data [24]. Economists have conceptualized privacy interests in personal data as a pieces of property for several years because commodified data privacy interests are convenient subjects for market-based models, and market solutions are deemed preferable to government regulation [25]. Propertizing personal information would take advantage of the extant market in personal information, and give members of the public some control, which they currently lack, over the traffic in personal data [26].

The collection and dissemination of personal information can be mutually beneficial for both individuals and companies [27]. The first-party cookies are commonly used by e-commerce companies for identification purposes. First-party cookies offer a more efficient online experience by allowing websites to register user activity. Cookies provide users with a personalized and efficient browsing experience and enable websites to take note of these preferences [28].

E-commerce business can record a user's browsing history across multiple sites and advertise based on his or her preferences. Third-party tracking methods allow companies with whom the user is not interacting to similarly monitor online activity and tailor advertisements.

Due to tailored marketing and advertising, companies and third parties derive significant economic benefit from collecting and distributing users' personal information. Businesses extract value from observing market trends, and more specifically, by aggregating personal information. Compiling personally identifiable information benefits businesses because it raises the probability that advertising will translate into sales, and it cuts the expense of advertising to uninterested consumers. Data collection therefore facilitates a cost-efficient advertising model that is increasingly necessary to remain competitive [29]. In addition to these benefits from tailored marketing and advertising, the collection of personal information can produce further economic gains through its dissemination. Companies amass individual profiles which include information such as education levels, occupation height, weight, political affiliation, ethnicity, race, hobbies, and net worth. These digital dossiers are commonly and freely sold to other companies. As a consequence of each of the strategies, businesses can realize concrete economic benefits from gathering and selling users' personal information within the bounds of any applicable privacy laws [30].

6. Trade of Personal Information

6.1 The Right of Informational Self-Determination

Human dignity, personality, freedom, and autonomy have been identified as ground for a right to privacy and personal data protection. People could not finally dispose their own personal information, unless they have a legal system to authorize the disposition. Individuals should be able to get some benefit from their personal information, if an individual possesses ownership of his / her personal information,

Alan F. Westin defined privacy as [31]:

The claim of individuals, group, or institutions to determine for themselves when, how, and to what extent information about them is communicated to others. (…) [It is] the desire of People to choose freely under what circumstances and to what extent they will expose themselves, their attitude and their behavior to others.

In 1983, the German Federal Constitutional Court defined "a right to informational self-determination." in the population census decision. The Court stated that the technical development regarding the modern processing of data had become so sophisticated that average citizen was unable to understand it. The data processing is risking human dignity, personality, and self-determination as constitutional value. The automated data processing of personal data in particular constituted such a danger in the view of the Court. Part of the freedom of personal development was the freedom to decide how, when and where to act in a certain way. If the individual did not know if his/her actions were monitored and if he or she could not pre-estimate the knowledge of his or her communication partner about individual's private data, this person would very likely refrain from exercising his/her right to free self-determination [32].

The right of personality aims to protect the individual from new dangers for his/her personality and can therefore be interpreted according to these new dangers. Part of the right of personality thus had to be a right to informational self-determination [33]. In the German Court, the right to data protection is authority of the individual to decide for himself, on the basis of the idea of self-determination, when and within what limits facts about his personal life shall be disclosed.

6.2 Exploit of Personal Information by Subject

The personal information protection law would not prohibit the final disposition of personal information by the information subject. The law would not prohibit transferring, disclosing, and providing personal information by the subject to others, including sale of the information.

The principle of individual autonomy assumes that parties enter into contracts voluntarily, guaranteeing them a considerable degree of freedom to enter into contractual obligations. This principle is also recognized in relation to constitutional law, meaning that freedom of contract even prevails when the contract sees to fundamental human rights that are accorded protection under the Constitution [34]. When applied to personal data, the constitutional recognition of privacy thus does not prevent individuals exploiting their privacy rights by using the instrument of freedom of contract. Individuals are free to negotiate the content of agreements to best suit their needs, and to ensure the most efficient exploitation of the economic value of their personal data.

6.3 Exploit of Personal Information by Possessor

Personal information as various behavioral information will be collected by the information system owned by the business entity and stored in a server owned by the same organization (including the Cloud). The users always use the service with IC card. The business entities would be the first collectors of the personal data, who should manage from the time the information is conceived through to its final disposition [35]. Privacy rights or obligations are related to the collection, use, disclosure, storage, and destruction of personal information, through the information (data) life cycle.

As for the personal information as behavioral information, the business operators would be not an owner but a manager and retainer. Therefore, the operators themselves could not sell the retained personal information, as they have no ownership of the information.

Certainly, the operators would be the owner of 'a personal information database,' and only the retainer of personal data stored in the physical database. The operators should be permitted to process the retained personal data within the organization only for customers' profit. The personal information protection law provides the notice of the use purpose at the acquisition. The customers should give no consent with collecting their own personal information, if they had been noticed about 'sell' within the purposes.

7. Conclusion

In recent years, concerning personal information, its importance has become higher than ever before in the past. It is an evaluation from the economic or business world to the last. It is said in the world that "personal information is gold mine" or "personal information is new oil." If that is true, we argue that personal information should be treated as a property for individuals and persons should have the ownership to their own personal information.

Until now, I have examined various issues concerning ownership of information, especially personal information. The meaning of ownership is that the person himself as information subject has exclusive control over his own personal information. If it is in that way, it seems that the information subject will become more conscious of "My personal information is mine." and will always become to be concerned with the dissemination of personal information on the one hand.

On the other hand, it is indispensable for a business entity to obtain the consent of the person himself, who is the owner of personal information, at the time when the entity uses and discloses the personal information, and the subsequent personal information processing becomes transparent through its life cycle (visualization). At the same time, it will prevent the use and provision of personal information for purposes other than collection purpose, and contribute to the improvement of compliance with the Personal Information Protection Law as the result.

Although this may be considered as a secondary outcome, it means that a so-called broker business will be standardized, so that inappropriate collection of personal information will drastically decrease. It can be expected that the broker can officially purchase the personal information from the information subject.

Personal information will require a new framework, upon which persons can exploit their own personal information for their own benefits. Persons can trade their own personal information on the framework. Individuals has an authority to license to mine data, in the case when organizations gather and mine their personal information. The mining process will be transferred to the smart device of the data subject. Then, the mining process will become most transparent.

References

[1] Cf., Nobuo Ikeda, Whose is Personal Information? (RIETI Discussion Paper Series 03-J-2003), p.3. (http://www.rieti.go.jp/jp/publications/dp/03j006.pdf).
[2] Cf., FTC Report (Docket No.160331306-630601) 2016, p.3.
[3] Cf., Kevin Kelly, *The Inevitable: Understanding the 12 Technological Forces That Will Shape Our Future*, Penguin 2016, pp. 237ff.
[4] Cf., Elspeth A. Brotherton, Big Brother Gets A Makeover: Behavioral Targeting and The Third-Party Doctrine, *Emory Law Journal*, Vol. 61:555, 2012, pp. 557ff.
[5] Cf., Nobuhiro Yamanaka, The Status Quo and Future of Protective Framework in Property Information, in:*Iwanami Course Modern Law Vol.10 Information and Law*, Iwanami 1997, pp.270ff.
[6] Cf., Kevin Kelly, *ibid.*, p.263.
[7] Vera Bergelson, It's Personal but Is It Mine? Toward Property Rights in Personal Information, University of California, Davis 2003, pp. 403ff.
[8] Kevin Kelley, *ibid.*, p.260.
[9] *Ibid.*, p.261.
[10] *Ibid.*
[11] Cf., ENISA(The European Union Agency for Network and Information Security), *Privacy Considerations of Online Behavioural Tracking*, [Deliverable- 2012-10-19], p.3.
[12] Cf., Kevin Kelly, *ibid.*, pp.244ff.
[13] Daniel J. Solove, *Understanding Privacy*, Harvard University Press 2008, p.26.
[14] Cf., Daniel J. Solove, *ibid.*
[15] *Ibid.*
[16] Cf., Nobuhiro Yamanaka, ibid.
[17] Cf., Andrew Murray, *Information Technology Law*, Oxford 2013, p.203.
[18] Cf., *ibid.*, p.11.
[19] A. Murray, *ibid.*, p.89.
[20] Cf., *ibid.*, pp. 86-87.

[21] Cf., "What we value." (https://www.dropbox.com/about)

[22] Cf., "Data Privacy" (https://aws.amazon.com/compliance/data-privacy-faq/?nc1=h_ls)

[23] Barbara J. Evans, Much Ado About Data Ownership, *Harvard Journal of Law & Technology*, Vol.25 No.1, 2011, p.88.

[24] Cf.,J.E.J. Prins, The Propertization of Personal Data and Identities, *Electronic Journal of Comparative Law*, Vol. 8.3, 2004, p.1.

[25] Jessica Litman, Information Privacy/Information Property, *Stanford Law Review*, Vol. 52:1283 2000, p.1289.

[26] Cf., ibid., p.1290.

[27] Patrick Myers, Protecting Personal Information: Achieving a Balance between User Privacy and Behavioral Targeting, *University of Michigan Journal of Law Reform*, Vol. 49 : 3, 2016, p.722.

[28] Cf., P. Myers, ibid.

[29] Ibid., p.723.

[30] Ibid.

[31] Cf., Alan F. Westin, Privacy and Freedom, New York: Atheneum 1967.

[32] Claudia Kodde, Germany's 'Right to be forgotten' – between the freedom of expression and the right to informational self-determination, *International Review of Law, Computers & Technology*, Vol. 30, Nos. 1-2, 17-31, p.20.

[33] Cf., Gabriel Stilman, The Right Our Personal Memories: Informational Self-Determination and the Right to Record and Disclose Our Personal Data, *Journal of Evolution & Technology*, Vol. 25 Issue 2, p.16.

[34] Cf., J.E.J. Prins, ibid., p.3.

[35] Cf., Tim Mather et al., *Cloud Security and Privacy*, O'Reilly 2009, p.146.

Chapter 2

The Asian Infrastructure Investment Bank and Building up a New Parallel International Financial System

Chris Czerkawski* and Osamu Kurihara**
*Faculty of Economic Sciences, Hiroshima Shudo University
1-1 Ozuka-Higashi 1-chome, Asaminami-ku, Hiroshima, Japan 731-3195
** Faculty of Information Design and Sociology, Hiroshima Kokusai Gakuin University
20-1 Nakano 6 –chome, Aki-ku, Hiroshima, Japan 739-0321

Abstract

In this paper the growth of the newly formed Asian Infrastructure Investment Bank is discussed in view of the parallel, to the World Bank and the Asian Development Bank, new international lending structure initiated and managed largely by China. The deficiencies of the existing system are presented as well as the expected and prospective advantages for the new international investment group and its members.

Key words:
AIIB, IMF, ADB, World Bank, China, America, Europe, Poland, Financial System

1. Introduction

There is a steady replacement of the West's international financial system, its control and dominance with one centered around China's new international financial system. A financial system designed to support not just itself, but everything from the Asian Pacific to the Eastern doorstep of Europe and more. The first and second decades of the XXI century saw a number of activities, on the part of China, which indicate its intention to set up a parallel international financial system independent from the US and Japanese dominance. The major ones included;

- An alternative international payment system to SWIFT. The Society for Worldwide Interbank Financial Telecommunication (SWIFT) provides a network that enables financial institutions worldwide to send and receive information about financial transactions in a secure, standardized and reliable environment. The China-based The Cross-Border Inter-Bank Payment System (CIPS) is a payment system which, offers clearing and settlement services for its participants' in cross-border RMB payments and trade.
- Foreign central banks can participate in the Chinese inter-bank bond market. Also China has announced that foreign central banks will shortly be able to participate in the Chinese 'onshore' foreign exchange market.
- Precious metals markets are open to international participation through the Shanghai International Gold exchange. Stock markets are already open to international participation through the Hong Kong – Shanghai stock connect program.
- The AIIB (The Asian Infrastructure Investment Bank) has been established to focus on supporting infrastructure construction in the Asia-Pacific region.
- A gold fund with an initial capital of Yuan 100 Billion (USD$ 16 Billion) has been established, with the specific objective of building up the sovereign gold reserves of the BRICS (Brazil, Russia, India, China and South Africa) and SCO (Shanghai Cooperation Organization) countries. This resulted, among others in the establishment of Chinese and Russian credit card systems, which are settled in Yuan and the Ruble. The extension of the above is the multiple bi-lateral currency swap agreements for the settlement of trade in Yuan have been signed with over 30 countries including the UK, Germany, France and Switzerland, without using the US Dollar.

In 2001 China, along with Russia, established the SCO (The Shanghai Cooperation Organization), which is a political and economic organization that initially comprised of China, Russia, Kyrgyzstan, Kazakhstan, Tajikistan, and Uzbekistan. In July 2015 the SCO decided to admit India and Pakistan as full SCO members. Observer states include Mongolia, Iran, Belarus and Afghanistan. China has been gradually opening its markets to international participation on a slow and gradual basis that will see it evolve from a closed market to one that will be integrated fully into the international financial system. There was also an extensive cooperation of the BRICS countries with SCO economies with several major investment projects initiated.[1]

---

[1] The construction of long distance, high-speed railway routes, connecting those countries that lie within the Eurasian continent. Auto-routes will be constructed in parallel with the high speed train routes. The construction of suitably placed international airports. The laying of secure, and independent, high speed communications lines, on both land and undersea, so as to provide secure, independent, internet communications for the BRICS and SCO countries. The development of local infrastructures, and industrial zones within the SCO and BRICS countries. See, China's Development of a Parallel International Financial System, 2016.

2. The AIIB and the US Response

The establishment of the Asian Infrastructure Investment Bank (AIIB) was announced before the October 2013 APEC meeting in Bali and was motivated by the huge demand for infrastructure financing and huge demand for productive economic infrastructure, especially in the emerging economies of Asia. The Asian Development Bank (ADB) estimates that developing Asian economies need to invest US$8 trillion from 2010 to 2020, just to keep pace with expected infrastructure needs. The supply of savings, much of which is generated in Asia, is more than adequate to begin to fill some of the demand for infrastructure.

In the period of 2013-2015 the creation of the Chinese-sponsored Asian Infrastructure Investment Bank (AIIB) has caused considerable attention in the USA and Japan. Some view the establishment of the AIIB as a challenge to the supremacy of the post-World War II Bretton Woods order. Others see it as another symbol of shifting regional power in Asia and have deep concerns about the AIIB's willingness to adhere to international safeguards and open procurement.

China became the world's second largest economy a new global political and economic order with the relatively declining USA and Japan is emerging, the result of new economic realities and one cannot expect to change these economic realities by force or by arguing. But if the response to the AIIB remains antagonistic one a dysfunctional global system or a global order that is distinctly not optimal or even self-destructive.

So far the US response to the growing international economic position of China was to take actions based on the idea that the world economy is an antagonistic game and that if the US-led world economy is to prosper then there is a need to preserve US share and reduce China's. If US and Japan see China's gains as coming at their expense, there will be another actions designed to limit China's influence. These actions not only will ultimately prove futile, but will also undermine confidence in the U.S. and its position of leadership in world economy. An example of this misguided policy may be the so-called Trans-Pacific Partnership, a proposed free-trade agreement among the U.S., Japan, and several other Asian countries which excluded China. It is seen by many as a way to tighten the links between the U.S. and certain Asian countries, at the expense of links with China. There is a huge and dynamic Asia trade and finance mechanism and the Trans-Pacific Partnership looks like an attempt to cut China out of this US-dominated mechanism. More recent example is the US attempt to oppose China increasing its voting rights in line with their GDP and the share in international trade. When the other G-20 nations agree that it is time that the leadership of international economic organizations be determined on the basis of merit, not nationality, the U.S. insists that the old order is good enough, that the World Bank, for instance, should continue to be headed by an American.[2]

The idea that a Chinese dominated institution could provide an additional channel for Chinese influence on the policies of its neighbours has some support in the history of the World Bank and the ADB. Internal US government assessments over decades concluded that its position in multilateral institutions was a source of political influence. Some, based on quantitative evidence, suggest that Japan has at times leveraged its informal influence at the ADB, particularly over the office of the President, to generate support for Japan's candidacy for temporary positions at the United Nations Security Council.

Finally, the U.S. supported by Japan has sought to weaken China's efforts to channel more assistance to developing countries through newly created multilateral institutions in which China would have a large, perhaps dominant role. The need for trillions of dollars of investment in infrastructure has been widely recognized and providing that investment is well beyond the capacity of the World Bank and existing multilateral institutions. What is needed is not only a more inclusive governance regime at the World Bank but also more capital. On both scores, the U.S. opposed both proposals. When China was trying to create an Asian Infrastructure Fund, working with a large number of other countries in the region the U.S. argued and pressured its partners not to join.

3. Criticism of the Existing International Funding Infrastructure

There are in fact many similarities between the AIIB and the existing multilateral finance institutions like the World Bank and Asian Development Bank (ADB). The AIIB has a similar governing body to existing multilateral banks, including an international board of governors, board of directors, and board of management. However, the AIIB governance structure will be leaner. The World Bank's resident board is criticized as being both costly ($70 million a year) and inefficient. Mindful of these criticisms of counterpart institutions, the AIIB has established its board of directors as non-resident. Board members will correspond electronically and meet physically as needed.

The main differences between the AIIB and other development banks are mostly related to its mission/mandate: while the World Bank and the ADB have a focus on projects in the most underdeveloped economies poverty-focused objective, the AIIB will only invest in infrastructure. AIIB will invest in all countries, regardless of their development stage. AIIB is

---

[2] Another example of the US negative attitude to China: when China, together with France and other countries supported by an International Commission of Experts appointed by the president of the U.N., suggested that the new international reserve currency be created, the U.S. blocked the effort.

not as decentralized as the World Bank or ADB. Its structure is relatively small with only 500-600 staff, compared to ADB which is six times this size, and World Bank which is 20 times this size.

The existing infrastructure lending provided mostly by the World Bank and the Asian Development Bank has been subject to extensive criticism.

In particular, the World Bank is in need of a new strategy. Lending has declined in recent years, driven by low capital inputs from World Bank members and increased competition from regional development banks and private institutions. Commitments from the International Bank for Reconstruction and Development the branch of the World Bank that loans to middle-income countries averaged more than $25 billion per year during the 1980s and 1990s. But support has since declined to around $15 billion per year, although 2014 saw an increase to $18.6 billion.[3]

Lack of adequate, stable resources—the result of low capital infusions and inconsistent capital increases—has been a continuing problem. The proliferation of ad-hoc trust funds—which began as a way to co-finance specific projects but are now mostly focused on global public goods that cross borders, such as climate change or public health initiatives shows the inadequacy of the World Bank's traditional lending instruments to solve the emerging complex global problems.

The Asian Development Bank is facing similar challenges. The United States is the second largest shareholder in the Asian Development Bank, behind Japan; China is number three. The combined capital base of the World Bank and ADB is less than $400 billion, not enough to meet growing infrastructure investment needs in developing Asia-Pacific nations.

The more detailed criticism includes a whole range of issues but they generally refer to the actual approaches adopted by the World Bank and the IMF in formulating their policies. This includes the social and economic impact these policies have on the population of debter nations.

Critics of the World Bank and the IMF are concerned about the conditionalities imposed on borrower countries. The World Bank and the IMF often attach loan conditionalities based on what is termed the 'Washington Consensus', focusing on liberalization—of trade, investment and the financial sector , deregulation and privatisation of nationalized industries. Often the conditionalities are attached without due regard for the borrower countries' individual circumstances and the prescriptive recommendations by the World Bank and IMF fail to resolve the economic problems within the debtor countries.

IMF conditionalities may additionally result in the loss of a state's authority to govern its own economy as national economic policies are predetermined under the structural adjustment packages. There are doubts about the types of development projects funded by the IBRD

---

[3] Bank for Reconstruction and Development, Annual Report, 2015.

(International Bank for Reconstruction and Development) and the IDA (International development Agency). Many infrastructural projects financed by the World Bank Group have social and environmental implications for the populations in the affected areas and criticism has centred around the ethical issues of funding such projects.[4]

Critics of the World Bank and the IMF expressed also doubts about the World Bank research, training and publishing activities. Decisions are made and policies implemented by leading industrialized countries the G7 because they represent the largest donors without much consultation with poor and developing countries. It further shows the links between tremendous ongoing and rising debt and poverty in the developing countries which results in marginalization of a vast majority of people around the world. Another criticism of the World Bank shows that its beneficiaries are often the wealthy people in western nations and the transnational corporations, while the majority of people in the world do not benefit from their funding projects.

The current policies of the IMF and the World Bank favor the implementation of free-market policies, such as trade liberalization, as the best solution to a country's economic problems. Most of the underdeveloped countries do not have the institutions that developed economies have built over time to properly regulate a market economy. Yet a market economy is forced on these countries as a condition of receiving the loans they applied for. Often the result is an even worse combination of wealth gaps, increasing poverty and environmental exploitation when their economy hasn't even improved. From this viewpoint the conditionality of the loans is viewed as the cause of the several failures - in East Asia, in Russia, in Latin America - of the IMF and World Bank to succeed in their missions of global economic stability and poverty eradication. Contrary to their expectations, IMF and the WB bailouts and loans give sometimes countries excuses not to make needed reforms and prolong economic backwardness while building up enormous levels of debt.

4. The Chinese Rationale for the AIIB

It seems a foregone conclusion that China will use the new bank to expand its influence at the expense of America and Japan. China's decision to fund a new multilateral bank rather than give more to the existing ones reflects also its disappointment with the very slow pace of global

---

[4] For example, World Bank-funded construction of hydroelectric dams in various countries have resulted in the displacement of indigenous peoples of the area. There are also concerns that the World Bank working in partnership with the private sector may undermine the role of the state as the primary provider of essential goods and services, such as healthcare and education, resulting in the shortfall of such services in countries badly in need of them.

economic governance reform. The same motivation supported the New Development Bank (NDB) established by the BRICS (Brazil, Russia, India, China and South Africa). Although China is the biggest economy in Asia, the ADB is dominated by Japan; Japan's voting share is more than twice China's and the bank's president has always been Japanese.

From this perspective the Asian Infrastructure Investment Bank is in just one of new components of international financial institutions in which China is taking a leadership position. Both the AIIB as well as NDB will operate in development lending with funding major infrastructure projects. With planned subscribed capitalization of over $100 billion every year this bank can instantly overtake the existing World Bank landing capacity.

The NDB, its structure and policies tend to favor the founding BRICS members, and any contributions from new members may not reduce the BRICS' voting shares below 55 percent or increase the new members' shares beyond 7 percent of the total voting shares. The ADB has similar minimum regional representations. The protected dominance in voting shares, along with a requirement that the president and vice president come from BRICS countries are likely to discourage other large economies from joining.

In contrast, the Asian Infrastructure Investment Bank is more open, with 57 founding members, compared to five for the BRICS bank. AIIB's Articles of Agreement specify an open procurement policy, which means non-AIIB members can provide goods and services for AIIB-funded projects. However, China will be the largest shareholder and host the headquarters of the AIIB.

In terms of investment demand, the AIIB and NDB are complementary to the existing lending institutions. The unanswered question is which type of projects these new development banks will support, and that is determined by the standards they employ for project approval. If these institutions adopt strong standards that safeguard people and the environment, they will support new development projects with a positive impact on borrowing nations and regions. High environmental and social standards at the AIIB and NDB could even push existing international lending institutions to tighten their own project standards and streamline their processes to become more efficient. On the other hand, if the AIIB and NDB adopt standards that are not sufficiently rigid they may risk funding problematic projects such as hydroelectric dams that may devastate the local environment or coal plants that accelerate global warming.

Several features make the AIIB unique: China is the main shareholder and has the most votes. The American-dominated World Bank, European-dominated IMF, and Japanese-dominated ADB have not given China enough room to play an influential role in the global economy nor have these institutions responded to China's push for more infrastructural investments. While China accounts for roughly 10 percent of the global economy, its voting power in the Bretton Woods institutions remains at 5 percent.

The AIIB is part of China's broader regional development strategy paralleled by the Belt and

Road Initiative (BRI), which aspires to develop cooperation among countries in Asia, Africa, and Europe through an elaborate network of land and sea infrastructure known as the Silk Road Economic Belt and the Maritime Silk Road. In theory the BRI will benefit 63 percent of the global population and contribute $2.1 trillion to global GDP.

China expects that the BRI will boost its economy by creating access to new markets and that the AIIB will be one of several sources of financing for the BRI. These expectations may however not fully realize because China's slowing economic growth and a falling foreign exchange reserve. Successful Funding both initiatives (BRI and AIIB) may yet prove too demanding and difficult.[5]

Two features of the AIIB make it particularly distinctive from the existing international development banks:

1. AIIB is much more representative of the South and gives developing nations a bigger voice. At least 75 percent of share votes are allocated for Asia-Pacific member states. This provides smaller Asian countries with the voice they do not have in other multilateral banks.
2. AIIB aims to promote greater efficiency. Slow project design, loan preparation, complex and complicated compliance procedures, and lengthy procurement processes are not infrequent in existing multilateral banks. The AIIB is committed to a simpler internal review and assessment process to approve loans more quickly. The AIIB's non-resident governance structure is also intended to reduce the transaction costs that are now associated with the resident boards of the existing institutions

5. The AIIB and the New Silk Road

Probably the most important long-term motive behind the establishment of the AIIB is the idea of building a new Silk Road between China and Europe. The Silk Road or Silk Route was an ancient network of trade routes that were central to cultural interaction through regions of the Asian continent connecting the West and East from China to the Mediterranean Sea.

The Silk Road derives its name from the lucrative trade in Chinese silk carried out along its length, beginning during the Han dynasty (207 BCE – 220 CE). The Central Asian sections of the trade routes were expanded around 114 BCE by the Han dynasty, largely through the missions and explorations of the Chinese imperial envoy, Zhang Qian. The Chinese took great

---

[5] The AIIB's first 5-year president, Jin Liqun, a Chinese national and former vice minister in China's Ministry of Finance, also served terms as an alternate executive director at the World Bank and vice president at the ADB.

interest in the safety of their trade products and extended the Great Wall of China to ensure the protection of the trade route.

The on-going project of the New Silk Road between China and Europe is a novelty with potentially far-reaching consequences. Indeed a great physical integration is taking place between central Asia and Europe. China has already invested in the New Silk Road and this is only the beginning of larger financial investments. Like the ancient Silk Road, it will involve land and maritime routes.

The interest of China and Europe in the Silk Road seems obvious. With the EU being China's biggest trading partner, a logistical route that improves economic integration between the Chinese industrial base and the European one is not in need of a sophisticated explanation. With this transcontinental logistical project, China is trying to develop industrial hubs in the interior of the country, which is an area with great economic potential and will likely be the future engine of growth. While trains now take less than two weeks to go from central China to Europe, with the new Silk Road, the journey time will be much reduced.

The new land route between Europe and China is not going to benefit only the "extremities" of the logistical route, but it is likely to have positive effects for the countries in between. The new Silk Road will bring widespread regional benefits and will likely increase the importance of the lands between the two economic giants. Thus, many Asian states may maximize their unique geographical position and with the right strategy their position can be transformed into an economic and political asset.

China's motivation behind the AIIB proposal is best explained in the context of its 'Silk Road economic belt' and '21st century maritime Silk Road' (together, 'one belt, one road') initiatives.[6]

While some scholars regard the Chinese initiative as a reaction to the United States 'new Silk Road' initiative to create a regional market for Afghanistan, China's proposal has its own

---

[6] Chinese President Xi Jinping proposed a Silk Road economic belt on a visit to Kazakhstan in September 2013, and a 21st century maritime Silk Road in Indonesia the following month, simultaneously with the AIIB proposal. In his capacity as chair of China's leading economic policy group, Xi Jinping has explicitly instructed policymakers that the 'primary task' of the AIIB is to provide capital for these initiatives ('Xi Stresses Implementing Central Economic Policies,' Xinhua, February 10, 2015). In addition to the AIIB, China has created a new $40 billion 'Silk Road fund' ('China to Speed up Construction of New Silk Road,' China Daily, November 6, 2014) and injected a further $31 billion in China's policy banks to support the initiative ('Policy Banks Linked to 'Belt and Road' Plans Said to Get US$ 31 Bln,' Caixin Online, July 21, 2015).

economic roots, particularly in the wake of the global financial crisis and recession in the North Atlantic which had limited China's potential for continued export-led growth.[7]

The fundamental assumption of the Silk Road proposal was that transport costs and connectivity, not tariffs, had become the major obstacle to intra-regional trade. Asian highway and railway networks were advocated as a means of reducing this barrier. A trans-Asian rail network depended on completing rail links from China to South and Southeast Asia through Myanmar and Laos, and to Central Asia through Kyrgyzstan. The highway network would connect central and southern China with the rest of Asia. The strategic implications of a Silk Road strategy for China were outlined by a some authors.[8]

Some of the obstacles for the initiative as outlined by Gan included: China's geography, the reality that some of the key countries on land routes were poor and required financial assistance, and the fact that over the previous two decades many organizations had encouraged the revitalization of the Silk Road, but there had not been a decisive platform through which to coordinate and resolve key issues.[9]

In addition to physical connectivity (including transport networks, but also energy and communications), the Silk Road initiative provides for policy coordination (including intergovernmental macro policy exchange), behind-the-border trade and investment facilitation, financial integration and people-to-people bonds. Additionally, it is linked to detailed development strategies for each of China's regions. The AIIB is just one of many financial integration initiatives by China aimed at promoting the Silk Road initiative, which includes regional bond markets, bilateral currency swaps and the internationalization of the yuan.

The strategic significance of building a land-based trade links with Europe in competition to the existing sea-based trade links established by the old colonial powers of England, Holland, France and more recently by the USA has not been ignored by the West. China's maritime Silk Road initiative was interpreted by some foreign commentators as a 'string of pearls' strategy to

---

[7] In 2009, the Asian Development Bank Institute published a working paper calling for a modern or restored 'Silk Road' to help Asia meet its potential. The article was translated into Chinese and published in a journal edited by the Chinese Academy of Social Sciences (Bhattacharyay, 2009b).

[8] According to Gan (Gan 2010) the potential benefits include : expanding markets for Chinese exports, improving security for China's energy imports via overland routes, increasing China's soft power through greater cultural and tourism exchanges, contributing to regional economic integration, and improving China's regional security.

[9] A joint action plan issued in March 2015 by China's National Development and Reform Commission, the Ministry of Foreign Affairs, and the Ministry of Commerce ('Vision and Actions on Jointly Building Belt and Road,' Xinhua, March 28, 2015) provided the authoritative plan for developing the Silk Road, which includes, but is broader than hard infrastructure.

displace the United States' strategic dominance over key energy and trade routes through Southeast Asia and the Indian ocean.[10]

There was also a concern that a Chinese-led institution would 'promote a version of China's state capitalism, not transparent markets' ('China Trounces U.S.,' Wall Street Journal, March 20, 2015) among its borrowers. Under this view, Asia's infrastructure deficit was not a financing problem, but rather could be explained in terms of a weak institutional environment for investment. The concern with the AIIB was that offering an alternative window to the ADB and World Bank would weaken their capacity to enforce their own policy conditionality, and therefore eroding their influence.[11]

The United States argued that the AIIB may not have the transparency, good governance and standards consistent with existing multilateral lenders. Consistent with the theory of policy conditionality in multilateral institutions (Stone 2008; McKeown 2009), stronger governance would restrict the ability of China to rely on informal mechanisms to meet its strategic goals that might not be common with other shareholders. The United States' emphasis on consistency with the standards of other multilateral banks was intended to reduce the scope of the AIIB to compete with the ADB and WB, while allowing reservations regarding the AIIB to be made in terms of the impact on developing countries, rather than being contrary to US strategic interests.

6. The Governance of the AIIB

Similar to other regional development banks, there are special entitlements for regional members which will firmly establish the AIIB as a regionally dominant institution, even if it is not a China dominant institution. The definition of the 'region' in the AIIB Articles is similar to that used by the ADB, and is based on the UN country classifications for Asia and Oceania. In the AIIB, regional members will always hold at least 75 per cent of the total capital stock (unless agreed by the members with 75 per cent of total capital stock). And nine of the 12

---

[10] See, 'Beijing Eyes Closer Ties,' The Korea Herald, July 3, 2014. Sometimes, the AIIB was seen as a war chest to 'bribe leaders from Dili to Ulaanbaatar' ('Buying Countries for Influence,' Korea Joong Ang Daily, 12 May 2014), although the strength of this argument is blunted by the existence of alternative, much less transparent, channels than for China to trade aid for policy support. More subtly, the concern that AIIB funds would be used to pursue China's strategic objectives was at least one of the objections put by Australia's foreign minister in arguing against Australia's early participation in the bank ('Division Over Bank,' The Conversation, 19 October 2014).

[11] See, Lim, D. Y. M., and Vreeland, J. R. 2013. "Regional Organizations and International Politics: Japanese Influence over the Asian Development Bank and the UN Security Council" World Politics 65 (1): 34–72.

members of the Board of Directors will represent regional members. Of the 57 prospective founding members of the AIIB, 37 are from the region. By way of comparison, there are 67 members of the ADB with 48 from the region.

Unlike the other development banks, the AIIB Articles allow for non-sovereign members from countries that are members of the AIIB. This, for example, allows Taiwan to join the Bank. While its initial application to join was rejected, the mainland remains open to Taiwan joining under an acceptable name *('Mainland Welcomes Taiwan Joining AIIB,' Xinhua, April 13, 2015)*. This provision allowing non-sovereign members also leaves opens the possibility of Chinese (and other countries') institutions becoming a member of the AIIB.

Capital allocations are based on 'the relative share of the global economy of members (based on GDP) within the regional and non-regional groupings, with the understanding that GDP share is indicative only for non-regional members'. This means that should Japan decide to join the AIIB, it would be a regional member and its share of the capital stock would be based on Japan's relative GDP. By contrast, should the United States join, its relative GDP would only be an indicative guide.

The voting arrangements for the AIIB will consist of basic votes (12 per cent of total votes will be shared equally between members, a similar arrangement exists in the other development banks to increase the voting power of small members); founding members votes (each founding member will be allocated 600 Founding Member Votes); and votes aligned with each members share of the capital stock in the Bank.

As the largest shareholder in the AIIB, China has by far the largest voting share at 26.06 per cent, followed at a distance by India (7.51 percent); Russia (5.93 percent) and Germany (4.15 percent). China's voting power in the AIIB is currently significantly larger than the United States' 15.02 percent voting share in the World Bank and Japan's 12.84 per cent voting share in the ADB.

While China does not have a formal veto power over project-level decisions, its 26.06 voting share in the AIIB gives it effective veto over major decisions requiring a super majority of 75 per cent. This is similar to the US veto over World Bank decisions requiring an 85 percent super majority. The decisions in the AIIB where China has a veto power include: increasing the bank's capital and increasing the capital subscription.[12]

China has more control over the appointment of the President of the AIIB than the US has in the World Bank and Japan in the ADB. China has a veto power over the appointment of the AIIB President whereas the influence of the US in the World Bank and Japan in the ADB

---

[12] China offered to give up veto powers in exchange for European participation ('China Forgoes Veto Power at New Bank to Win Key European Nations' Support' the Wall Street Journal, 23, March, 2015), it enjoys veto power that goes beyond that enjoyed by major shareholders in other development banks.

depends on informal arrangements. Given the resentment among emerging markets and developing countries over the convention that the President of the World Bank is always an American and the head of the IMF always is a European, China could have taken the moral high ground by highlighting that the appointment of the AIIB President should be based on merit, regardless of nationality. However China followed the ADB precedent and the AIIB Articles say that the President must be a national of one of the bank's members.[13]

China's ability to maintain significant veto powers is a reflection of its dominant financial power. It could also mean that for some prospective members, governance considerations were not their primary consideration, notwithstanding their public comments. That China has sought extensive veto power may also suggest that it does not yet fully appreciate that its influence does not depend solely on its voting power combined with veto provisions. As has been evident in the World Bank and the ADB since their inception, the major shareholder can have a significant influence informally. This can be more effective than the blunt instrument of vetoing decisions that are supported by the majority of members.

China has maintained significant flexibility for future direction of the AIIB. Despite its name, the bank is not restricted to infrastructure investment. Its formal role is to use its resources to promote public and private investment in the region and support 'harmonious economic growth,' in particular but not exclusively through investment in infrastructure.

While the AIIB's authorized capital is US$100 billion, it can also accept 'special funds' to increase its resources as well as administer funds held in trust for other parties. This is broadly consistent with the arrangements for the development banks. The AIIB can also administer trust funds that are separate from its balance sheet. Its methods of operation are wide ranging and the recipients of its financing need not be members of the Bank. As such, the statutes of the Bank do not limit China's capacity to use the AIIB to directly pursue its economic and political interests should this be its motivation.

Similar to the other development banks, the AIIB will have a three-layer governance structure involving a Board of Governors, a 12 member Board of Directors and management/staff. The most distinguishing aspect, and one that could either enhance the efficiency of the bank or alternatively be a weak link in its governance arrangements, is the absence of a fulltime, resident board of directors.

Prospective members of the AIIB who had doubts over its governance arrangements and feared it would largely be a vehicle for promoting China's interests would have supported a

---

[13] At the sixth Chief Negotiators' meeting in August 2014, negotiators considered formal nominations from China and Russia to serve as the President-designate of the bank. Mr. Jin Liqun, the former Chinese Vice Minister of Finance and state-owned financial executive, who had fronted the negotiations for the bank was the consensus choice (Asian Infrastructure Investment Bank Interim Multilateral Secretariat).

fulltime resident board for the same reasons the United States insisted on full time boards in the World Bank and IMF, namely to be a political check on every decision taken.

The AIIB adoption of a non-resident board opens the possibility of a more effective board that provides strategic oversight and direction to the bank, as well as holding management accountable for its performance. If this is achieved, it will be a major advance on the arrangements in the World Bank and ADB. But for a part-time, nonexecutive board to be effective, the roles, responsibilities and expectations of the board and management has to be clearly defined. Management should have operational freedom and discretion, but must be fully accountable to shareholders through the board for its performance. But the potential downside of the non-resident board is that it can take an excessive approach to the performance of the bank. It will be critical for every director to take their responsibilities seriously and play an active role in controlling the performance of the bank. All shareholders in the AIIB will have the responsibility of ensuring that the non-resident board does provide effective management of the institution.

7. Potential for Growth of the AIIB

The Bank has 37 member states (all "Founding Members") and was proposed as an initiative by the government of China. The initiative gained support from 37 regional and 20 non-regional Prospective Founding Members (PFM), all of which have signed the Articles of Agreement that form the legal basis for the bank. The bank started operation after the agreement came into force on 25 December 2015, after ratifications were received from 10 member states holding a total number of 50 percent of the initial subscriptions of the Authorized Capital Stock. On 25 December 2015, the Articles of Agreement came into force. On 16 January 2016, the board of governors of the bank convened its inaugural meeting in Beijing and declared the bank open for business. Jin Liqun was elected as the bank's president for a five-year term. 17 states (Australia, Austria, Brunei, China, Georgia, Germany, Jordan, Luxembourg, Mongolia, Myanmar, the Netherlands, New Zealand, Norway, Pakistan, Singapore, South Korea and the United Kingdom) together holding 50.1 percent of the initial subscriptions of Authorized Capital Stock, had deposited the instrument of ratification for the agreement, triggering entry into force, and making them all founding members and making the Articles of Agreement, operational. Twelve other states followed, taking the amount of Authorized Capital Stock held by the 29 members of the bank to 74 percent.

There could be several potential obstacles to the smooth and dynamic growth of the AIIB. The constraints on investment, especially attracting private investment in infrastructure, include problems of project selection and preparation, implementation risks, the need to translate sound economic rates of return into financial returns, and intermediation challenges.

China needs far better links to its neighbours: the supply of cheap factory labour from the countryside is being eroded and labour costs are rising rapidly, creating an urgent need to re-orient supply chains. The opening of Myanmar makes it possible to meet this need and allow more economies at various stages of development to participate in international production networks in line with their evolving comparative advantage.

Following China's decision to set up the AIIB, consultations are likely to take place around the Asia Pacific, encouraging more governments as well as private investors to become foundation shareholders. Potential investors in the AIIB will want to be assured that the management of the new bank will be of high quality, preferably selected on a competitive basis, and will be overseen by independent, commercially experienced directors. Sound procedures for project selection, designing financing plans and tendering for project implementation can be based on those developed by existing multilateral development banks.

It should also be possible to clarify that the AIIB will operate on commercial principles. Subsidizing the capital costs of some infrastructure can be justified by externalities that are created, but these subsidies should be injected by the governments of the economies which expect to benefit. The world does not need yet another window for overseas development assistance.

The first planned investment projects are huge and of great strategic value to the prospective participants – The Trans ASEAN Gas Pipeline (TAEG) and the Trans-ASEAN Electricity Grid (TAEG). The TAEG is estimated to cost US$6 billion, the TAGP $7 billion. Their combined $13 billion cost amounts to about 13% of the AIIB's $100 billion capital. Together, the TAGP, TAEG and Kunming-Singapore Railway offer a regional economic development template for China and Southeast Asia. The three projects — and particularly the TAGP — could lead to enough mutual confidence for China and her Southeast Asian neighbours to agree on Joint Development Areas (JDAs) for oil and gas in the South China Sea. Deepening gas, electricity and train connections between the Chinese and ASEAN economies will also speed up regional decarbonization of energy markets. This will generate economic wealth. It can also help break the ice between China and her Southeast Asian neighbors over hot button South China Sea territorial issues.

The AIIB should be able to attract shareholding from Asia Pacific governments committed to their new APEC Framework on Connectivity, as well as from some private sources. If APEC governments on both sides of the Pacific participate in the new infrastructure development bank, the AIIB could be transformed into an Asia Pacific Infrastructure Investment Bank, which could invest in projects to upgrade connectivity among all Asia Pacific economies.

To have a significant impact on the need for economic infrastructure, the AIIB would have to expand as rapidly as it can acquire the necessary expertise. In time, its impact on the region could be greater than the ADB or the World Bank, depending on whether those institutions decide to rediscover their capacity to finance productive infrastructure on commercial terms. The AIIB will create new competition for the World Bank and the ADB, but the new bank will also have a strong incentive to cooperate with them. Using the expertise of experienced development banks is the most efficient way, and perhaps the only way, to build the capacity of the new bank to assess and implement projects successfully. There is growing expectation that the membership in the AIIB would bring strategic and long term benefits to the European countries.

Well-prepared negotiations (such as consultations with experts experienced in global financial institutions, such as the IMF) and Chinese determination to create an effective investment mechanism based on economic efficiency make the AIIB attractive for Poland. For this country, a willingness to be a founding member of the bank is a clear message to China and other Asian countries about a readiness to develop bilateral relations, which is one of Poland's foreign policy goals.

Although the AIIB will probably be focused on projects only in Asia (but China is considering not limiting the geographical scope of the bank's operation), membership could create better conditions for Polish companies to enter the Asian market, and offer an opportunity to take part in infrastructural projects, probably as sub-contractors. This could be beneficial not only in terms of access to investment funds. The AIIB's participation in projects, through its assessment or verification of their relevance, and then through granting loans, could minimize a project's risk significantly, and enhance its credibility, including among contractors, providing guarantees, and so on, thus making a given project more predictable and safer for Polish firms. It might also be the right way to overcome the lack of knowledge about business partners and a particular country, which is one of the main barriers for Polish companies entering non-European markets. What is more, participation in such projects enables Polish enterprises to gain experience in conducting complex projects ("learning by doing") and cooperation with foreign partners, which could be useful in their future activities.

It is still an open question to what extent Poland will take advantage of the development opportunities provided by the AIIB. There was a view that Poland's accession to the AIIB should depend on the contracts it could obtain. Poland particularly hopes to improve its trade balance with China, which has been negative for many years (Poland exports about EUR 2 billion to China and imports about EUR 19 billion). Involvement in the AIIB is supposed to ease the access of Polish companies to infrastructure projects to get first-hand information on investments the AIIB wants to support. Poland also hopes to make it easier for Polish companies to access Asian markets through the AIIB structures.

For Poland, joining the AIIB is also an investment in the future, because European Union cohesion funds are gradually drying up. Being a member of a financial institution with global impact should help Poland influence the bank's activity, and could highlight projects Poland cares about.

The financial guarantees provided by the AIIB, which should translate into improved security for the activities of Polish companies on the Asian markets, are also important. Besides China, the AIIB will also operate in Central Asia and the Caucasus, where Polish companies are already present.

Poland could also use its membership in the AIIB to develop an entirely new strategy for eastern markets, and particularly China. Until recently, few believed that China would be able to so quickly establish a completely new financial institution of international importance, and that Poland would be a member.

The potential for growth of the AIIB is difficult to overestimate. The bank's creation is also widely discussed in China, where it is treated as a prestigious success in the face of the recent economic troubles like the slump on the local stock market, growing internal debt, capital flight, falling foreign exchange reserves and generally pessimistic macroeconomic data.

References

[1] Asian Development Bank. 2015. "ASEAN Infrastructure Fund Overview—Asian Development Bank." Accessed 29 March 2016. http://www.adb.org/site/aif/overview.

[2] Asian Infrastructure Investment Bank Interim Multilateral Secretariat. 2015a. "Asian Infrastructure Investment Bank Articles of Agreement." http://www.aiibank.org/uploadfile/.

[3] Bhattacharyay, Biswa N. 2010. Estimating Demand for Infrastructure in Energy, Transport, Telecommunications, Water and Sanitation in Asia and the Pacific: 2010–2020. ADBI Working Paper Series No 248. September 2010.

[4] Bhattacharyay, Biswa N., and Prabir De. 2009a, "Restoring Asian Silk Route: Towards the Vision of an Integrated Asia." Journal of Contemporary Asia-Pacific Studies 3: 37–56.

[5] Bhattacharyay, Biswa N., and Prabir De. 2009b. Restoring the Asian Silk Route—Toward the Vision of an Integrated Asia. ADBI Working Paper Series No. 140. June 2009.

[6] Callaghan, Mike and Paul Hubbard: The Asian Infrastructure Investment Bank:Multilateralism on the Silk Road, China Economic Journal, 2016, Vol. 9 No 2, 116-139.

[7] Dutt, Nitish. 2001. "The US and the Asian Development Bank: Origins, Structure and Lending Operations." Journal of Contemporary Asia 31 (2): 241–61.

[8] Fallon, Theresa. 2015. "The New Silk Road: Xi Jinping's Grand Strategy for Eurasia." American Foreign Policy Interests 37 (3): 140–47.

[9] Gan, Nectar and Li Jing. (2016) "China's climate envoy bullish on hitting reduction goal for 2020", 23 February 2016. South China Morning Post,
http://www.scmp.com/news/china/policies-politics/article/1916025/chinas-climate-envoy-

bullish-hitting-reduction-goal/.

[10] Kilby, Christopher. 2006. "Donor Influence in Multilateral Development Banks: The Case of the Asian Development Bank." Review of International Organizations 1 (2): 173–95.

[11] Lim, Daniel Y. M., and Vreeland, James R. 2013. "Regional Organizations and International Politics: Japanese Influence over the Asian Development Bank and the UN Security Council." World Politics 65 (1): 34–72.

[12] McKeown, Timothy J. 2009. "How U.S. Decision-Makers Assessed Their Control of Multilateral Organizations, 1957–1982." Review of International Organizations 4 (3): 269–91.

[13] New Asian Infrastructure and Investment Bank Breaks Ground: What You Need to Know, Alma Freeman Interview for Asia Foundation, Asia Foundation.org/2016/01/27

[14] Rodney, Don, and Ong Junio. 2014. "Asian Infrastructure Investment Bank: An Idea Whose Time Has Come?" The Diplomat.

[15] Rodrik, Dani. 1995. "Why Is There Multilateral Lending?" In Proceedings of the Annual World Bank Conference in Development Economics, 167–205.

[16] World Bank. 2015. World Bank Acknowledges Shortcomings in Resettlement Projects, Announces Action Plan to Fix Problems. Press Release No 2015/332/ECR. Accessed 29 March 2016.

[17] Zoellick, Robert B. 2006. "Whither China: From Membership to Responsibility?" The DISAM Journal 28 (2): 94–98.

Chapter 3

Application of Environmental Economic Evaluation to Forest Conservation Policies in Sabah, Malaysia

Hiroshi Hasegawa
Faculty of Human Environmental Studies, Hiroshima Shudo University
1-1-1 Ozuka-higashi, Asaminami-ku, Hiroshima 731-3195 JAPAN

Abstract

Among various forest conservation policies, the current study has taken up the forest certification project and the clean development mechanism (CDM) project, to apply the environmental economic evaluation system. The forest certification system is expected not only to control illegal logging but also to contribute to maintain the ecosystem service, while the CDM projects have positive effects not only on air quality by absorbing CO_2 and producing O_2 but also on total ecosystem as well.

In particular, the study has researched on potential monetary valuation methods to internalize environmental benefits and costs through cost-benefit analysis of these projects, as trying evaluations of natural ecosystem in Sabah including the Kinabalu National Park (UNESCO world natural heritage) as well as the Deramakot Forest Reserve Area. Finally, ecosystem service of the tropical forest (natural forest, production forest, and farmland) has been estimated for Sabah, with some political implication.

Key Words:
Forest Certification, Clean Development Mechanism (CDM), Environmental Economic Evaluation, Cost Benefit Analysis, Contingent Valuation Method (CVM), Corporative Social Responsibility (CSR)

1. Introduction

Figure 1 shows relationship between forest conservation policies and their evaluation systems. Among them, the current research takes up the Forest Certification project and the Clean Development Mechanism (CDM) project for afforestation and reforestation, to apply the environmental economic evaluation system. In particular, I have studied what kind of roles the environmental economic evaluation performs for internalization of environmental benefits and costs through cost-benefit analysis of these projects, as trying evaluations of natural ecosystem in Sabah including the Kinabalu Park as well as the Deramakot Forest Reserve Area.

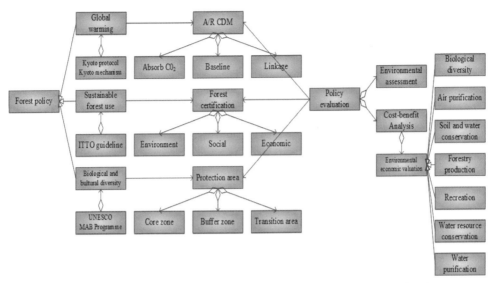

Figure 1. Relationship between Forest Conservation Policies and Evaluation Systems

2. Necessity of Environmental Economic Evaluation for Forest Policies

In carrying out the project as forest policy, calculating environmental values provides objective evaluation standards. It will support in preserving good forest ecosystem, formulating regulations/laws for forest preservation, zoning nature preservation areas and controlling land use for amenity preservation. Further, it can provide basic data to carry out public or private projects, which have a high economic efficiency from the environmental standpoints. The social loss occurs as precious forest resources decrease. Environmental economic evaluation can make contributions to the policies as follows ;

(1) Switch from policies only for economic growth by plantation or clear-cutting toward policies with environmental preservation functions such as water resources conservation and flood control,

(2) Promotion of policies which increase environmental values at the expense of efficient and fair operation/maintenance costs,

(3) Development of policies which improve overall social welfare considering public services such as amenity, biodiversity and local culture, not only for national economic growth or private sector's profits, and

(4) Formulation of policies actively aiming at environment-oriented land use and social structure for urban area with little natural resources.

3. Cost-benefit Analysis

The cost-benefit analysis is a technique to prioritize policies or projects by evaluating social costs and benefits in monetary terms, and comparing the cost with validity. Public infrastructure or private-sector projects have been usually evaluated only with the direct benefits and costs that are so-called "internal economic effects". However, when the target policies/projects are more concerned with environmental impacts or services, it is also needed to internalize the "external effects" of environment and natural resources. If such environmental damages and contribution are estimated as social costs and benefits, it would be possible to duly evaluate the policies/projects not only from the viewpoints of economic efficiency but also from social and environmental ones through the analysis. Table 1 shows a cost-benefit analysis model to calculate a typical evaluation parameter "Net Present Value" for forest policies.[8] Calculating value of the external benefit (Be) and the external cost (Ce) can realize economic internalization of environmental aspects, leading to fair and social evaluation of the forest policies.

Table 1. Cost-benefit Analysis Model for Forest Policy

$$NPV = Bd + Be - Cd - Cp - Ce$$

NPV = net present value
Bd = direct benefit from the forest policy
Be = external benefit (including environmental services)
Cd = direct cost to implement the forest policy
Cp = cost for counter-measures to prevent environmental loss
Ce = external cost (including unavoidable environmental damage)

4. Application of Environmental Economic Evaluation to Forest Certification Project

4.1 Background of Forest Certification Project

The competition with non-certified cheap woods hinders the spread of forest certification system. Under the system, marketable woods and their commercial usage have been limited due to their youngness. Therefore, it is a task to manufacture various marketable products using the certified woods. Prices of the certified products are higher than non-certified ones, although quality is not different between them. So the problem is how to appeal to consumers for environmental significance attributed to the certified products.

At the Deramakot Forest Reserve Area managed by Sabah Forestry Department, tree-cutting have been controlled with the RIL (Reduced Impact Logging) method which is a model for sustainable forest management. It minimizes the environmental damage relying on natural regeneration function and duly considering biodiversity in the forest. Because of such background, the RIL area was first in Sabah certified as sustainable management forest by FSC (Forest Stewardship Council) in 1997[6].

However, the forest certification system has not been commonly applied in Sabah, because the system necessitates extra techniques and additional cost for preliminary survey and forest management. Economic benefit covering such additional cost is uncertain and environmental contribution is not recognized in wood market. Commercial forests in Sabah have been mostly logged in a short period with a cost-saving productive method. In addition, impacts on society and culture have to be evaluated as management change of commercial forests and setting-up of reserve area affect employment opportunity and life resources for local people.

4.2 Cost-benefit Analysis of Forest Certification Project

Table 2 presents typical elements to be included into the cost-benefit analysis model. Improvement of public service functions as well as reduction of environmental and social impacts are required to obtain the forest certificate. Compared with non-certified forests, the certified forests therefore need additional cost to monitor environmental and social impacts on logging area. The model has to cover such additional costs and benefits, reflecting local people's values for project impacts on social and cultural aspects.

Table 2. Typical Costs and Benefits of Forest Certification Project

Bd = value of certificated woods
Be = social and environmental benefit (improvement of biodiversity, flood control, water resources conservation, creation of local employment, etc.)
Cd = direct cost for certification procedure, forest management, logging, etc.
Cp = cost for environmental and social conservation (monitoring, counter-measures, etc.)
Ce = unavoidable social and environmental damage (degraded biodiversity, income reduction, etc.)

4.3 Cost for Certification

Cd varies depending on the size of forests. For example, the cost to obtain the certificate is US$0.01-1.3/ha/year under the FSC system while that for Swiss imported woods under the CoC (Chain-of-Custody) system is estimated from US$500 to 1% of the wood price. In case of the SGS which is a FSC certification organization, the cost of certification is US$4,000-100,000/case depending on forest area.[27] Because the direct cost for certification is thus a financially large burden to private foresters, external social and environmental benefits from the certification system should be clarified to wood products consumers so that the higher prices of the certified woods could be well acceptable in market.

4.4 Price of Certified Woods

Be is reflected to the price of certified woods and processed products, so that the certified products are sold with 10-20% higher market prices than non-certification products.[20] These prices will further increase for profitability with a small demand because marketable species, diameter and age are limited. If the consumers purchase more Malaysian certified woods, it will help to reduce illegal logging and excessive deforestation in Malaysia. In addition, the wood-mileage evaluation should be reflected on the international and domestic market prices to promote environment-oriented forestry all over the world.

5. Application of Environmental Economic Evaluation to CDM Project

5.1 Background of CDM Project

The CDM projects have positive effects not only on air quality by absorbing CO_2 and producing O_2 but also on total ecosystem. They also contribute in improving flood control function and water resource conservation as usual afforestation projects. But, at the same time, afforestation/reforestation activities will have negative impacts on natural ecosystem and local community when mono-species plantation of fast-growing or exotic trees is introduced.

A difference to the CDM projects from the usual afforestation activities is additional cost for acquisition of the credit. Its example is the cost to monitor and prevent the "linkage", which means incremental CO_2 emission at the tree-cutted agricultural area newly cultivated by farmers who are forced to move from the CDM project sites. As such, social environmental consideration is strictly required under the CDM projects. When the CDM system is introduced in Sabah with a large population and natural environment, impacts of the projects should be fully assessed.

5.2 Cost-benefit Analysis of CDM Project

In addition to benefit from air purification function of CO_2 absorption, other Be and Ce should also be internalized for evaluation of the CDM project. And monitoring and preventive costs for the linkage are to be included as Cp. Values of forestry resources are usually estimated through market prices. When these values are increased or reduced, they are regarded as Bd or Cd respectively. But, if local people consume forest resources for fuel materials, building materials and food not through the market, they should be evaluated as Be or Ce to be internalized into the cost-benefit analysis model. In addition, social benefit or cost accrues from the CDM project's impact on local people, such as employment opportunity and community disturbance by the forest management. Typical costs and benefits of the CDM project is shown in Table 3.

Table 3. Typical Costs and Benefits of CDM Project

Bd = increased wood products
Be = absorbed CO_2, flood control, water resources conservation, local employment, etc.
Cd = cost of afforestation management (investigation, monitoring, afforestation, logging, road maintenance, etc.)
Cp = cost of social and environmental preservation measures
Ce = unavoidable social environmental damage (degraded biodiversity mono-plantation of fast-growing or exotic species such as eucalyptus, influence to traditional culture, etc.)

5.3 Credit Period

Because the credit period affects the credit price, the credit period is the important matter for the entrepreneurs. In COP9, the credit period was set to 60 years at the longest (renewable 20 years twice) or 30 years (no renewable). This relatively longer period has been determined, considering difference of growth period by species and area. However, unlike power station construction or energy-saving projects, afforestation does not have permanence to absorb CO_2 in the future. It is a problem that CO_2 will be emitted again when trees are cut or caught in fires.

6. Monetary Evaluation Methods for Environmental Values

In actually applying the cost-benefit analysis models presented in the previous chapters, elements more unfamiliar and difficult to evaluate in monetary terms are Ce and Be. So, in this and following chapters, methodological framework to evaluate typical environmental values ("cost" when it is lost, and "benefit" when it is conserved or improved) is studies, and actual measurement is tried for natural forest, commercial forest and agricultural land in Sabah. Environmental functions are major targets under the current study. The main purpose to apply the monetary evaluation methods is to quantitatively measure the benefits. Envisaged benefits

could be largely classified into 9 categories as follows :
1) Fostered water resources,
2) Conserved water quality,
3) Erosion and flood control capacity,
4) Air purification,
5) Aesthetic and recreational amenity,
6) Biodiversity services
7) Forestry resources,
8) Fishery resources, and
9) Agricultural resources

Potential methods for estimating the monetary value of natural resources and environmental benefits are examined. The next table presents a menu of valuation techniques which have been developed so far in environmental/resource economics, as well as typical examples of the evaluated effects. These are largely divided into two categories (OVA and SVA), based on their extent of objectivity or subjectivity.

Table 4. Menu of Valuation Methods for Environmental Effects

Valuation Method	Typical Effects Valued
Objective Valuation Approaches (OVA)	
1) Change in Productivity	Productivity
2) Cost of Illness	Health (morbidity)
3) Human Capital	Health (mortality)
4) Replacement (Restoration) Cost	Capital assets, and natural resource assets
Subjective Valuation Approaches (SVA)	
1) Preventive (Mitigative) Expenditure	Health, productivity, capital assets, and natural resource assets
2) Hedonic Approaches	
- Property (Land) Value	Environmental quality, and productivity
- Wage Differential	Health
3) Travel Cost Method (TCM)	Natural resource assets, and touristic assets
4) Contingent Valuation Method (CVM)	Any effects including biological and aesthetic values
5) Conjoint Analysis	

Source : Economic Analysis of Environmental Impacts, ADB/WB, 1994

6.1 Objective Valuation Approaches

The first set of methods in the table, the Objective Valuation Approaches (OVA), are based on physical relationships that formally describe cause and effect relationships and provide objective measures of effects resulting from various causes. OVA use "damage functions" which relate the level of offending activity to the degree of physical damage to a natural or man-made asset, or to the degree of health impact. OVA in general provide measures of the gross benefits, in the sense of losses avoided, of preventive or remedial actions. The important assumptions for OVA are :

- The net value of averting damage is at least equal to the cost which would be incurred if the damage actually occurred ; and
- Rational individuals, in order to prevent some damage from occurring, would be willing to pay an amount less than or equal to the costs arising from the predicted level of environmental effects.

6.2 Subjective Valuation Approaches

In contrast to OVA, the second set of approaches in the table, the Subjective Valuation Approaches (SVA), are based on more subjective assessments of possible damage expressed in real or hypothetical market behavior. Using revealed behavior involves examination of real markets for goods or services which are affected by environmental impacts, such as air or water pollution, in which people actually make trade offs between the environmental impact and other goods or income. In other cases environmental impacts cannot be valued, even indirectly, through market behavior. The alternative is to construct hypothetical markets for various options to reduce environmental damages, and to ask directly a sample of people to express how much they would be willing to pay for various reductions in environmental impacts. These are the so-called "Contingent Valuation Methods" (CVM) and "Conjoint Analysis".[1]

7. Applicable Evaluation Framework

The selection of a particular method of measurement obviously depends on what is being measured. Selection procedure starts with any environmental impact and determines whether or not there is measurable change in production, or if the primary effect of the impact is change in environmental quality.[9] According to availability of necessary data for monetary calculation, the more applicable evaluation methods for the above-mentioned 9 kinds of benefits brought from the forest ecosystem could be selected as below.

7.1 Fostered Water Resources

It is assumed that development water discharge (incremental water discharge usable during the dry season) is equal to an average outflow of groundwater fostered by incremental vegetation. Therefore, benefit of the water fostering function of the incremental vegetation is evaluated with costs necessary to obtain the same development discharge from irrigation dams (construction and O&M costs of irrigation dams).[11]

Increased water resources → Change in environmental quality → Human habitat
→ **Replacement Cost Method**
[Benefit] = [Incremental vegetation] × [Average unit groundwater outflow of vegetation]
× [(Annual construction cost of irrigation dam per unit development discharge)
+ (Annual O&M cost of irrigation dam per unit development discharge)]

Increased water resources → Measurable change in production → Non-distorted market prices
→ **Change in Productivity Method**
[Benefit] = [Incremental vegetation area] × [Fostered groundwater per unit vegetation]
× [Contribution rate of unit groundwater to each sectoral production]

Natural vegetation in the watershed fosters groundwater for use in the watershed area and the downstream. And the fostered water flows into rivers and lakes, contributing to stabilization of discharged water amount there. So, loss of the vegetation affects the groundwater utilization and river discharge, decreasing products of agricultural and fishery sectors using water as key input. These industrial production losses can be taken as value of the water fostering function of the vegetation.

7.2 Conserved Water Quality

The value of water quality is assumed to be equivalent to the incremental cost of treating the water so that it is suitable for downstream uses. The level of treatment depends on the downstream use. For example, irrigation water does not require the same level of purity as drinking water, so the cost of treating water for use in agriculture would be less than drinking water supply. The incremental cost could be calculated as the extra alum or lime, filter capacity, treatment plant operation costs, etc. needed to treat the excess water pollutants.

> Conserved or improved water quality → Change in environmental quality → Water quality
> → **Replacement Cost Method** or **Preventive Expenditure Method**
> [Benefit by preventive expenditure method]
>   = [Reduced water pollutants]
>   ×[Unit cost for construction and O&M of water filter plant to remove the pollutants]

7.3 Erosion and Flood Control Capacity

In case there is stripped area without vegetation in the watershed, severe erosion would occur under heavy rainfall and its downstream water quality is degraded. So value of the vegetation's erosion control function is evaluated using construction costs of check dams to control and mitigate the washed-away soil.

> Strengthened erosion control capacity → Change in environmental quality → Water quality
> → **Replacement Cost Method** or **Preventive Expenditure Method**
> [Benefit by preventive expenditure method]
>   = [Amount of soil erosion without vegetation]
>   ×[Unit cost for check dam construction to control or mitigate the washed-away soil]

Watershed degradation contributes to increased flooding in two ways. First, tree cutting and other land disturbance reduce the water holding capacity of the soil, causing larger peak flows of drainage after rain storms. Second, the sediment that erodes from the stripped or disturbed land fills the beds of rivers and lakes, allowing flood water to rise above the river and lake banks. The value of flood damage resulting from watershed degradation could be estimated as the value of the incremental amount of increased flooding or decreased flood control capacity.

> Strengthened flood control capacity → Change in environmental quality → Human habitat
> → **Replacement Cost Method**
> [Benefit] = [Reduced cost to rehabilitate damages due to mud-slide and flooding]
>   = [Cost to restore damaged land and building] + [Cost to remove mud and water]
>   + [Repair cost of paddy dikes] + [Cost to rebuild or relocate damaged infrastructure]
>   + [Other expenditure in rehabilitation]

When land and buildings are damaged, the measure of damage should be calculated as the cost to restore them to their original condition. The restoration activities might include removal of mud and dust, repairing of buildings and paddy dikes, and finding temporary accommodation while the buildings are being repaired. Roads, bridges, pipelines, electrical power lines and other public infrastructure could be damaged by mud slides and flooding associated with land disturbance activities in the watershed. The value of the damage in these cases could be calculated as cost to rebuild or relocate the damaged infrastructure.

The next equation reflects that the loss of revenue from lost farm production is a value of the strengthened erosion- and flood-control capacity when agricultural land is covered by mud slides.

Strengthened erosion and flood control capacity
　　→ Measurable change in agricultural production → Non-distorted market prices
　　　　　　　　　　　　　　　　　　　　　　　　→ **Change-in-Productivity Method**
[Benefit] = [Agricultural area protected from erosion]
　　　　　　　　　×[Incremental products] ×[Unit market price of product]

7.4 Air Purification

Oxygen supply function of the incremental vegetation is evaluated by calculating the oxygen weight discharged from the vegetation based on the existing research data, which is multiplied by unit market price of the industrial oxygen. And amount of CO_2 absorbed by the incremental vegetation is estimated for calculation of a total cost to remove them alternatively. This total cost is regarded as an economic value of the air purification function of the incremental vegetation.

Improved air quality → Change in environmental quality → Air quality
　　　　　　　　　　　　　　　　　　　　　　　　→ **Replacement Cost Method**
[Benefit] = [Amount of incremental vegetation]
　　　　　　×{[(Annual net O_2 discharge per vegetation)×(Unit market price of O_2)]
　　　　　　　+ [(Annual net CO_2 absorption net vegetation)×(Unit removal cost of CO_2)]}

7.5 Aesthetic & Recreational Amenity, and Biodiversity Services

The value of the aesthetic quality of the natural environment is difficult to calculate in monetary terms, because it depends on the subjective preference of each individual person. One approach to assigning a monetary value to aesthetic qualities is to estimate how much the people living in and around the area would pay to preserve them (willingness to pay, WTP). The cumulative regional WTP could be interpreted to be equal to the overall value of restoring the aesthetic quality of the environment. In addition, It is likely that Malaysian and international tourists who visit the National Park would also be willing to pay some small amount of money such as a surcharge on hotel room rates for preserving the aesthetic quantities of the Park.[14]

Aesthetic and biodiversity quality → Change in environmental quality
　　　　　　　　　　　　　　　　→ Aesthetics, biodiversity → **Contingent Valuation Method**
[Non-use benefit including existence value]
　　= [Average WTP of non-use value of local households]
　　　　×[Number of local households]
　　　　　+ [Average WTP of non-use value of tourists]×[Number of tourists]

Tourism accounts for a part of the trade of goods and services in and around the National Park. A majority of tourists visiting the Park could be classified as "Adventure and Eco-tourists" enjoying the natural landscape of the area.[5]

> Conserved or improved aesthetic quality → Change in environmental quality → Recreation
> → **Travel-Cost Method** or **Contingent Valuation Method**
> [Use-benefit by travel cost method]
> = [Average travel cost of tourists] × [Incremental number of tourists]
> + [Average travel cost of local visitors] × [Incremental number of local visitors]
> Where [Travel cost] = [Transportation fee] + [Time cost] + [Opportunity cost of stay]
> [Use-benefit by contingent-valuation method]
> = [Average WTP of use value of local households] × [Number of local households]
> + [Average WTP of use value of tourists] × [Number of tourists]

> Conserved or improved aesthetic quality → Measurable change in tourism production
> Non-distorted market prices → **Change in Productivity Method**
> [Benefit] = [Incremental tourists due to environmental improvement or conservation]
> × [Incremental net profit of tourism sector per tourist]

7.6 Improved Forestry Resources

Forests provide several valuable goods and services, including wood products, flood control by stabilizing soil, aesthetic quality and habitat for wildlife. Potential methods for calculating the value of the loss of flood control and aesthetic quality are mentioned in the above sections, respectively. The value of loss of timber and other wood products could be estimated as the overall income that would be derived from harvesting, processing, and selling the products on a sustainable logging on land of similar area, tree-types, proximity to roads and factories, etc. where watershed management has been well done.[12]

> Improved forestry resources → Measurable change in forestry production
> → Non-distorted market prices → **Change in Productivity Method**
> [Benefit] = [Incremental forest land] × [Amount of incremental forest goods]
> × [Unit market price of forest goods]

7.7 Conserved or Improved Fishery Resources

Siltation of river/lake beds and other fish habitat is the main source of environmental damage that poor watershed management causes to fishery resources. Top soil is eroded during heavy rain, and the sediment drains into these sensitive aquatic areas decreasing their ability to support fish life. The value of the damage to fishery resources might be estimated as the loss of fishing income caused by the siltation of fish habitat. The loss of fishing income might be estimated directly or indirectly. If historical records were available, it might be possible to directly estimate the reduction in fishing income. But these results might be unreliable because such factors as improved fishing techniques and boats, increase in the sale price of fish, and increases in the number of people who work in the fishing industry must all be considered. In addition, this direct estimate might unfairly bias against the watershed management, because the other factors such as over-harvesting and pollution from the inland fishery itself might have contributed to the decline in fishing.[4] Consequently, an indirect method of comparison would probably give better results.

Conserved or improved fishery resources → Measurable change in fishery production
→ Non-distorted market prices → **Change in Productivity Method**
[Benefit] = [Improved or conserved water area]
×[Amount of incrementally caught fish and other fishery products]
×[Unit market price of such fishery products]

7.8 Improved or Conserved Agricultural Resources

The extension program of agroforestry technology would increase productivity of the existing agricultural land. This could be a major benefit, so that the incremental agricultural products between with-project and without-project are evaluated with non-distorted market prices.[3]

Improved agricultural resources → Measurable change in agricultural production
→ Non-distorted market prices → **Change in Productivity Method**
[Benefit] = [Amount of incremental agricultural products]
×[Unit market price of the agricultural products]

8. Results of Economic Evaluation for Natural Ecosystem in Sabah

In accordance with the existing data and information available, the most appropriate evaluation methods were selected and economic values for various environmental functions have been measured for such typical ecosystems in Sabah as natural forest, commercial forest and agricultural land. As shown in Table 5, annual overall value of the natural forest seems much higher than the other two ecosystems, although their non-use value of biodiversity services could not be calculated due to lack of data.

Table 5. Economic Values of Environmental Functions

Environmental Functions	Evaluation Methods	Economic Value (RM/ha/year in 2003 price)		
		Natural Forest	Commercial Forest	Agricultural Land
1. Fostered water resources	Replacement cost	91	102	21
2. Conserved water quality	Preventive-expenditure	29,693	7,423	Not related
3. Erosion & flood control	Replacement cost, Change-in-productivity	21,391	5,348	Not related
4. Air purification (including CO_2 absorption)	Replacement cost	24,006	27,828	Little data
5. Aesthetic & recreational amenity	Travel cost	8,735	Not related	Not related
6. Biodiversity services (non-use)	Contingent valuation	112,024,000	Little data	Little data
7. Forestry resources	Change-in-productivity	Not related	51~89	Not related
8. Agricultural resources	Change-in-productivity	Not related	Not related	1,917~19,940
9. Improved fishery resources	Change-in-productivity	1.45	0.36	Not related

"6. Biodiversity services" for the natural forest has been calculated with statistical data (Table 6) collected through questionnaire survey to tourists and local residents around the Kinabalu Park. In order to measure the value for the commercial forest and agricultural land, another questionnaire survey should be carried out to apply the contingent valuation method, furthermore "conjoint analysis" which had been also tried under the current study but resulting in statistically insignificant outputs unfortunately.

Table 6. Average Value for Biodiversity Services

Subject	Unit	Foreign Tourists	Malaysian Tourists	Local Residents
Number of Samples	person	97	76	24
1. Biodiversity of natural forest	$/ha/year	58	10	5
2. Biodiversity of commercial forest	$/ha/year	37	9	6
3. Average value for flora	$/species/year	0.9	0.2	0.1

Note) US$ 1＝RM 3.8

9. Contribution to Forest Policy/Project by Environmental Economic Evaluation

CO_2-absorption function of forest resources is expected as incentive to prevent decrease of a tropical forest. Actually, the forest certification, CDM and ISO14001 has become powerful systems to implement so-called "corporative social responsibility"(CSR). However, the CDM project and the forest certification project should not be managed only as CO_2 absorption source, but also for sustainable forest management. For example, further environmental consideration should be taken such as targeting secondary forests rather than natural forests when a plantation expands.

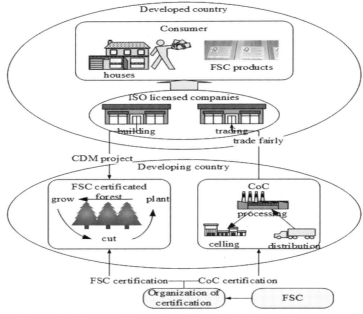

Figure 2. Structural Example of Sustainable Forest Management

As Figure 2 shows, additional value can be added to the certified woods by means of putting the certification labels because of the recent activation of green consumerism. Private foresters can improve their social images through selling eco-friendly certified products. The certified forests help prevent environmental destruction by afforestation managed with technical standards regulating logging methods, tree species and maintenance of logging roads for biodiversity and security of the employment. Environmental value of the certified woods has already been internalized, for example setting the price of certified woods at 20% higher than the non-certified woods.

In activating more and more such environment-oriented forestry systems, the environmental economic evaluation approach focused in this study is quite useful clarifying the objective environmental values of the systems and persuading both foresters and consumers to be actively involved into the sustainable forestry and environmental conservation.

References

[1] Bennett, J.W., and Carter, M., "Prospects for Contingent Valuation : Lessons from the South-East Forests", *Australian Journal of Agricultural Economics*, Australian Agricultural and Resource Economics Society, Vol.37(02), pp.1207-1254 (1993)

[2] Dartmouth Flood Observatory, "Global Flood Detection, Mapping, and Measurement", http://www.dartmouth.edu/~floods/index.html

[3] DASM, "Agricultural Statistics of Sabah 2000-2001" (2002)

[4] Department of Fisheries, Sabah, "Statistic of Agriculture, Livestock and Fisheries Sector", Sabah (1994)

[5] Department of Wildlife and National Parks, Peninsular Malaysia, http://www.wildlife.gov.my/

[6] Deramakot Forest Reserve, "Implementation of Reduced Impact Logging (RIL) in Sabah", (2001)

[7] Dixon, J.A., et al., "Economic Analysis of the Environmental Impacts of Development Projects", Asian Development Bank (1986)

[8] Dixon, J.A., et al., "Economic Analysis of Environmental Impacts", ADB/WB, Earthscan Publications Ltd, London (1994)

[9] Dixon, J.A., and Hufschmidt, M.M., "Economic Valuation Techniques for the Environment : A Case Study Workbook", Johns Hopkins University Press (1986)

[10] DSMS, "Yearbook of Statistics Sabah 2003" (2004)

[11] Fleming, W.M., "Phewa Tal Catchment Management Program : Benefits and Costs of Forestry and Soil Conservation in Nepal", Forest and Watershed Development and Conservation in Asia and the Pacific, East-West Environment and Policy Institute, Honolulu, pp.217-288 (1983)

[12] Forest Department Sarawak, http://www.forestry.sarawak.gov.my/forweb/homepage.htm

[13] Harashina, S., et al., "Sustainability Assessment", Gakugei Shuppansha (2015)

[14] Hasegawa, H., "Economic Assessment of Environmental Impacts", Tokyo Shuppan (1988)

[15] Hensher, D. A., and Johnson, L.W., "Applied Discrete-Choice Modelling", John Wiley and Sons, p.52 (1981)

[16] International Labor Office, "Labor Cost in Manufacturing", http://laborsta.ilo.org/

[17] JICA, "The Study on Critical Land and Protection Forest Rehabilitation at Tondano Watershed in Indonesia" (2002)

[18] Kitayama, K., " Actual Vegetation of Mount Kinabalu Park" (1991)

[19] Ma, A.N., "Environmental Management for the Palm Oil Industry", Palm Oil Development, Vol.30, pp.1-10 (2000)

[20] Mannan, S., et al., "The Sabah Forestry Department Experience from Deramakot Forest Reserve : Five Years of Practical Experience in Certified Sustainable Forest Management" Sabah Forestry Department (2002)

[21] Mannan, S., and Awang, Y., "Sustainable Forest Management in Sabah", Seminar on Sustainable Forest Management (1997)

[22] Ministry of Plantation Industries and Commodities, Malaysia, "Statistics on Commodities 2007" (2008)

[23] Ministry of Plantation Industries and Commodities, Malaysia, http://www.wildlife.gov.my/

[24] MPIM, "Statistics on Commodities 2001" (2001)

[25] Research Institute for Humanity and Nature, "Sustainability and Biodiversity Assessment on Forest Utilization Options" (2007)

[26] Ruitenbeek, J. H., "Modeling Economy-Ecology Linkages in Mangroves : Economic Evidence for Promoting Conservation in Bintuni Bay, Indonesia", *Ecological Economics*, Elsevier, Vol.10(3), pp.233-247 (1994)

[27] Sabah Forestry Department, "Annual Report 2001" (2000)

[28] Sabah Wildlife Department, http://www.sabah.gov.my/jhl/

Chapter 4

A Comparative Study on Grouping Methods for an Adaptive Differential Evolution

Setsuko Sakai and Tetsuyuki Takahama***
Faculty of Commercial Sciences, Hiroshima Shudo University
1-1 Ozuka-Higashi 1-chome, Asaminami-ku, Hiroshima, JAPAN 731-3195
*** Graduate School of Information Sciences, Hiroshima City University*
4-1 Ozuka-Higashi 3-chome, Asaminami-ku, Hiroshima, JAPAN 731-3194

Abstract

Differential Evolution (DE) has been successfully applied to various optimization problems. The performance of DE is affected by algorithm parameters such as a scaling factor F and a crossover rate CR. Many studies have been done to control the parameters adaptively. One of the most successful studies on controlling the parameters is JADE. In JADE, the values of each parameter are generated according to one probability density function (PDF) which is learned by the values in success cases where the child is better than the parent. However, search performance might be improved by learning multiple PDFs for each parameter based on some characteristics of search points. In this study, search points are divided into plural groups according to some criteria and PDFs are learned by parameter values in success cases for each group. Objective values and distances from a reference point, which is the best search point or the centroid of search points, are adopted as the criteria. The effect of JADE with group-based learning is shown by solving thirteen benchmark problems.

Key Words:

Adaptive differential evolution, Group-based learning, Differential evolution, Evolutionary algorithms

1. Introduction

Optimization problems, especially nonlinear optimization problems, are very important and frequently appear in the real world. There exist many studies on solving optimization problems using evolutionary algorithms (EAs). Differential evolution (DE) is an EA proposed by Storn and Price [1]. DE has been successfully applied to optimization problems including non-linear, non-differentiable, non-convex and multimodal functions [2–4]. It has been shown that DE is a very fast and robust algorithm.

The performance of DE is affected by algorithm parameters such as a scaling factor F, a crossover rate CR and population size, and by mutation strategies such as a rand strategy and a best strategy. Many studies have been done to control the parameters and the strategies. One of the most successful studies on controlling the parameters is JADE (adaptive DE with optional external archive) [5]. In JADE, the values of parameters F and CR are generated according to the corresponding probability density function (PDF) and a child is created from the parent using the generated values. The values in success cases, where the child is better than the parent, are used to learn the PDFs. As for F, a location parameter of Cauchy distribution is learned, the scale parameter is fixed and values of F are generated according to the Cauchy distribution. As for CR, a mean of normal distribution is learned, the standard deviation is fixed and values of CR are generated according to the normal distribution. However, search performance might be improved by learning multiple PDFs for F and CR based on some characteristics of search points.

In this study, group-based learning of the PDFs is proposed. Search points are divided into plural groups according to some criteria and the PDFs are learned by parameter values in success cases for each group. The criteria include objective values and distances from a reference point such as the best search point or the centroid of search points. The effect of JADE with group-based learning is shown by solving thirteen benchmark problems.

In Section 2, related works are described. DE and JADE are briefly explained in Section 3. In Section 4, JADE with group-based learning is proposed. The experimental results are shown in Section 5. Finally, conclusions are described in Section 6.

2. Related Works

The performance of DE is affected by control parameters such as the scaling factor F, the crossover rate CR and the population size N, and by mutation strategies such as the rand strategy and the best strategy. Many researchers have been studying on controlling the parameters and the strategies. The methods of the control can be classified into some categories as follows:

The methods of controlling algorithm parameters can be classified into some categories as follows:

(1) selection-based control: Strategies and parameter values are selected regardless of current search state. CoDE (composite DE) [6] generates three trial vectors using three strategies with randomly selected parameter values from parameter candidate sets and the best trial vector will head to the survivor selection.

(2) observation-based control: The current search state is observed, proper parameter values are inferred according to the observation, and parameters and/or strategies are dynamically controlled. FADE (Fuzzy Adaptive DE) [7] observes the movement of search points and the change of function values between successive generations, and controls F and CR. DESFC (DE with Speciation and Fuzzy Clustering) [8] adopts fuzzy clustering, observes partition entropy of search points, and controls CR and the mutation strategies between the rand and the species-best strategy. LMDE (DE with detecting Landscape Modality) [9–11] detects the landscape modality such as unimodal or multimodal using the change of the objective values at sampling points which are equally spaced along a line. If the landscape is unimodal, greedy parameter settings for local search are selected. Otherwise, parameter settings for global search are selected.

(3) success-based control: It is recognized as a success case when a better search point than the parent is generated. The parameters and/or strategies are adjusted so that the values in the success cases are frequently used. It is thought that the self-adaptation, where parameters are contained in individuals and are evolved by applying evolutionary operators to the parameters, is included in this category. DESAP (DE with Self-Adapting Populations) [12] controls F, CR and N self-adaptively. SaDE (Self-adaptive DE) [13] controls the selection probability of the mutation strategies according to the success rates and controls the

mean value of CR for each strategy according to the mean value in success case. jDE (self-adaptive DE algorithm) [14] controls F and CR self-adaptively. JADE(adaptive DE with optional external archive) [5] and MDE_pBX (modified DE with p-best crossover) [15] control the mean or power mean values of F and CR according to the mean values in success cases. CADE (Correlation-based Adaptive DE) [16] introduces the correlation of F and CR to JADE.

In the category (1), useful knowledge to improve the search efficiency is ignored. In the category (2), it is difficult to select proper type of observation which is independent of the optimization problem and its scale. In the category (3), when a new good search point is found near the parent, parameters are adjusted to the direction of convergence. In problems with ridge landscape or multimodal landscape, where good search points exist in small region, parameters are tuned for small success and big success will be missed. Thus, search process would be trapped at a local optimal solution. In JADE, as for a mean value of F a weighted mean value by the value of F is used to generate larger F than a usual mean value and it is succeeded to reduce the problem of the convergence.

In this study, we propose to improve JADE in the category (3) by introducing group-based learning of the PDFs.

3. Optimization by Differential Evolution

3.1 Optimization Problems

In this study, the following optimization problem with lower bound and upper bound constraints will be discussed.

$$\begin{aligned} \text{minimize} \quad & f(\boldsymbol{x}) \\ \text{subject to} \quad & l_i \leq x_i \leq u_i, \ i = 1, \ldots, D, \end{aligned} \quad (1)$$

where $\boldsymbol{x} = (x_1, x_2, \cdots, x_D)$ is a D dimensional vector and $f(\boldsymbol{x})$ is an objective function. The function f is a nonlinear real-valued function. Values l_i and u_i are the lower bound and the upper bound of x_i, respectively. Let the search space in which every point satisfies the lower and upper bound constraints be denoted by $\mathfrak{S}$.

3.2 Differential Evolution

DE is an evolutionary algorithm proposed by Storn and Price [1, 17]. DE has been successfully applied to the optimization problems including non-linear, non-differentiable, non-convex and multimodal functions. It has been shown that DE is fast and robust to these functions [3].

In DE, initial individuals are randomly generated within given search space and form an initial population. Each individual contains D genes as decision variables. At each generation or iteration, all individuals are selected as parents. Each parent is processed as follows: The mutation operation begins by choosing several individuals from the population except for the parent in the processing. The first individual is a base vector. All subsequent individuals are paired to create difference vectors. The difference vectors are scaled by a scaling factor F and added to the base vector. The resulting vector, or a mutant vector, is then recombined with the parent. The probability of recombination at an element is controlled by a crossover rate CR. This crossover operation produces a child, or a trial vector. Finally, for survivor selection, the trial vector is accepted for the next generation if the trial vector is better than the parent.

There are some variants of DE that have been proposed. The variants are classified using the notation DE/*base*/*num*/*cross* such as DE/rand/1/bin and DE/rand/1/exp.

"*base*" specifies a way of selecting an individual that will form the base vector. For example, DE/rand selects an individual for the base vector at random from the population. DE/best selects the best individual in the population.

"*num*" specifies the number of difference vectors used to perturb the base vector. In case of DE/rand/1, for example, for each parent x^i, three individuals x^{r1}, x^{r2} and x^{r3} are chosen randomly from the population without overlapping x^i and each other. A new vector, or a mutant vector x' is generated by the base vector x^{r1} and the difference vector $x^{r2} - x^{r3}$, where F is the scaling factor.

$$x' = x^{r1} + F(x^{r2} - x^{r3}) \tag{2}$$

"*cross*" specifies the type of crossover that is used to create a child. For example, 'bin' indicates that the crossover is controlled by the binomial crossover using a constant crossover rate, and 'exp' indicates that the crossover is controlled by a kind of two-point crossover using exponentially decreasing the crossover rate. Figure 1 shows the binomial and exponential crossover. A new child x^{child} is generated from the parent x^i and the mutant vector x', where CR is a crossover rate.

```
binomial crossover DE/·/·/bin
  j_rand=randint(1,D);
  for(k=1; k≤D; k++) {
    if(k == j_rand || u(0,1) < CR) x_k^child=x'_k;
    else x_k^child=x_k^i;
  }
exponential crossover DE/·/·/exp
  k=1; j=randint(1,D);
  do {
    x_j^child=x'_j;
    k=k+1; j=(j+1)%D;
  } while(k ≤ D && u(0,1) < CR);
  while(k ≤ D) {
    x_j^child=x_j^i;
    k=k+1; j=(j+1)%D;
  }
```

Figure 1. Binomial and exponential crossover operation, where randint$(1,D)$ generates an integer randomly from $[1, D]$ and $u(l, r)$ is a uniform random number generator in $[l, r]$.

The algorithm of DE is as follows:

Step1 Initialization of a population. Initial N individuals $P = \{x^i, i = 1, 2, \cdots, N\}$ are generated randomly in search space and form an initial population.

Step2 Termination condition. If the number of function evaluations exceeds the maximum number of evaluation $FE_{\max}$, the algorithm is terminated.

Step3 DE operations. Each individual x^i is selected as a parent. If all individuals are selected, go to Step4. A mutant vector x' is generated according to Eq. (2). A trial vector (child) is generated from the parent x^i and the mutant vector x' using a crossover operation shown in Figure 1. If the child is better than or equal to the parent, or the DE operation is succeeded, the child survives. Otherwise the parent survives. Go back to Step3 and the next individual is selected as a parent.

Step4 Survivor selection (generation change). The population is organized by the survivors. Go back to Step2.

Figure 2 shows a pseudo-code of DE/rand/1.

```
DE/rand/1()
{
// Initialize an population
 P=N individuals generated randomly in 𝔖;
 for(t=1; FE ≤ FE_max; t++) {
  for(i=1; i ≤ N; i++) {
// DE operation
   x^{r1}=Randomly selected from P(r1 ≠ i);
   x^{r2}=Randomly selected from P(r2 ∉ {i,r1});
   x^{r3}=Randomly selected from P(r3 ∉ {i,r1,r2});
   x'=x^{r1}+F(x^{r2} − x^{r3});
   x^{child}=trial vector is generated from x^i and x'
         by the crossover operation;
// Survivor selection
   if(f(x^{child}) ≤ f(x^i)) z^i=x^{child};
   else                     z^i=x^i;
   FE=FE+1;
  }
  P={z^i, i = 1, 2, ···, N};
 }
}
```

Figure 2. The pseudo-code of DE, FE is the number of function evaluations.

3.3 JADE

In JADE, the mean value of the scaling factor μ_F and the mean value of the crossover rate μ_{CR} are learned to define two PDFs, where initial values are $\mu_F=\mu_{CR}=0.5$. The scaling factor F_i and the crossover rate CR_i for each individual x^i are independently generated according to the two functions as follows:

$$F_i \sim C(\mu_F, \sigma_F) \quad (3)$$
$$CR_i \sim N(\mu_{CR}, \sigma_{CR}^2) \quad (4)$$

where F_i is a random variable according to a Cauchy distribution $C(\mu_F, \sigma_F)$ with a location parameter μ_F and a scale parameter $\sigma_F=0.1$. CR_i is a random variable according to a normal distribution $N(\mu_{CR}, \sigma_{CR}^2)$ of a mean μ_{CR} and a standard deviation $\sigma_{CR}=0.1$. CR_i is truncated to $[0, 1]$ and F_i is truncated to be 1 if $F_i > 1$ or regenerated if $F_i \leq 0$. The location μ_F and the mean μ_{CR} are updated as follows:

$$\mu_F = (1-c)\mu_F + cS_{F2}/S_F \quad (5)$$
$$\mu_{CR} = (1-c)\mu_{CR} + cS_{CR}/S_N \quad (6)$$

where S_N is the number of success cases, S_F, S_{F^2} and S_{CR} are the sum of F, F^2 and CR in success cases, respectively. A constant c is a weight of update in (0,1] and the recommended value is 0.1.

JADE adopts a strategy called "current-to-pbest" where an intermediate point between a target vector and a randomly selected point from top individuals is used as a base vector. A mutation vector is generated by current-to-pbest without archive as follows:

$$\bm{m} = \bm{x}^i + F_i(\bm{x}^{pbest} - \bm{x}^i) + F_i(\bm{x}^{r2} - \bm{x}^{r3}) \tag{7}$$

where $\bm{x}^{pbest}$ is a randomly selected individual from the top $100p\%$ individuals. When an external archive is adopted, a mutant vector is generated by current-to-pbest with archive as follows:

$$\bm{m} = \bm{x}^i + F_i(\bm{x}^{pbest} - \bm{x}^i) + F_i(\bm{x}^{r2} - \widetilde{\bm{x}}^{r3}) \tag{8}$$

where $\widetilde{\bm{x}}^{r3}$ is selected randomly from the union of the current population and the archive. The archive is initialized to be empty. Defeated parents by the children are added to the archive. If the number of archived individuals exceeds the maximum archive size, randomly selected individuals are removed from the archive to keep the maximum archive size. The archive provides information about the progress direction and is also capable of improving the diversity of the population.

In order to satisfy bound constraints, a child that is outside of the search space $\mathfrak{S}$ is moved into the inside of $\mathfrak{S}$. In JADE, each outside element of the child is set to be the middle between the corresponding boundary and the element of the parent as follows:

$$x_j^{child} = \begin{cases} \frac{1}{2}(l_j + x_j^i), & \text{if } x_j^{child} < l_j \\ \frac{1}{2}(u_j + x_j^i), & \text{if } x_j^{child} > u_j \end{cases} \tag{9}$$

This operation is applied when a new point is generated by JADE operations.

4. Proposed Method

4.1 Group-based learning

In this study, a population of individuals $\{\bm{x}^i \mid i = 1, 2, \cdots, N\}$ is divided into K groups according to a criterion, where N is the number of individuals and K is the number of groups. All individuals are sorted according to the criterion and the rank r_i $(r_i = 1, 2, \cdots, N)$ is assigned to each individual $\bm{x}^i$. The following criteria are adopted:

Objective Objective value of each individual is used as the criteria. The rank of the best individual, who has the best objective value, is 1. In case of $K = 2$, the individuals are divided into good individuals (group id 1) and bad individuals (group id is 2).

Dbest The distance between the best individual and each individual is used as the criteria. The rank of the best individual is 1 because the distance is zero. In case of $K=2$, the individuals are divided into near individuals from the best individual (group id is 1) and far individuals from it (group id is 2).

Dcentroid The distance between the centroid of all individuals and each individual is used as the criteria. In case of $K=2$, the individuals are divided into near individuals from the centroid (group id is 1) and far individuals from it (group id is 2).

Random The group ids are randomly selected from $[1, K]$. This criterion is added to see whether group learning without any criterion is effective or not.

The group id of x^i, $group(x^i)$ is defined as follows:

$$group(x^i) = \left\lceil \frac{r_i}{N} K \right\rceil \quad (10)$$

In order to realize group-based learning using parameter control of JADE, the following equations are adopted for each group $k = 1, \cdots, K$.

$$F_i \sim C(\mu_F^k, \sigma_F) \quad (11)$$
$$CR_i \sim N(\mu_{CR}^k, \sigma_{CR}^2) \quad (12)$$
$$\mu_F^k = (1-c)\mu_F^k + cS_{F^2}^k/S_F^k \quad (13)$$
$$\mu_{CR}^k = (1-c)\mu_{CR}^k + cS_{CR}^k/S_N^k \quad (14)$$

where μ_F^k is the location of Cauchy distribution for F in group k, μ_{CR}^k is the mean of normal distribution for CR in group k. S_N^k is the number of success cases in group k, where the better child than the parent is generated. S_F^k, $S_{F^2}^k$ and S_{CR}^k are the sum of F_i, F_i^2, CR_i at success cases in group k, respectively. As well as JADE, CR_i is truncated to $[0, 1]$ and F_i is truncated to be 1 if $F_i > 1$ or regenerated if $F_i \leq 0$.

4.2 Algorithm

The algorithm of JADE with group-based learning can be described as follows:

Step0 Parameter setup. A criterion for grouping is specified. The location values of scaling factor μ_F^k=0.5 and the mean values of crossover rate μ_{CR}^k=0.5 ($k = 1, 2, \cdots, K$). The scale parameter σ_F=0.1 and the standard deviation σ_{CR}=0.1.

Step1 Initialization of the individuals. N individuals $\{x^i | i = 1, 2, \cdots, N\}$ are generated randomly in search space $\mathfrak{S}$ and form an initial population.

Step2 Termination condition. If the number of function evaluations exceeds the maximum number of evaluations $FE_{\max}$, the algorithm is terminated.

Step3 Initialization for each generation. The individuals are sorted according to a specified criterion and the ranks of x^i, $r_i, i = 1, 2, \cdots, N$, are obtained. The list of success cases S^k is made empty ($k = 1, 2, \cdots, K$).

Step4 DE operation with adaptive parameters. For each individual x^i, the group id $k = group(x^i)$ is obtained according to Eq. (10). The scaling factor F_i is generated according to the Cauchy distribution for group k as Eq. (11). The crossover rate CR_i is generated according to the normal distribution for group k as Eq. (12). DE/current-to-pbest/1/bin is executed and a new child is generated.

Step5 Survivor selection. If the child is better than the parent, the operation is treated as a success case and the child becomes a survivor. The successful pair of parameter values (F_i, CR_i) is added to success cases S^k. Otherwise, the parent x^i becomes a survivor. Go back to Step 4 until all individuals are processed.

Step6 Learning of parameters. The locations of the scaling factor μ_F^k and the means of crossover rate μ_{CR}^k are updated using S^k ($k = 1, 2, \cdots, K$) according to Eqs. (13) and (14).

Step7 Go back to Step2.

Figure 3 shows the pseudo-code of the proposed method. Lines starting with '+' shows the modified lines from original JADE.

```
JADE/current-to-pbest/1/bin with group learning()
{
+  μ_F^k = μ_CR^k=0.5  (1≤k≤K);
   σ_F = σ_CR=0.1;
// Initialize a population
   P=N individuals generated randomly in 𝔖;
   FE=FE+N;
   for(t=1; FE < FE_max; t++) {
+      S^k = φ  (1≤k≤K);
+      sort P and obtain rank values r_i;
       for(i=1; i≤N; i++) {
+         k=group(x^i);
+         CR_i = μ_CR^k + N(0, σ_CR^2);
          if(CR_i < 0)  CR_i=0;
          else if(CR_i > 1)  CR_i=1;
          do {
+            F_i=μ_F^k + C(0, σ_F);
          } while(F_i ≤ 0);
          if(F_i > 1)  F_i = 1;
          x^pbest = Randomly selected from top 100p% in P;
          x^r1 = Randomly selected from P(r1 ∉ {i});
          x^r2 = Randomly selected from P(r2 ∉ {i,r1});
          m^i = x^i+F_i(x^pbest − x^i)+F_i(x^r1 − x^r2);
          x^child=generated from x^i and m^i
                 by binomial crossover as a trial vector;
          FE=FE+1;
// Survivor selection
          if(f(x^child) < f(z)) {
             z^i = x^child;
             S^k = S^k ∪ {(F_i,CR_i)};  // a success case is added to S^k
          }
          else z^i = x^i;
       }
       P = {z^i};
+      for(k=1; k≤K; k++) {
+         if(|S^k| > 0) {
+            μ_F^k = (1−c)μ_F^k + c∑_{F_i∈S^k} F_i^2/∑_{F_i∈S^k} F_i;
+            μ_CR^k = (1−c)μ_CR^k + c∑_{CR_i∈S^k} CR_i/|S^k|;
          }
+      }
   }
}
```

Figure 3. The pseudo-code of proposed method

A Comparative Study on Grouping Methods for an Adaptive Differential Evolution

5. Numerical Experiments

In this paper, well-known thirteen benchmark problems are solved.

5.1 Test Problems

The 13 scalable benchmark functions are shown in Table 1 [5]. Every function has an optimal objective value 0. Some characteristics are briefly summarized as follows: Functions f_1 to f_4 are continuous unimodal functions. The function f_5 is Rosenbrock function which is unimodal for 2- and 3-dimensions but may have multiple minima in high dimension cases [18]. The function f_6 is a discontinuous step function, and f_7 is a noisy quartic function. Functions f_8 to f_{13} are multimodal functions and the number of their local minima increases exponentially with the problem dimension [19].

5.2 Conditions of Experiments

Experimental conditions are same as JADE as follows: Population size $N = 100$, initial location for scaling factor $\mu_F = 0.5$ or $\mu_F^k = 0.5$ and initial mean for crossover rate $\mu_{CR} = 0.5$ or $\mu_{CR}^k = 0.5$, the pbest parameter $p=0.05$, and the learning parameter $c=0.1$.

Independent 50 runs are performed for 13 problems. The number of dimensions for the problems is 30 ($D=30$). Each run stops when the number of function evaluations (FEs) exceeds the maximum number of evaluations $FE_{\max}$. In each function, different $FE_{\max}$ is adopted.

Three grouping criteria of Objective, Dbest and Dcentroid are examined.

5.3 Experimental Results

Table 2 and 3 show the experimental results on JADE, Objective, Dbest, Dcentroid and Random in case of $K=2$ and $K=3$, respectively. The mean value and the standard deviation of best objective values in 50 runs are shown for each function. The maximum number of evaluations is selected for each function and is shown in column labeled $FE_{\max}$. The best result among algorithms is highlighted using bold face fonts. Also, Wilcoxon signed rank test is performed and the result for each function is shown under the mean value. Symbols '+', '−' and '=' are shown when a grouping criterion is significantly better than JADE, is significantly worse than JADE, and is not significantly different from JADE, respectively. Symbols '++' and '−−' are shown when the significance level is 1% and '+' and '−' are shown when the significance level is 5%.

In case of $K=2$, Objective attained best mean results in 8 functions f_1, f_4, f_5, f_6, f_9, f_{10}, f_{12} and f_{13} out of 13 functions, Dbest attained a best result in the function f_8, Dcentroid attained a best result in function f_2, Random attained a best result in the function f_{11}, and JADE attained best results in 2 functions f_3 and f_7. Also, Objective attained significantly better results than JADE in 8 functions f_1, f_6, f_8, f_9, f_{10}, f_{11}, f_{12} and f_{13}. Dbest attained significantly better results than JADE in 3 functions f_8, f_9 and f_{10}, and significantly worse results than JADE in 2 functions f_3 and f_4. Dcentroid attained significantly better results than JADE in 5 functions f_2, f_6, f_9, f_{12} and f_{13}, and significantly worse results than JADE in a function f_4. Random attained a significantly better result than JADE in a function f_2. Thus, it is thought that Objective is the best method among 4 methods and Dcentroid is the second best method.

In case of $K=3$, Objective attained best mean results in 6 functions f_1, f_2, f_4, f_9, f_{10} and f_{12}, Dbest attained best results in 2 functions f_8 and f_{11}, Dcentroid attained best results in 2 functions f_6 and f_{13}, Random attained a best result in the function f_5, and JADE attained best results in 2 functions f_3 and f_7. Also, Objective attained significantly better results than JADE in 8 functions f_1, f_2, f_6, f_8, f_9, f_{10}, f_{12} and f_{13}. Dbest attained significantly better results than JADE in 6 functions f_2, f_6, f_8, f_9, f_{12} and f_{13}, and a significantly worse result than JADE in the function f_4. Dcentroid attained significantly better results than JADE in 6 functions f_2, f_6, f_9, f_{10}, f_{12} and

Table 1. Test functions of dimension D. These are sphere, Schwefel 2.22, Schwefel 1.2, Schwefel 2.21, Rosenbrock, step, noisy quartic, Schwefel 2.26, Rastrigin, Ackley, Griewank, and two penalized functions, respectively [20]

Test functions	Bound constraints
$f_1(\boldsymbol{x}) = \sum_{i=1}^{D} x_i^2$	$[-100, 100]^D$
$f_2(\boldsymbol{x}) = \sum_{i=1}^{D} |x_i| + \prod_{i=1}^{D} |x_i|$	$[-10, 10]^D$
$f_3(\boldsymbol{x}) = \sum_{i=1}^{D} \left(\sum_{j=1}^{i} x_j \right)^2$	$[-100, 100]^D$
$f_4(\boldsymbol{x}) = \max_i \{|x_i|\}$	$[-100, 100]^D$
$f_5(\boldsymbol{x}) = \sum_{i=1}^{D-1} \left[100(x_{i+1} - x_i^2)^2 + (x_i - 1)^2 \right]$	$[-30, 30]^D$
$f_6(\boldsymbol{x}) = \sum_{i=1}^{D} \lfloor x_i + 0.5 \rfloor^2$	$[-100, 100]^D$
$f_7(\boldsymbol{x}) = \sum_{i=1}^{D} i x_i^4 + rand[0, 1)$	$[-1.28, 1.28]^D$
$f_8(\boldsymbol{x}) = \sum_{i=1}^{D} -x_i \sin \sqrt{|x_i|} + D \cdot 418.98288727243369$	$[-500, 500]^D$
$f_9(\boldsymbol{x}) = \sum_{i=1}^{D} \left[x_i^2 - 10 \cos(2\pi x_i) + 10 \right]$	$[-5.12, 5.12]^D$
$f_{10}(\boldsymbol{x}) = -20 \exp \left(-0.2 \sqrt{\frac{1}{D} \sum_{i=1}^{D} x_i^2} \right) - \exp \left(\frac{1}{D} \sum_{i=1}^{D} \cos(2\pi x_i) \right) + 20 + e$	$[-32, 32]^D$
$f_{11}(\boldsymbol{x}) = \frac{1}{4000} \sum_{i=1}^{D} x_i^2 - \prod_{i=1}^{D} \cos \left(\frac{x_i}{\sqrt{i}} \right) + 1$	$[-600, 600]^D$
$f_{12}(\boldsymbol{x}) = \frac{\pi}{D} [10 \sin^2(\pi y_1) + \sum_{i=1}^{D-1} (y_i - 1)^2 \{1 + 10 \sin^2(\pi y_{i+1})\} + (y_D - 1)^2] + \sum_{i=1}^{D} u(x_i, 10, 100, 4)$ where $y_i = 1 + \frac{1}{4}(x_i + 1)$ and $u(x_i, a, k, m) = \begin{cases} k(x_i - a)^m & x_i > a \\ 0 & -a \leq x_i \leq a \\ k(-x_i - a)^m & x_i < -a \end{cases}$	$[-50, 50]^D$
$f_{13}(\boldsymbol{x}) = 0.1[\sin^2(3\pi x_1) + \sum_{i=1}^{D-1} (x_i - 1)^2 \{1 + \sin^2(3\pi x_{i+1})\} + (x_D - 1)^2 \{1 + \sin^2(2\pi x_D)\}] + \sum_{i=1}^{D} u(x_i, 5, 100, 4)$	$[-50, 50]^D$

Table 2. Experimental results on 13 functions ($K=2$)

	FE_{max}	JADE	Objective	Dbest	Dcentroid	Random
f_1	100,000	3.59e-38 ± 2.3e-37	**5.56e-42 ± 1.1e-41** ++	5.50e-40 ± 1.9e-39 =	3.36e-40 ± 9.5e-40 =	2.26e-39 ± 7.4e-39 =
f_2	100,000	5.69e-17 ± 2.5e-16	8.08e-16 ± 4.6e-15 =	4.05e-17 ± 1.6e-16 =	**5.49e-18 ± 1.2e-17** ++	7.13e-18 ± 2.7e-17 +
f_3	200,000	**4.73e-22 ± 9.9e-22**	1.46e-21 ± 6.8e-21 =	1.87e-21 ± 5.5e-21 −	1.15e-21 ± 3.8e-21 =	1.40e-21 ± 5.8e-21 =
f_4	200,000	1.85e-09 ± 8.0e-09	**1.46e-09 ± 4.7e-09** =	2.80e-09 ± 5.4e-09 −−	4.28e-09 ± 1.1e-08 −−	1.89e-09 ± 4.5e-09 =
f_5	300,000	5.78e-01 ± 3.5e+00	**7.97e-02 ± 5.6e-01** =	2.39e-01 ± 9.5e-01 =	3.99e-01 ± 1.2e+00 =	1.59e-01 ± 7.8e-01 =
f_6	10,000	3.02e+00 ± 1.3e+00	**1.78e+00 ± 1.2e+00** ++	2.62e+00 ± 1.3e+00 =	2.18e+00 ± 1.2e+00 ++	3.10e+00 ± 1.2e+00 =
f_7	300,000	**6.04e-04 ± 2.4e-04**	7.11e-04 ± 2.3e-04 =	6.94e-04 ± 2.4e-04 =	6.13e-04 ± 2.1e-04 =	6.79e-04 ± 2.5e-04 =
f_8	100,000	2.37e+00 ± 1.7e+01	2.46e-05 ± 3.1e-05 ++	**2.43e-05 ± 2.4e-05** ++	2.83e-05 ± 1.9e-05 =	4.22e-05 ± 6.5e-05 =
f_9	100,000	1.01e-04 ± 3.9e-05	**5.64e-05 ± 2.8e-05** ++	7.72e-05 ± 3.9e-05 =	6.78e-05 ± 3.3e-05 ++	9.65e-05 ± 4.6e-05 =
f_{10}	50,000	9.20e-10 ± 6.4e-10	**4.22e-10 ± 3.0e-10** ++	6.23e-10 ± 3.7e-10 ++	7.68e-10 ± 6.5e-10 =	8.35e-10 ± 1.1e-09 =
f_{11}	50,000	1.15e-08 ± 6.9e-08	1.97e-04 ± 1.4e-03 +	5.42e-04 ± 2.9e-03 =	1.98e-04 ± 1.4e-03 =	**1.75e-09 ± 1.2e-08** =
f_{12}	50,000	2.40e-16 ± 1.6e-15	**4.99e-18 ± 2.6e-17** ++	1.21e-17 ± 4.7e-17 =	1.65e-17 ± 6.4e-17 +	5.99e-17 ± 5.6e-16 =
f_{13}	50,000	1.15e-16 ± 2.2e-16	**2.17e-17 ± 5.1e-17** ++	3.61e-16 ± 1.5e-15 =	4.54e-17 ± 1.2e-16 ++	7.46e-17 ± 1.9e-16 =
+			8	3	5	1
=			5	8	7	12
−			0	2	1	0

Table 3. Experimental results on 13 functions ($K=3$)

	$FE_{\max}$	JADE	Objective	Dbest	Dcentroid	Random
f_1	100,000	3.59e-38 ± 2.3e-37	**3.49e-41 ± 1.1e-40** ++	1.48e-39 ± 7.9e-39 =	3.55e-40 ± 1.7e-39 =	4.51e-39 ± 2.5e-38 =
f_2	100,000	5.69e-17 ± 2.5e-16	**1.99e-18 ± 4.8e-18** ++	7.08e-18 ± 3.1e-17 ++	6.12e-18 ± 2.5e-17 ++	3.59e-17 ± 2.3e-16 +
f_3	200,000	**4.73e-22 ± 9.9e-22**	7.39e-22 ± 1.9e-21 =	9.50e-22 ± 2.6e-21 =	8.57e-22 ± 3.6e-21 =	2.39e-21 ± 1.5e-20 =
f_4	200,000	1.85e-09 ± 8.0e-09	**1.48e-09 ± 3.6e-09** =	5.41e-09 ± 1.9e-08 --	4.50e-09 ± 8.1e-09 --	3.13e-09 ± 1.3e-08 =
f_5	300,000	5.78e-01 ± 3.5e+00	7.26e-01 ± 3.5e+00 =	3.99e-01 ± 1.2e+00 =	3.99e-01 ± 1.2e+00 =	**2.39e-01 ± 9.5e-01**
f_6	10,000	3.02e+00 ± 1.3e+00	1.98e+00 ± 1.1e+00 ++	2.40e+00 ± 1.0e+00 ++	**1.84e+00 ± 1.1e+00** ++	2.82e+00 ± 1.1e+00 =
f_7	300,000	**6.04e-04 ± 2.4e-04**	6.80e-04 ± 2.2e-04 =	7.02e-04 ± 2.3e-04 =	6.91e-04 ± 1.9e-04 =	6.76e-04 ± 2.1e-04 =
f_8	100,000	2.37e+00 ± 1.7e+01	1.18e+01 ± 3.6e+01 +	**2.34e-05 ± 2.0e-05** +	4.74e+00 ± 2.3e+01 =	4.74e+00 ± 2.3e+01 =
f_9	100,000	1.01e-04 ± 3.9e-05	**5.95e-05 ± 3.0e-05** ++	6.52e-05 ± 3.1e-05 ++	6.46e-05 ± 3.7e-05 ++	1.00e-04 ± 4.8e-05 =
f_{10}	50,000	9.20e-10 ± 6.4e-10	**3.41e-10 ± 3.1e-10** ++	7.83e-10 ± 1.0e-09 =	6.00e-10 ± 5.6e-10 ++	7.61e-10 ± 8.6e-10 =
f_{11}	50,000	1.15e-08 ± 6.9e-08	3.46e-04 ± 1.7e-03 =	**5.03e-10 ± 3.5e-09** =	2.96e-04 ± 1.4e-03 =	1.48e-04 ± 1.0e-03 +
f_{12}	50,000	2.40e-16 ± 1.6e-15	**1.37e-18 ± 5.5e-18** ++	2.36e-18 ± 3.8e-18 ++	2.64e-18 ± 6.9e-18 ++	6.13e-18 ± 2.0e-17 +
f_{13}	50,000	1.15e-16 ± 2.2e-16	1.69e-17 ± 7.5e-17 ++	3.60e-17 ± 9.4e-17 ++	**1.42e-17 ± 2.2e-17** ++	4.26e-17 ± 8.2e-17 ++
+			8	6	6	4
=			5	6	6	9
−			0	1	1	0

f_{13}, and a significantly worse result than JADE in the function f_4. Random attained significantly better results than JADE in 4 functions f_2, f_{11}, f_{12} and f_{13}. Thus, it is thought that Objective is the best method among 4 methods and Dbest and Dcentroid are the second best methods. Also, it is thought that the number of groups K=3 is better than K=2 because better statistic results are shown in Dbest, Dcentroid and Random.

Figures 4 to 16 and Figures 17 to 29 show the change of best objective value found, F and CR over the number of function evaluations in case of K=2 and K=3, respectively.

In case of K=2, Random learned nearly same parameter values as those of JADE in almost all functions except for smaller values of CR in f_7. Smaller values of F and CR than those of JADE for group 1 and larger values of F and CR than those of JADE for group 2 are learned by Objective, Dbest and Dcentroid in f_1, f_2, f_{10}, f_{11}, f_{12} and f_{13}. Smaller values of F for group 1, larger values of F for group 2, and nearly same values of CR as those of JADE for group 1 and 2 are learned in f_3, f_4, f_5 and f_6. In f_7, parameter values of F and CR for group 1 are smaller than those of JADE, and parameter values for group 2 are nearly same as those of JADE. In f_8 and f_9, parameter values of F and CR for group 1 and group 2 are nearly same as those of JADE. Generally in Objective, Dbest and Dcentroid, it is thought that parameters for individuals in group 1 are controlled to intensify convergence and parameters for individuals in group 2 are controlled to keep divergence.

In case of K=3, Random learned nearly same parameter values as those of JADE in almost all functions except for smaller values of CR in f_7. Smaller values of F and CR for group 1, a little smaller values of F and larger values of CR for group 2, and larger values of F and CR than those of JADE for group 3 are learned by Objective, Dbest and Dcentroid in f_1, f_2, f_{10}, f_{11}, f_{12} and f_{13}. Smaller values of F for group 1, nearly same values of F for group 2, and larger values of F for group 3, and nearly same values of CR as those of JADE for all groups are learned in f_3, f_4, f_5 and f_6. In f_7, smaller values of F for group 1, nearly same values of F for group 2, larger values of F for group 3, and smaller values of CR for all groups are learned. In f_8 and f_9, parameter values of F and CR for all groups are nearly same as those of JADE. Generally in Objective, Dbest, and Dcentroid, it is thought that parameters for individuals in group 1 are controlled to intensify convergence, parameters for individuals in group 2 are controlled to realize nearly same control of JADE, and parameters for individuals in group 3 are controlled to keep divergence.

6. Conclusion

In this study, group-based learning of algorithm parameters is proposed, where individuals are divided into plural groups according to some criteria and the parameters are learned for each group. Three criteria including the objective value for each individual, the distance between the best individual and each individual, and the distance between the centroid of individuals and each individual are proposed and tested.

DE with group learning is applied optimization of various 13 functions including unimodal functions, a function with ridge structure, multimodal functions. It is shown that proposed method is effective compared with JADE. Especially, the criterion using the objective value is most effective among three criteria. Also, it is shown that parameters for good individuals are controlled to intensify convergence and parameters for bad individuals are controlled to keep divergence.

In the future, we will apply group-based learning to other adaptive optimization algorithms including differential evolution and particle swarm optimization.

Acknowledgment

This study is supported by JSPS KAKENHI Grant Numbers 26350443.

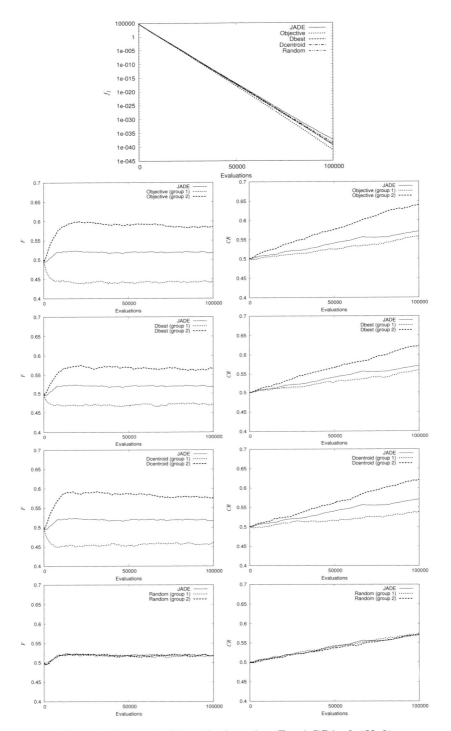

Figure 4. The graph of the objective value, F and CR in f_1 ($K=2$)

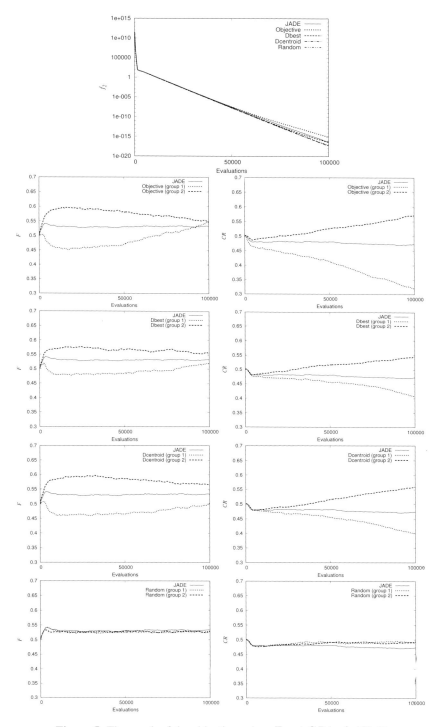

Figure 5. The graph of the objective value, F and CR in f_2 ($K=2$)

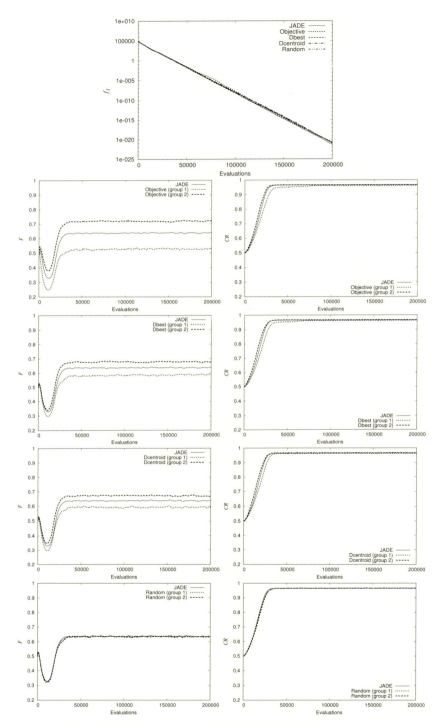

Figure 6. The graph of the objective value, F and CR in f_3 (K=2)

A Comparative Study on Grouping Methods for an Adaptive Differential Evolution 67

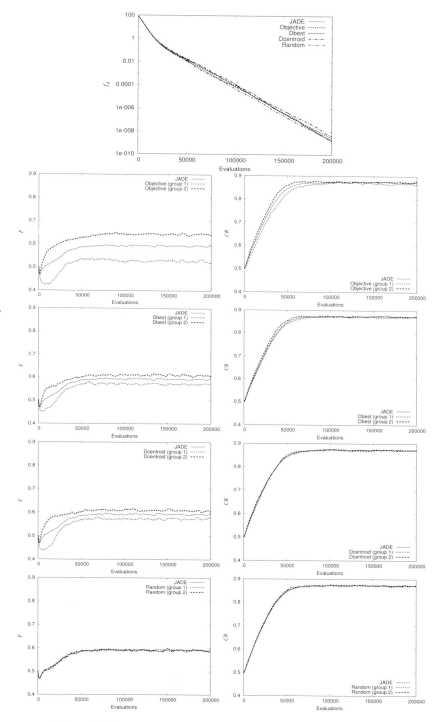

Figure 7. The graph of the objective value, F and CR in f_4 (K=2)

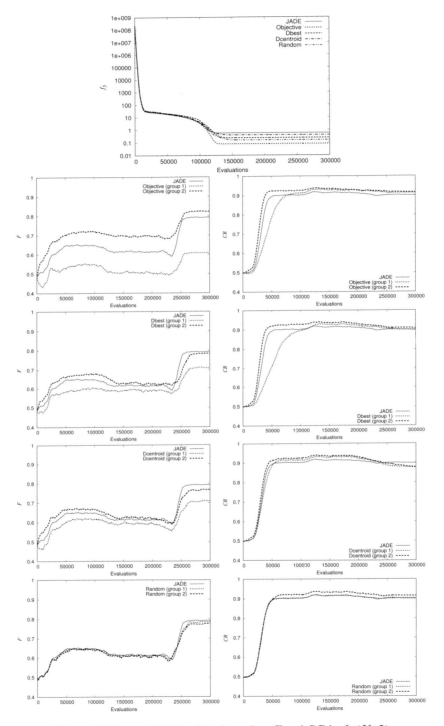

Figure 8. The graph of the objective value, F and CR in f_5 (K=2)

A Comparative Study on Grouping Methods for an Adaptive Differential Evolution

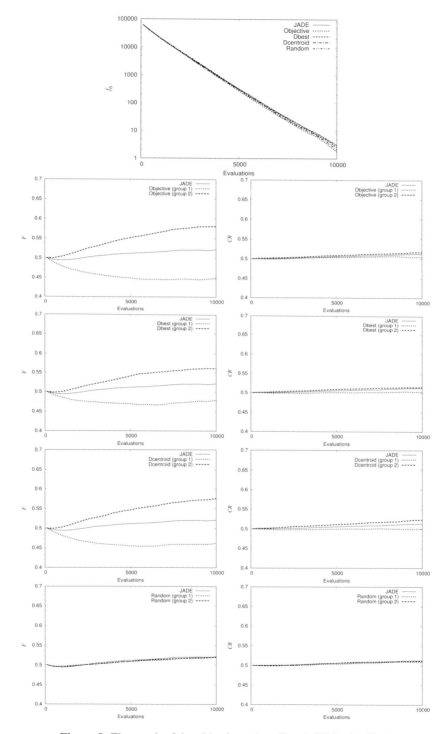

Figure 9. The graph of the objective value, F and CR in f_6 ($K=2$)

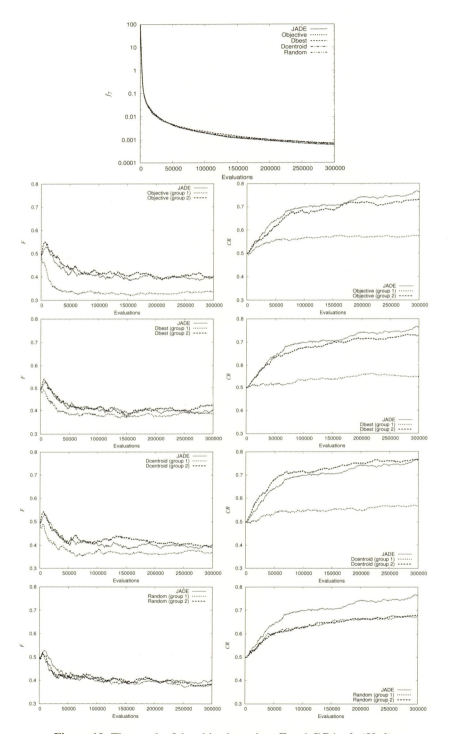

Figure 10. The graph of the objective value, F and CR in f_7 (K=2)

A Comparative Study on Grouping Methods for an Adaptive Differential Evolution 71

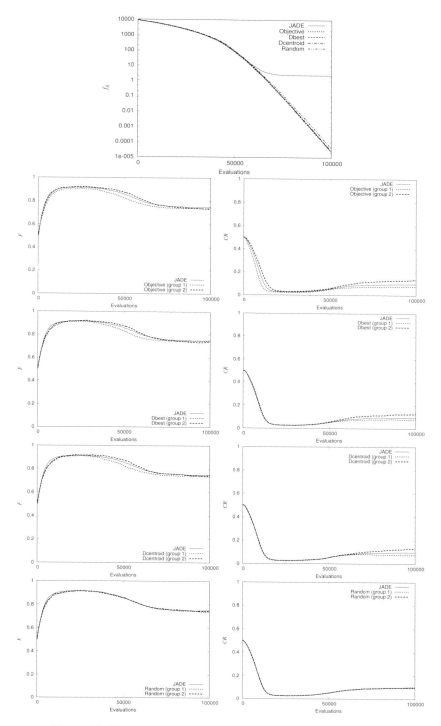

Figure 11. The graph of the objective value, F and CR in f_8 ($K=2$)

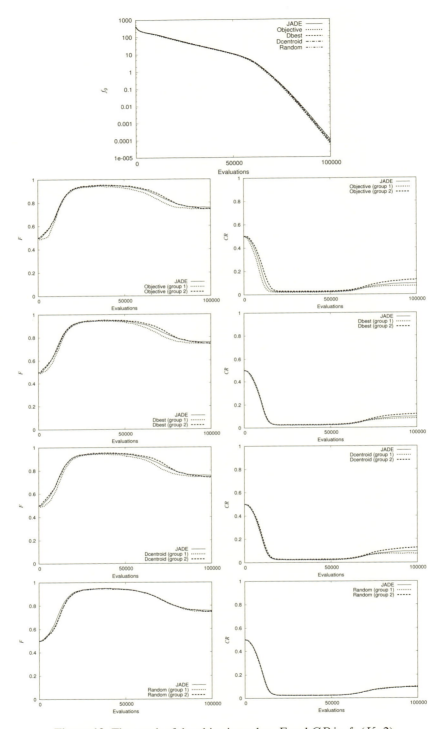

Figure 12. The graph of the objective value, F and CR in f_9 ($K=2$)

A Comparative Study on Grouping Methods for an Adaptive Differential Evolution 73

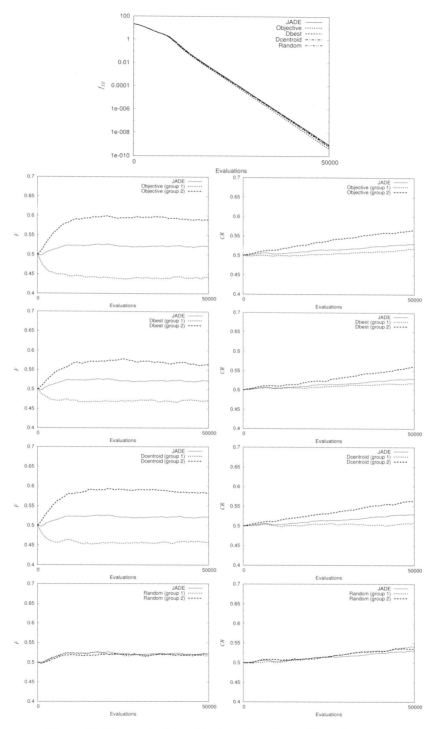

Figure 13. The graph of the objective value, F and CR in f_{10} ($K=2$)

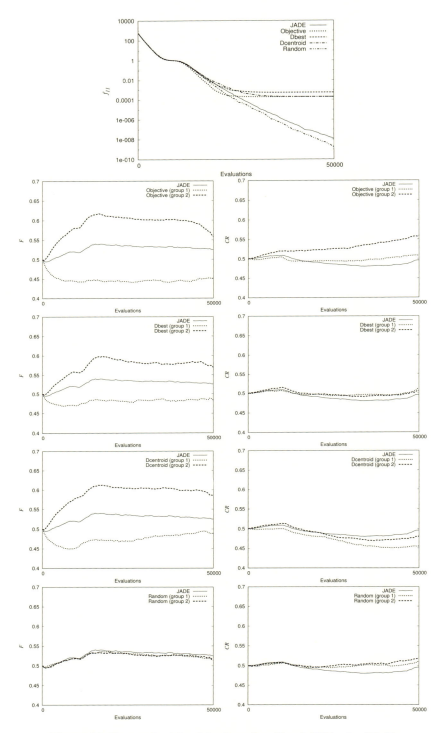

Figure 14. The graph of the objective value, F and CR in f_{11} (K=2)

A Comparative Study on Grouping Methods for an Adaptive Differential Evolution 75

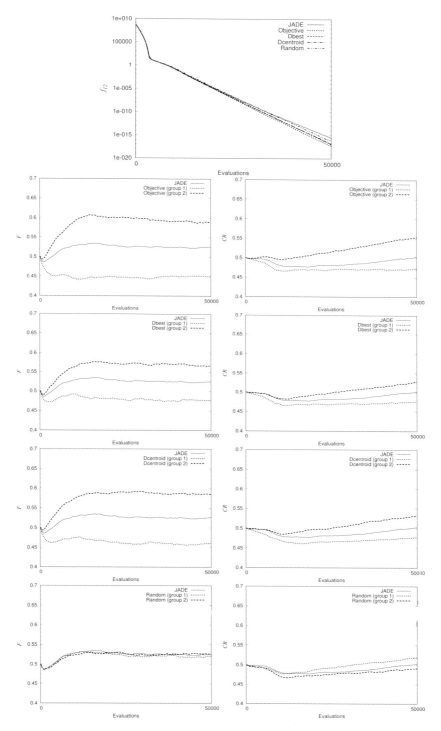

Figure 15. The graph of the objective value, F and CR in f_{12} (K=2)

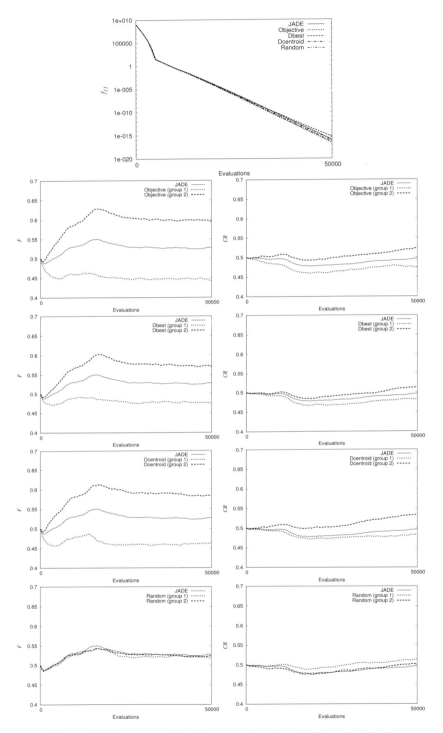

Figure 16. The graph of the objective value, F and CR in f_{13} ($K=2$)

A Comparative Study on Grouping Methods for an Adaptive Differential Evolution 77

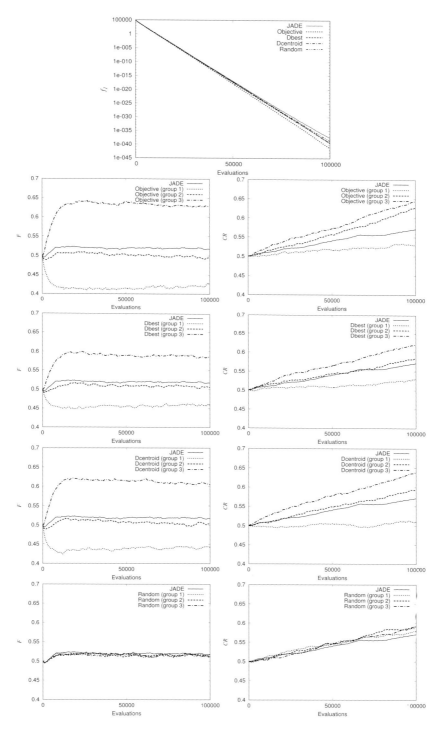

Figure 17. The graph of the objective value, F and CR in f_1 ($K=3$)

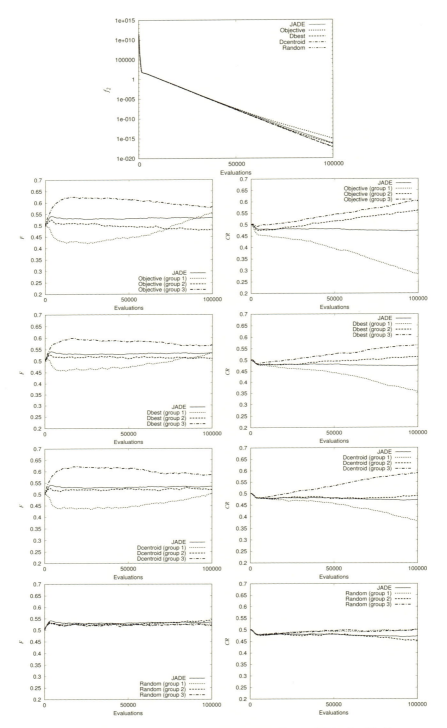

Figure 18. The graph of the objective value, F and CR in f_2 ($K=3$)

A Comparative Study on Grouping Methods for an Adaptive Differential Evolution 79

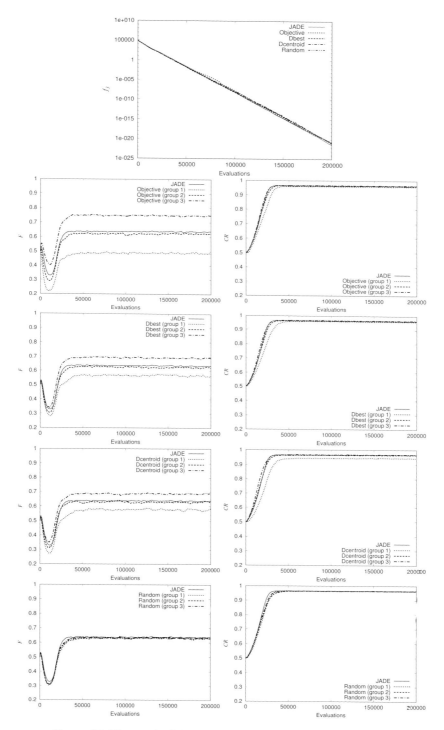

Figure 19. The graph of the objective value, F and CR in f_3 ($K=3$)

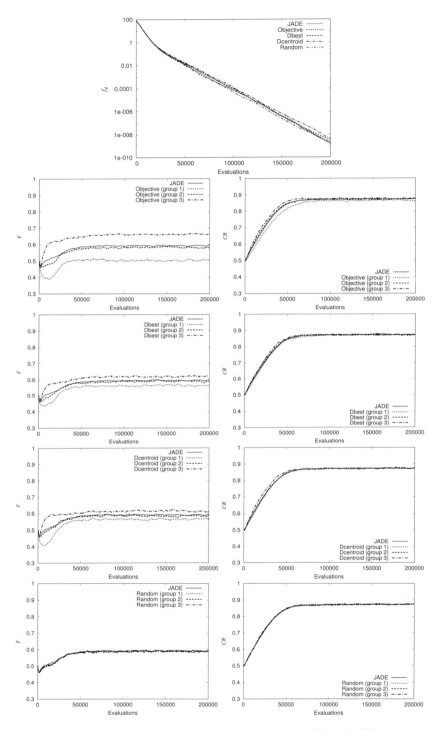

Figure 20. The graph of the objective value, F and CR in f_4 (K=3)

A Comparative Study on Grouping Methods for an Adaptive Differential Evolution

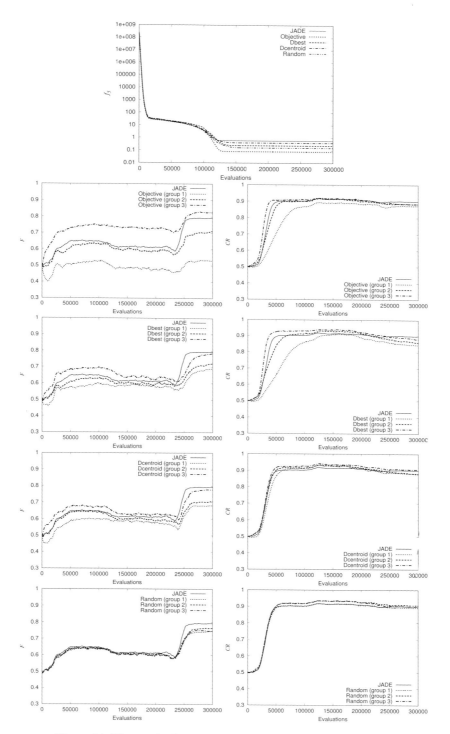

Figure 21. The graph of the objective value, F and CR in f_5 ($K=3$)

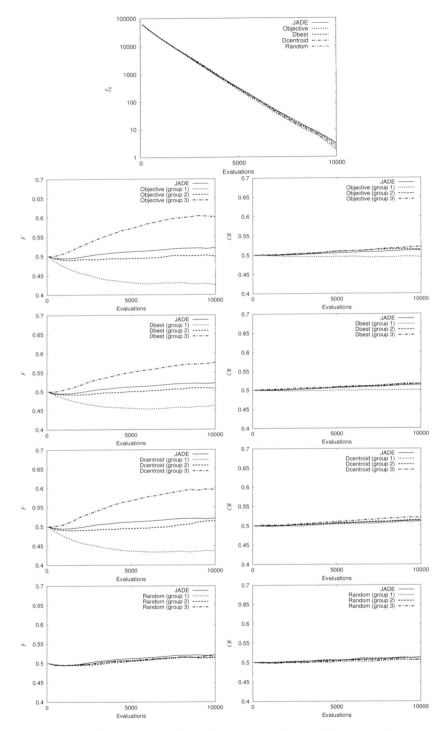

Figure 22. The graph of the objective value, F and CR in f_6 ($K=3$)

A Comparative Study on Grouping Methods for an Adaptive Differential Evolution 83

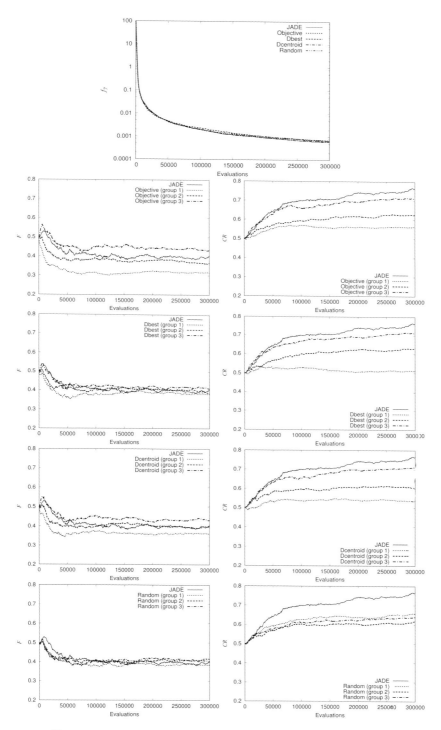

Figure 23. The graph of the objective value, F and CR in f_7 ($K=3$)

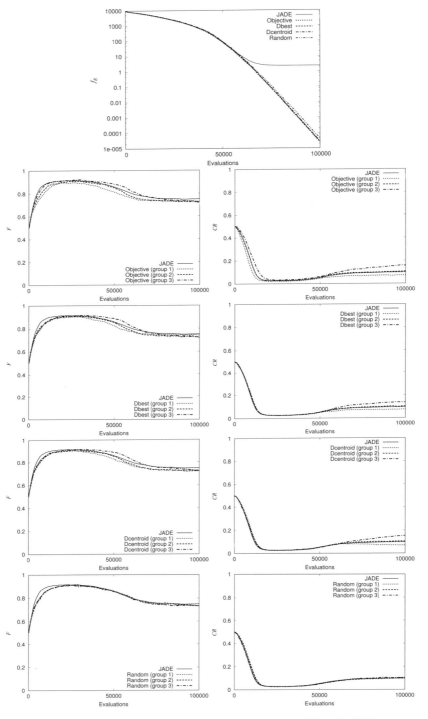

Figure 24. The graph of the objective value, F and CR in f_8 (K=3)

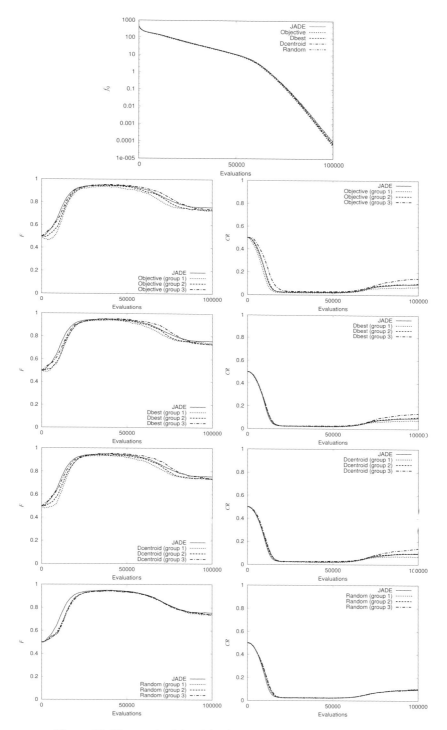

Figure 25. The graph of the objective value, F and CR in f_9 ($K=3$)

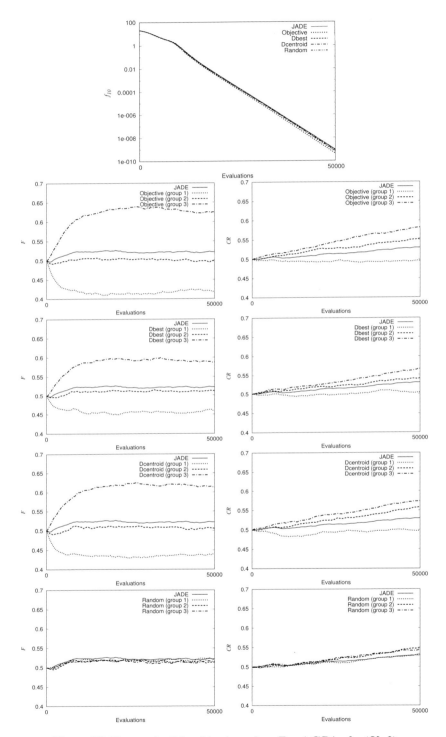

Figure 26. The graph of the objective value, F and CR in f_{10} (K=3)

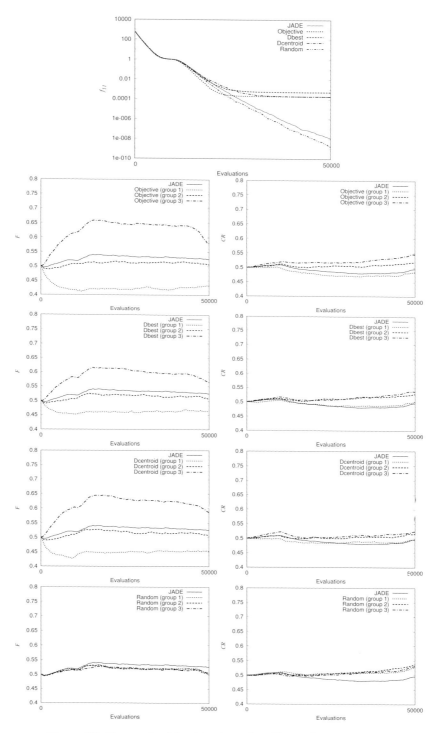

Figure 27. The graph of the objective value, F and CR in f_{11} ($K=3$)

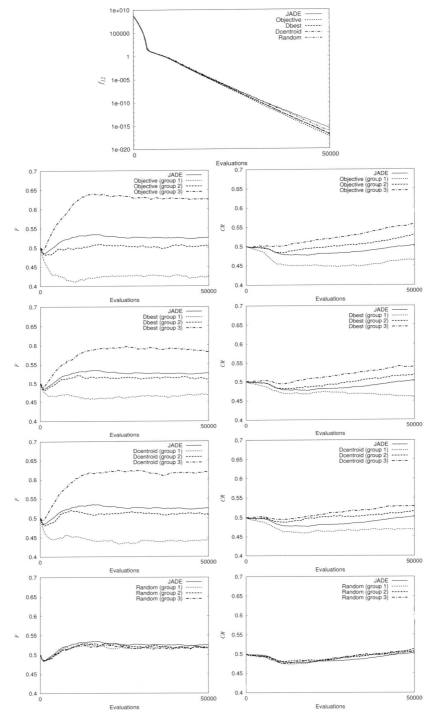

Figure 28. The graph of the objective value, F and CR in f_{12} (K=3)

A Comparative Study on Grouping Methods for an Adaptive Differential Evolution

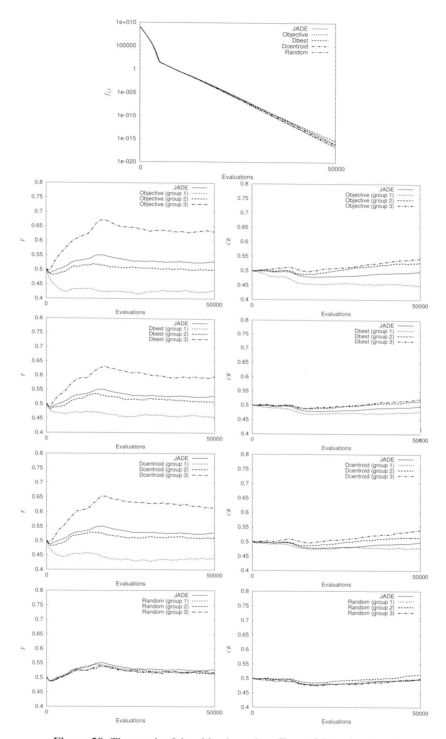

Figure 29. The graph of the objective value, F and CR in f_{13} ($K=3$)

References

[1] Storn, R. and Price, K., "Differential Evolution – A Simple and Efficient Heuristic for Global Optimization over Continuous Spaces", *Journal of Global Optimization*, Vol. 11, pp. 341–359 (1997).

[2] Price, K., Storn, R. and Lampinen, J. A., *Differential Evolution: A Practical Approach to Global Optimization*, Springer (2005).

[3] Chakraborty, U. K. (ed.), *Advances in Differential Evolution*, Springer (2008).

[4] Das, S. and Suganthan, P., "Differential Evolution: A Survey of the State-of-the-Art", *IEEE Transactions on Evolutionary Computation*, Vol. 15, No. 1, pp. 4–31 (2011).

[5] Zhang, J. and Sanderson, A. C., "JADE: Adaptive Differential Evolution With Optional External Archive", *IEEE Transactions on Evolutionary Computation*, Vol. 13, No. 5, pp. 945–958 (2009).

[6] Wang, Y., Cai, Z. and Zhang, Q., "Differential Evolution With Composite Trial Vector Generation Strategies and Control Parameters", *IEEE Transactions on Evolutionary Computation*, Vol. 15, No. 1, pp. 55–66 (2011).

[7] Liu, J. and Lampinen, J., "A Fuzzy Adaptive Differential Evolution Algorithm", *Soft Computing*, Vol. 9, No. 6, pp. 448–462 (2005).

[8] Takahama, T. and Sakai, S., "Fuzzy C-Means Clustering and Partition Entropy for Species-Best Strategy and Search Mode Selection in Nonlinear Optimization by Differential Evolution", *Proc. of the 2011 IEEE International Conference on Fuzzy Systems* (2011), pp. 290–297.

[9] Takahama, T. and Sakai, S., "Differential Evolution with Dynamic Strategy and Parameter Selection by Detecting Landscape Modality", *Proc. of the 2012 IEEE Congress on Evolutionary Computation* (2012), pp. 2114–2121.

[10] Takahama, T. and Sakai, S., "Large Scale Optimization by Differential Evolution with Landscape Modality Detection and a Diversity Archive", *Proc. of the 2012 IEEE Congress on Evolutionary Computation* (2012), pp. 2842–2849.

[11] Sakai, S. and Takahama, T., "Large Scale Optimization by Adaptive Differential Evolution with Landscape Modality Detection and a Diversity Archive", *Journal of Business Studies*, Vol. 58, No. 3, pp. 55–77 (2012).

[12] Teo, J., "Exploring Dynamic Self-Adaptive Populations in Differential Evolution", *Soft Computing*, Vol. 10, No. 8, pp. 673–686 (2006).

[13] Qin, A., Huang, V. and Suganthan, P., "Differential Evolution Algorithm With Strategy Adaptation for Global Numerical Optimization", *IEEE Transactions on Evolutionary Computation*, Vol. 13, No. 2, pp. 398–417 (2009).

[14] Brest, J., Greiner, S., Boskovic, B., Mernik, M. and Zumer, V., "Self-Adapting Control Parameters in Differential Evolution: A Comparative Study on Numerical Benchmark Problems", *IEEE Transaction on Evolutionary Computation*, Vol. 10, No. 6, pp. 646–657 (2006).

[15] Islam, S. M., Das, S., Ghosh, S., Roy, S. and Suganthan, P. N., "An Adaptive Differential Evolution Algorithm With Novel Mutation and Crossover Strategies for Global Numerical Optimization", *IEEE Transactions on Systems, Man, and Cybernetics, Part B: Cybernetics*, Vol. 42, No. 2, pp. 482–500 (2012).

[16] Takahama, T. and Sakai, S., "An Adaptive Differential Evolution Considering Correlation of Two Algorithm Parameters", *Proc. of the Joint 7th International Conference on Soft Computing and Intelligent Systems and 15th International Symposium on Advanced Intelligent Systems (SCIS&ISIS2014)* (2014), pp. 618–623.

[17] Storn, R. and Price, K., "Minimizing the Real Functions of the ICEC'96 Contest by Differen-

tial Evolution", *Proc. of the International Conference on Evolutionary Computation* (1996), pp. 842–844.

[18] Shang, Y.-W. and Qiu, Y.-H., "A Note on the Extended Rosenbrock Function", *Evolutionary Computation*, Vol. 14, No. 1, pp. 119–126 (2006).

[19] Yao, X., Liu, Y., and Lin, G., "Evolutionary Programming Made Faster", *IEEE Transactions on Evolutionary Computation*, Vol. 3, pp. 82–102 (1999).

[20] Yao, X., Liu, Y., Liang, K.-H. and Lin, G., "Fast Evolutionary Algorithms", Ghosh, A. and Tsutsui, S. (eds.), *Advances in Evolutionary Computing: Theory and Applications*, New York, NY, USA: Springer-Verlag New York, Inc., pp. 45–94 (2003).

Chapter 5

Generators of Irreducible Components of Harmonic Polynomials in the Case of $\mathfrak{so}(d,2)$

Ryoko Wada* and Yoshio Agaoka**
**Faculty of Economic Sciences, Hiroshima Shudo University,
1-1 Ozuka-Higashi 1-chome, Asaminami-Ku, Hiroshima, Japan 731-3195,
**Department of Mathematics, Graduate School of Science, Hiroshima University,
1-1 Kagamiyama 1-chome, Higashi-Hiroshima, Japan 739-8521.*

Abstract

Classical harmonic polynomials on $\mathbf{C}^d$ are generalized to several vector spaces from the Lie algebraic viewpoint by Kostant-Rallis. In their formulation, the case $\mathbf{C}^d$ corresponds to the real rank 1 Lie algebra $\mathfrak{so}(d,1)$. In the series of papers we further investigate harmonic polynomials corresponding to the Lie algebras $\mathfrak{su}(d,1)$, $\mathfrak{sp}(d,1)$ and $\mathfrak{f}_{4(-20)}$, etc. that are also real rank 1. In this paper we consider harmonic polynomials for the real rank 2 case $\mathfrak{so}(d,2)$, and determine the generators of irreducible components of harmonic polynomials for the principal part. Further, we give an algorithm to obtain generators of lower irreducible components, give some examples, and state several conjectures for future studies. We also give reproducing kernels of the lower irreducible components of harmonic polynomials in some cases.

Key Words:

Harmonic polynomial, Spherical harmonics, Reproducing kernel, Special function

1. Introduction

This paper is a continuation of our previous studies [8], [9], [10].

Let $\mathfrak{g}$ be a complex semisimple Lie algebra and let $\mathfrak{g}_\mathbf{R}$ be a noncompact real form of $\mathfrak{g}$. We fix a maximal compact subalgebra $\mathfrak{k}_\mathbf{R}$ of $\mathfrak{g}_\mathbf{R}$, and let $\mathfrak{g}_\mathbf{R} = \mathfrak{k}_\mathbf{R} + \mathfrak{p}_\mathbf{R}$ be a Cartan decomposition of $\mathfrak{g}_\mathbf{R}$. We denote by $\mathfrak{g} = \mathfrak{k} + \mathfrak{p}$ its complexification.

In [6], [7] we considered the reproducing formulas of the harmonic polynomials in the cases where $\mathfrak{g}_\mathbf{R}$'s are of real rank 1, and in [8], we considered the case $\mathfrak{g}_\mathbf{R} = \mathfrak{so}(d,2)$, which is the case of the classical real rank 2. We explicitly gave the $\mathfrak{k}_\mathbf{R}$-irreducible decomposition of the space of harmonic polynomials of degree ≤ 4, including their generators, and showed the reproducing formulas for some cases.

In [9], we gave the $\mathfrak{k}_\mathbf{R}$-irreducible decomposition of the space of harmonic polynomials of general dimension in the case $\mathfrak{g}_\mathbf{R} = \mathfrak{so}(d,2)$ and give the examples of reproducing formulas of harmonic polynomials of degree ≤ 4. In the paper [10], we gave an algorithm to obtain the generators of irreducible components of the space of harmonic polynomials for the case $\mathfrak{g}_{\mathbf{R}} = \mathfrak{so}(d, 2)$, and proved the structure theorem of the $\mathfrak{k}_{\mathbf{R}}$-irreducible decomposition of the space of polynomials on $\mathfrak{p}$. Explicit decomposition and generators are listed up for degree ≤ 5. Also, we gave the reproducing formulas of the principal part of the spaces of harmonic polynomials of degree ≤ 5.

In this paper, we give the explicit form of the generators of "principal" irreducible components of the space of polynomials on $\mathfrak{p}$ (which are automatically harmonic), and further give an algorithm to obtain generators of "lower" irreducible components of the space of harmonic polynomials. In a sense, their generators are uniquely determined, but their explicit forms are quite complicated as stated in §5. For future studies, we give in §6 several conjectures concerning the explicit form of the generators of lower irreducible components of harmonic polynomials. Further, we give some examples of reproducing kernels of lower part of harmonic polynomials of degree ≤ 5 in §7.

2. Preliminaries

In this section we fix several notations and review some definitions. For details, see our previous papers [8], [9], [10].

Let $\mathfrak{g}$ be a complex semisimple Lie algebra, and let $\mathfrak{g} = \mathfrak{k} + \mathfrak{p}$, $\mathfrak{g}_{\mathbf{R}} = \mathfrak{k}_{\mathbf{R}} + \mathfrak{p}_{\mathbf{R}}$ be direct sum decompositions, which we state in Introduction. We put $K = \exp \mathrm{ad}\, \mathfrak{k} \subset GL(\mathfrak{p})$ and $K_{\mathbf{R}} = \exp \mathrm{ad}\, \mathfrak{k}_{\mathbf{R}}$.

Let $S(\mathfrak{p})$ be the symmetric algebra on $\mathfrak{p}$, and let S be the space of polynomials on $\mathfrak{p}$. For $X \in \mathfrak{p}$ we denote by $\partial(X)$ the differential operator defined by

$$(\partial(X)f)(Y) = \frac{d}{dt} f(Y + tX)\,|_{t=0} \qquad (f \in S,\, Y \in \mathfrak{p}).$$

The linear mapping $X \mapsto \partial(X)$ naturally extends to an isomorphism of $S(\mathfrak{p})$ onto the algebra of all differential operators on $\mathfrak{p}$ with complex coefficients. For $f \in S$ and $g \in K$, we define an element $\rho(g)f$ of S by $\rho(g)f(X) = f(g^{-1}X)$ for $X \in \mathfrak{p}$. Let J denote the ring of K-invariant polynomials on $\mathfrak{p}$ and we put $J_+ = \{f \in J \,;\, f(0) = 0\}$.

Let $I(\mathfrak{p})$ be the set of K-invariants of $S(\mathfrak{p})$ and we put

$$I_+(\mathfrak{p}) = \{u \in I(\mathfrak{p}) \,;\, \partial(u)1 = 0\},$$

i.e., $I_+(\mathfrak{p})$ is the set of K-invariants without constant term.

According to the definition in [4], a polynomial $f \in S$ is harmonic if and only if $\partial(u)f = 0$ for any $u \in I_+(\mathfrak{p})$. We denote by S_n the space of homogeneous polynomials on $\mathfrak{p}$ of degree n, and $\mathcal{H}_n$ the space of homogeneous harmonic polynomials of degree n, where n is a non-negative integer. Remark that K acts on S_n and $\mathcal{H}_n$. We regard $K_{\mathbf{R}} \subset K$ and $\mathfrak{p}_{\mathbf{R}} \subset \mathfrak{p}$ in the following. For more details on harmonic polynomials of $\mathfrak{p}$, see [2], [4].

Now we consider the case $\mathfrak{g} = \mathfrak{so}(d+2, \mathbf{C})$ and $\mathfrak{g}_{\mathbf{R}} = \mathfrak{so}(d, 2)$. From now on we assume $d \geq 4$. For $z, w \in \mathbf{C}^d$ we put $z \cdot w = {}^t z w$, $z^2 = z \cdot z$, $w^2 = w \cdot w$. The natural action of the special orthogonal group $SO(d)$ on $\mathbf{C}^d$ preserves this product. Then we have

$$\mathfrak{k} = \left\{ \begin{pmatrix} A & 0 \\ 0 & B \end{pmatrix} \in M(d+2, \mathbf{C}) \, ; \, A \in \mathfrak{so}(d, \mathbf{C}), \, B \in \mathfrak{so}(2, \mathbf{C}) \right\},$$

$$\mathfrak{p} = \left\{ \begin{pmatrix} 0 & X \\ {}^tX & 0 \end{pmatrix} \in M(d+2, \mathbf{C}) \, ; \, X \text{ is a complex } d \times 2 \text{ matrix} \right\},$$

$$K_{\mathbf{R}} = \left\{ \mathrm{Ad} \begin{pmatrix} A & 0 \\ 0 & B \end{pmatrix} \, ; \, A \in SO(d), \, B \in SO(2) \right\},$$

and $\mathfrak{g} = \mathfrak{k} + \mathfrak{p}$. For $\widetilde{X} = \begin{pmatrix} 0 & X \\ {}^tX & 0 \end{pmatrix} \in \mathfrak{p}$, and $g = \mathrm{Ad}\begin{pmatrix} A & 0 \\ 0 & B \end{pmatrix} \in K_{\mathbf{R}}$ ($A \in SO(d)$, $B \in SO(2)$) we have $g\widetilde{X} = \begin{pmatrix} 0 & AX^tB \\ {}^t(AX^tB) & 0 \end{pmatrix}$. For $\widetilde{X} = \begin{pmatrix} 0 & X \\ {}^tX & 0 \end{pmatrix} \in \mathfrak{p}$ with $X = (x \ y)$ ($x, y \in \mathbf{C}^d$), two polynomials

$$P(\widetilde{X}) = \frac{1}{2} \mathrm{Tr}\,(\widetilde{X}^2) = x^2 + y^2,$$

$$Q(\widetilde{X}) = \det({}^tXX) = x^2 y^2 - (x \cdot y)^2$$

give the generators of J. Then we have $\mathcal{H}_n = \{f \in S_n; P(D)f = Q(D)f = 0\}$, where

$$P(D) = \Delta_x + \Delta_y, \quad Q(D) = \Delta_x \Delta_y - \left(\sum_{j=1}^d \frac{\partial^2}{\partial x_j \partial y_j} \right)^2,$$

$$\Delta_x = \sum_{j=1}^d \left(\frac{\partial}{\partial x_j} \right)^2, \, \Delta_y = \sum_{j=1}^d \left(\frac{\partial}{\partial y_j} \right)^2.$$

For $\widetilde{X} = \begin{pmatrix} 0 & X \\ {}^tX & 0 \end{pmatrix} \in \mathfrak{p}$ with $X = (x \ y)$ ($x, y \in \mathbf{C}^d$), we put $\begin{pmatrix} z \\ w \end{pmatrix} = \begin{pmatrix} x + iy \\ x - iy \end{pmatrix} \in \mathbf{C}^{2d}$ and we define the linear bijective mapping $\Psi : \mathfrak{p} \longrightarrow \mathbf{C}^{2d}$ by $\Psi(\widetilde{X}) = \begin{pmatrix} z \\ w \end{pmatrix}$. We denote by $S_n(\mathbf{C}^{2d})$ the space of homogeneous polynomials on $\mathbf{C}^{2d}$ with degree n, and we put

$$\mathcal{H}_n(\mathbf{C}^{2d}) = \left\{ f\left(\begin{pmatrix} z \\ w \end{pmatrix}\right) \in S_n(\mathbf{C}^{2d}) \, ; \, \Delta_z \Delta_w f = 0 \text{ and } \sum_{j=1}^d \frac{\partial^2 f}{\partial z_j \partial w_j} = 0 \right\}.$$

Since we have $P(\widetilde{X}) = P \circ \Psi^{-1}\left(\begin{pmatrix} z \\ w \end{pmatrix}\right) = z \cdot w$ and $Q(\widetilde{X}) = Q \circ \Psi^{-1}\left(\begin{pmatrix} z \\ w \end{pmatrix}\right) = -\frac{1}{4}\{z^2w^2 - (z \cdot w)^2\}$, we can see that $f \in \mathcal{H}_n$ if and only if $f \circ \Psi^{-1} \in \mathcal{H}_n(\mathbf{C}^{2d})$. In the following we identify two spaces $\mathcal{H}_n$ and $\mathcal{H}_n(\mathbf{C}^{2d})$ through Ψ.

3. Irreducible Decomposition of S_n

In this section, we first review the $K_{\mathbf{R}}$-irreducible decomposition of the space S_n, following the notations in [8], [9], [10].

The Lie group $K_{\mathbf{R}}$ is isomorphic to the product group $SO(d) \times SO(2)$, and its irreducible representation space is symbolically expressed as $(p\Lambda_1 + q\Lambda_2) \otimes V_k$, where p, q are non-negative integers and $k \in \mathbf{Z}$.

Remind that the irreducible component $(p\Lambda_1 + q\Lambda_2) \otimes V_k$ in S_n is *principal* if $p + 2q = n$, and the remaining components are called *lower* components of S_n. We denote by P_n the direct sum of principal irreducible components of S_n, and by L_n the direct sum of subspaces of S_n consisting of lower components of S_n. For example, principal irreducible components of S_5 consists of 12 terms:

$$P_5 = (5\Lambda_1) \otimes (V_5 + V_3 + V_1 + V_{-1} + V_{-3} + V_{-5})$$
$$+ (3\Lambda_1 + \Lambda_2) \otimes (V_3 + V_1 + V_{-1} + V_{-3}) + (\Lambda_1 + 2\Lambda_2) \otimes (V_1 + V_{-1}),$$

while lower components of S_5 are given by

$$L_5 = \{(3\Lambda_1) + (\Lambda_1)\} \otimes (V_5 + V_3 + V_1 + V_{-1} + V_{-3} + V_{-5})$$
$$+ \{(3\Lambda_1) + (\Lambda_1 + \Lambda_2) + (\Lambda_1)\} \otimes (V_3 + V_1 + V_{-1} + V_{-3})$$
$$+ \{(3\Lambda_1) + (\Lambda_1 + \Lambda_2) + (\Lambda_1)\} \otimes (V_1 + V_{-1}).$$

Lower components of S_n are obtained from principal components and the following three polynomials

$$\{z^2\}, \quad \{z \cdot w\}, \quad \{w^2\}.$$

These are 1-dimensional irreducible subspaces of quadratic polynomials S_2, whose characters are respectively given by

$$(0) \otimes V_2, \quad (0) \otimes V_0, \quad (0) \otimes V_{-2}.$$

Then by making a tensor product of a principal component $(p\Lambda_1 + q\Lambda_2) \otimes V_k$ ($p + 2q = n - 2l$) of S_{n-2l} ($0 < l \leq n/2$) and an l-th product of the above three quadratic polynomials $(z^2)^s (z \cdot w)^t (w^2)^u$ ($s + t + u = l$), we obtain a lower irreducible component $(p\Lambda_1 + q\Lambda_2) \otimes V_{k+2s-2u}$ in S_n. We express this irreducible component of S_n symbolically as

$$(p\Lambda_1 + q\Lambda_2) \otimes V_{k+[s,t,u]}.$$

Any irreducible component of L_n can be obtained in this way, and the following decomposition theorem on S_n holds.

Theorem 3.1 ([10]). *The $SO(d) \times SO(2)$-irreducible decomposition of S_n is given by:*

$$S_n = \sum_{\substack{p+2q+2(s+t+u)=n, \\ p \geq 0, q \geq 0, \\ s \geq 0, t \geq 0, u \geq 0}} (p\Lambda_1 + q\Lambda_2) \otimes (V_{p+[s,t,u]} + V_{p-2+[s,t,u]} + \cdots + V_{-(p-2)+[s,t,u]} + V_{-p+[s,t,u]}),$$

where we consider $(p\Lambda_1 + q\Lambda_2) \otimes V_{k+[s,t,u]} = (p\Lambda_1 + q\Lambda_2) \otimes V_k$ in case $p + 2q = n$ and $s = t = u = 0$.

In addition, the irreducible decompositions of the principal part P_n and the lower part L_n are respectively given by:

$$P_n = \sum_{\substack{p+2q=n, \\ p \geq 0, q \geq 0}} (p\Lambda_1 + q\Lambda_2) \otimes (V_p + V_{p-2} + \cdots + V_{-(p-2)} + V_{-p})$$

and

$$L_n = \sum_{\substack{p+2q<n, \\ p \equiv n \,(\mathrm{mod}\,2), \\ p \geq 0, q \geq 0, \\ s+t+u=(n-p-2q)/2, \\ s \geq 0, t \geq 0, u \geq 0}} (p\Lambda_1 + q\Lambda_2) \otimes (V_{p+[s,t,u]} + V_{p-2+[s,t,u]} + \cdots + V_{-(p-2)+[s,t,u]} + V_{-p+[s,t,u]}).$$

Next, we review the $K_{\mathbf{R}}$-irreducible decomposition of the space of harmonic polynomials $\mathcal{H}_n$. First, remind that any polynomial in the principal component P_n is harmonic, and the multiplicity of any irreducible principal component is always 1 ([p.88; 10]).

We express the lower harmonic components in $\mathcal{H}_n$ as $\mathcal{L}\mathcal{H}_n$. Then we have the following theorem.

Theorem 3.2 ([9]). $K_{\mathbf{R}}$-*irreducible direct sum decomposition of the space* $\mathcal{L}\mathcal{H}_n$ *is symbolically given by*

$$\mathcal{L}\mathcal{H}_n = \sum_{\substack{p+2q \leq n-2, \\ p \geq 0, q \geq 0, \\ p \equiv n \,(\mathrm{mod}\,2)}} (p\Lambda_1 + q\Lambda_2) \otimes (V_{n-2q} + V_{n-2q-2} + \cdots + V_{n-2p-2q} + V_{-(n-2p-2q)} + \cdots + V_{-(n-2q-2)} + V_{-(n-2q)}).$$

The multiplicity of each irreducible component is at most 2, and the multiplicity 2 case occurs if and only if $p+2q \leq n-2$ and $p+q \geq n/2$ for the space V_k with $|k| \leq 2p+2q-n$.

Remind that the function $f(z_1, \cdots, z_d, w_1, \cdots, w_d)$ is harmonic if and only if

$$\sum_i \frac{\partial^2 f}{\partial z_i \partial w_i} = 0, \qquad \sum_{i,j} \frac{\partial^2}{\partial z_i^2}\left(\frac{\partial^2 f}{\partial w_j^2}\right) = 0.$$

4. Generators of Principal Components

As stated above, principal components P_n of S_n is automatically harmonic. In this section we explicitly give the generator of each component of P_n. The results are summarized in the following theorem.

Theorem 4.1. *The generator of the principal irreducible component*

$$(p\Lambda_1 + q\Lambda_2) \otimes V_k \subset P_n$$

with $p + 2q = n$ ($p \geq 0$, $q \geq 0$), $|k| \leq p$ and $k \equiv p \pmod{2}$ is given by

$$(z \cdot \alpha)^{(p+k)/2}(w \cdot \alpha)^{(p-k)/2}\{(z \cdot \alpha)(w \cdot \beta) - (z \cdot \beta)(w \cdot \alpha)\}^q$$

with $\alpha^2 = \alpha \cdot \beta = \beta^2 = 0$.

Alternatively, a non-zero polynomial

$$(z \cdot \alpha)^\lambda (w \cdot \alpha)^\nu \{(z \cdot \alpha)(w \cdot \beta) - (z \cdot \beta)(w \cdot \alpha)\}^\xi$$

with $\alpha^2 = \alpha \cdot \beta = \beta^2 = 0$ gives a generator of the principal irreducible component

$$((\lambda + \nu)\Lambda_1 + \xi\Lambda_2) \otimes V_{\lambda-\nu}$$

with degree $n = \lambda + \nu + 2\xi$.

To prove this theorem, we must prepare the following proposition, concerning the inner product of polynomials:

Proposition 4.2. *Assume* $i_1 + \cdots + i_d = a + \bar{a}$, $j_1 + \cdots + j_d = b + \bar{b}$. *Then*

$$\langle (z \cdot \alpha)^a (w \cdot \alpha)^b (z \cdot \beta)^{\bar{a}} (w \cdot \beta)^{\bar{b}}, z_1^{i_1} \cdots z_d^{i_d} w_1^{j_1} \cdots w_d^{j_d} \rangle$$
$$= a!\, b!\, \bar{a}!\, \bar{b}!\, [(\alpha_1 + \beta_1)^{i_1} \cdots (\alpha_d + \beta_d)^{i_d}]_{\alpha^a \beta^{\bar{a}}} \times [(\alpha_1 + \beta_1)^{j_1} \cdots (\alpha_d + \beta_d)^{j_d}]_{\alpha^b \beta^{\bar{b}}}.$$

Here the symbol $[F]_{\alpha^a \beta^{\bar{a}}}$ *etc. means the sum of monomials in F with total degree* a *with respect to* $\alpha_1, \cdots, \alpha_d$ *and total degree* $\bar{a}$ *with respect to* $\beta_1, \cdots, \beta_d$.

Proof. Clearly, by definition, we have

$$\langle (z \cdot \alpha)^a (w \cdot \alpha)^b (z \cdot \beta)^{\bar{a}} (w \cdot \beta)^{\bar{b}}, z_1^{i_1} \cdots z_d^{i_d} w_1^{j_1} \cdots w_d^{j_d} \rangle$$
$$= \langle (z \cdot \alpha)^a (z \cdot \beta)^{\bar{a}}, z_1^{i_1} \cdots z_d^{i_d} \rangle \langle (w \cdot \alpha)^b (w \cdot \beta)^{\bar{b}}, w_1^{j_1} \cdots w_d^{j_d} \rangle.$$

We have

$$\langle (z \cdot \alpha)^a (z \cdot \beta)^{\bar{a}}, z_1^{i_1} \cdots z_d^{i_d} \rangle$$
$$= \langle \sum \frac{a!}{a_1! \cdots a_d!} \frac{\bar{a}!}{\bar{a}_1! \cdots \bar{a}_d!} (\alpha_1 z_1)^{a_1} \cdots (\alpha_d z_d)^{a_d} (\beta_1 z_1)^{\bar{a}_1} \cdots (\beta_d z_d)^{\bar{a}_d}, z_1^{i_1} \cdots z_d^{i_d} \rangle$$
$$= \langle \sum \frac{a!}{a_1! \cdots a_d!} \frac{\bar{a}!}{\bar{a}_1! \cdots \bar{a}_d!} \alpha_1^{a_1} \cdots \alpha_d^{a_d} \beta_1^{\bar{a}_1} \cdots \beta_d^{\bar{a}_d} z_1^{a_1 + \bar{a}_1} \cdots z_d^{a_d + \bar{a}_d}, z_1^{i_1} \cdots z_d^{i_d} \rangle$$
$$= \sum \frac{a!}{a_1! \cdots a_d!} \frac{\bar{a}!}{\bar{a}_1! \cdots \bar{a}_d!} \alpha_1^{a_1} \cdots \alpha_d^{a_d} \beta_1^{\bar{a}_1} \cdots \beta_d^{\bar{a}_d} i_1! \cdots i_d!,$$

where the summation is taken over exponents with

$$a_1 + \cdots + a_d = a, \quad \bar{a}_1 + \cdots + \bar{a}_d = \bar{a}, \quad a_1 + \bar{a}_1 = i_1, \cdots, a_d + \bar{a}_d = i_d.$$

Since $\frac{i_1!}{a_1!\bar{a}_1!} = \binom{i_1}{a_1}$ etc., the above expression is equal to

$$a!\,\bar{a}!\sum \binom{i_1}{a_1}\cdots\binom{i_d}{a_d}(\alpha_1^{a_1}\beta_1^{\bar{a}_1})\cdots(\alpha_d^{a_d}\beta_d^{\bar{a}_d})$$
$$= a!\,\bar{a}!\sum{}'(\alpha_1+\beta_1)^{i_1}\cdots(\alpha_d+\beta_d)^{i_d},$$

where the symbol $\sum'$ implies that the sum is taken under the conditions

$$a_1+\cdots+a_d = a, \quad \bar{a}_1+\cdots+\bar{a}_d = \bar{a},$$

after expanding the powers $(\alpha_1+\beta_1)^{i_1}$ etc. into sum of monomials. This restriction implies that the sum is taken under the conditions that the total degree with respect to $\alpha_1,\cdots,\alpha_d$ is a and the total degree with respect to $\beta_1,\cdots,\beta_d$ is $\bar{a}$.

Similar formula holds for the inner product concerning $w_1,\ldots,w_d$, and thus we complete the proof of the proposition. q.e.d.

Example. We calculate the inner product

$$\langle (z\cdot\alpha)^3(w\cdot\alpha)^2(z\cdot\beta)(w\cdot\beta),\, z_1^2 z_2 z_3 w_1 w_2^2\rangle$$
$$= \langle (z\cdot\alpha)^3(z\cdot\beta),\, z_1^2 z_2 z_3\rangle\,\langle (w\cdot\alpha)^2(w\cdot\beta),\, w_1 w_2^2\rangle.$$

By direct calculations we have easily know that

$$\langle (z\cdot\alpha)^3(z\cdot\beta),\, z_1^2 z_2 z_3\rangle = 3!1!\,[(\alpha_1+\beta_1)^2(\alpha_2+\beta_2)(\alpha_3+\beta_3)]_{\alpha^3\beta^1}$$
$$= 6\,\alpha_1(\alpha_1\alpha_2\beta_3 + \alpha_1\alpha_3\beta_2 + 2\alpha_2\alpha_3\beta_1),$$

and

$$\langle (w\cdot\alpha)^2(w\cdot\beta),\, w_1 w_2^2\rangle = 2!1!\,[(\alpha_1+\beta_1)(\alpha_2+\beta_2)^2]_{\alpha^2\beta^1}$$
$$= 2\,\alpha_2(2\alpha_1\beta_2 + \alpha_2\beta_1).$$

Hence the inner product is equal to

$$12\,\alpha_1\alpha_2(\alpha_1\alpha_2\beta_3 + \alpha_1\alpha_3\beta_2 + 2\alpha_2\alpha_3\beta_1)(2\alpha_1\beta_2 + \alpha_2\beta_1).$$

We prepare one more proposition.

Proposition 4.3. *We put*

$$F = a!\,\bar{a}!\,(\alpha_1+\beta_1)^{i_1}\cdots(\alpha_d+\beta_d)^{i_d},$$
$$G = b!\,\bar{b}!\,(\alpha_1+\beta_1)^{j_1}\cdots(\alpha_d+\beta_d)^{j_d}.$$

Then we have the following equalities:
(1) *Assume* $i_1+\cdots+i_d+2 = a+\bar{a}$. *Then*

$$\langle (z\cdot\alpha)^a(z\cdot\beta)^{\bar{a}},\, (z^2)\, z_1^{i_1}\cdots z_d^{i_d}\rangle$$
$$= [F]_{\alpha^{a-2}\beta^{\bar{a}}}(\alpha^2) + 2[F]_{\alpha^{a-1}\beta^{\bar{a}-1}}(\alpha\cdot\beta) + [F]_{\alpha^a\beta^{\bar{a}-2}}(\beta^2).$$

(2) Assume $i_1 + \cdots + i_d + 1 = a + \bar{a}$, $j_1 + \cdots + j_d + 1 = b + \bar{b}$. Then
$$\langle (z \cdot \alpha)^a (w \cdot \alpha)^b (z \cdot \beta)^{\bar{a}} (w \cdot \beta)^{\bar{b}}, (z \cdot w) \, z_1^{i_1} \cdots z_d^{i_d} w_1^{j_1} \cdots w_d^{j_d} \rangle$$
$$= [F]_{\alpha^{a-1}\beta^{\bar{a}}} [G]_{\alpha^{b-1}\beta^{\bar{b}}} (\alpha^2) + [F]_{\alpha^{a-1}\beta^{\bar{a}}} [G]_{\alpha^b \beta^{\bar{b}-1}} (\alpha \cdot \beta)$$
$$+ [F]_{\alpha^a \beta^{\bar{a}-1}} [G]_{\alpha^{b-1}\beta^{\bar{b}}} (\alpha \cdot \beta) + [F]_{\alpha^a \beta^{\bar{a}-1}} [G]_{\alpha^b \beta^{\bar{b}-1}} (\beta^2).$$

(3) Assume $j_1 + \cdots + j_d + 2 = b + \bar{b}$. Then
$$\langle (w \cdot \alpha)^b (w \cdot \beta)^{\bar{b}}, (w^2) \, w_1^{j_1} \cdots w_d^{j_d} \rangle$$
$$= [G]_{\alpha^{b-2}\beta^{\bar{b}}} (\alpha^2) + 2[G]_{\alpha^{b-1}\beta^{\bar{b}-1}} (\alpha \cdot \beta) + [G]_{\alpha^b \beta^{\bar{b}-2}} (\beta^2).$$

Proof. We give an outline of the proof of (1). From the equality
$$(z^2) z_1^{i_1} \cdots z_d^{i_d} = z_1^{i_1+2} z_2^{i_2} \cdots z_d^{i_d} + z_1^{i_1} z_2^{i_2+2} z_3^{i_3} \cdots z_d^{i_d} + \cdots + z_1^{i_1} \cdots z_{d-1}^{i_{d-1}} z_d^{i_d+2},$$
the inner product in (1) is equal to
$$\langle (z \cdot \alpha)^a (z \cdot \beta)^{\bar{a}}, z_1^{i_1+2} z_2^{i_2} \cdots z_d^{i_d} \rangle + \langle (z \cdot \alpha)^a (z \cdot \beta)^{\bar{a}}, z_1^{i_1} z_2^{i_2+2} z_3^{i_3} \cdots z_d^{i_d} \rangle + \cdots .$$
We here apply Proposition 4.2. Then we know that it is equal to
$$a! \, \bar{a}! \, [(\alpha_1 + \beta_1)^{i_1+2} (\alpha_2 + \beta_2)^{i_2} \cdots (\alpha_d + \beta_d)^{i_d}$$
$$+ (\alpha_1 + \beta_1)^{i_1} (\alpha_2 + \beta_2)^{i_2+2} \cdots (\alpha_d + \beta_d)^{i_d} + \cdots]_{\alpha^a \beta^{\bar{a}}}$$
$$= [F\{(\alpha_1 + \beta_1)^2 + \cdots + (\alpha_d + \beta_d)^2\}]_{\alpha^a \beta^{\bar{a}}}$$
$$= [F\{(\alpha^2) + 2(\alpha \cdot \beta) + (\beta^2)\}]_{\alpha^a \beta^{\bar{a}}}.$$
Then the result follows immediately.

The remaining cases can be proved in the same way. q.e.d.

Example. By applying Proposition 4.3 (2), we calculate the inner product
$$\langle (z \cdot \alpha)^4 (w \cdot \beta), (z \cdot w)(z \cdot \gamma)^3 \rangle.$$
In this case we have
$$a = 4, \quad b = 0, \quad \bar{a} = 0, \quad \bar{b} = 1, \quad i_1 + \cdots + i_d = 3, \quad j_1 + \cdots + j_d = 0,$$
and
$$F = 24(\alpha_1 + \beta_1)^{i_1} \cdots (\alpha_d + \beta_d)^{i_d}, \quad G = 1,$$
where we express
$$(z \cdot \gamma)^3 = \sum \frac{3!}{i_1! \cdots i_d!} (\gamma_1 z_1)^{i_1} \cdots (\gamma_d z_d)^{i_d} = \sum \frac{3!}{i_1! \cdots i_d!} \gamma_1^{i_1} \cdots \gamma_d^{i_d} z_1^{i_1} \cdots z_d^{i_d}.$$
Thus, actually, F must be a sum of several terms appearing in $(z \cdot \gamma)^3$. In this case, among four terms in (2), the second term only remains, and we have
$$[F]_{\alpha^3 \beta^0} [G]_{\alpha^0 \beta^0} (\alpha \cdot \beta) = 24 \sum \frac{3!}{i_1! \cdots i_d!} \gamma_1^{i_1} \cdots \gamma_d^{i_d} [(\alpha_1 + \beta_1)^{i_1} \cdots (\alpha_d + \beta_d)^{i_d}]_{\alpha^3 \beta^0} (\alpha \cdot \beta)$$
$$= 24 \sum \frac{3!}{i_1! \cdots i_d!} \gamma_1^{i_1} \cdots \gamma_d^{i_d} \alpha_1^{i_1} \cdots \alpha_d^{i_d} (\alpha \cdot \beta)$$
$$= 24 \sum \frac{3!}{i_1! \cdots i_d!} (\alpha_1 \gamma_1)^{i_1} \cdots (\alpha_d \gamma_d)^{i_d} (\alpha \cdot \beta)$$
$$= 24(\alpha_1 \gamma_1 + \cdots + \alpha_d \gamma_d)^3 (\alpha \cdot \beta)$$
$$= 24(\alpha \cdot \gamma)^3 (\alpha \cdot \beta).$$

Now under these preparations, we give a proof of Theorem 4.1. We already explain a method to obtain the generator of each irreducible component of the principal part P_n in p.91~92 of [10].

We use the same notations as in [10], but here we use the space $\mathbf{C}^d$ instead of $\mathbf{C}^p$ in [10]. The $GL(d,\mathbf{C}) \times SO(2)$-irreducible component $T_{ab}V_k$ in S_{a+b} is generated by

$$(z \cdot \alpha)^{(a-b+k)/2}(w \cdot \alpha)^{(a-b-k)/2}\{(z \cdot \alpha)(w \cdot \beta) - (z \cdot \beta)(w \cdot \alpha)\}^b.$$

(Note that $|k| \leq a - b$ and $k \equiv a - b \pmod{2}$.) We must impose some conditions on α, β to obtain a generator of the $SO(d) \times SO(2)$-irreducible principal component

$$((a - b)\Lambda_1 + b\Lambda_2) \otimes V_k \subset T_{ab}V_k.$$

Conditions on α and β follows from the orthogonality, explained in p.92 [10]. To take out the principal irreducible component, we impose a condition that the space we are considering is orthogonal to any other remaining irreducible component. Each space $T_{cd}V_l$ contains a unique principal component, and if $(a, b, k) \neq (c, d, l)$, two spaces $T_{ab}V_k$ and $T_{cd}V_l$ are orthogonal. Hence it suffices to consider the orthgonality condition to lower parts of S_n.

As we already shown in [10], generators of lower part of S_n are expressed in the form

$$(z^2)^s(z \cdot w)^t(w^2)^u \times [\text{principal part of lower degree}]$$

for some $(s, t, u) \neq (0, 0, 0)$ (cf. Theorem 3.1 and the list in p.99~101 of [10]). Hence we have only to show that under the conditions $\alpha^2 = \alpha \cdot \beta = \beta^2 = 0$, the polynomial

$$(z \cdot \alpha)^\lambda (w \cdot \alpha)^\nu \{(z \cdot \alpha)(w \cdot \beta) - (z \cdot \beta)(w \cdot \alpha)\}^\xi$$

is orthogonal to

$$(z^2)^s(z \cdot w)^t(w^2)^u \times (z \cdot \gamma)^{\overline{\lambda}}(w \cdot \gamma)^{\overline{\nu}}\{(z \cdot \gamma)(w \cdot \delta) - (z \cdot \delta)(w \cdot \gamma)\}^{\overline{\xi}}$$

with $(s, t, u) \neq (0, 0, 0)$. But this fact follows immediately from Proposition 4.3, since all inner products are expressed in the form $(\alpha^2)F_1 + (\alpha \cdot \beta)F_2 + (\beta^2)F_3$ for some polynomials F_1, F_2, F_3.
c.e.d.

Remark. In several cases some of α^2, $\alpha \cdot \beta$, β^2 do not appear in inner products. But we may impose redundant conditions on generators of irreducible components, since irreducible components are generated only by one non-zero element, and the pair $(\alpha, \beta) \neq (0, 0)$ satisfying $\alpha^2 = \alpha \cdot \beta = \beta^2 = 0$ always exists in case $d \geq 4$.

5. Generators of Lower Harmonic Components

Remind that the lower harmonic components $\mathcal{LH}_n \subset \mathcal{H}_n$ are given by

$$\mathcal{LH}_n = \sum_{\substack{p+2q \leq n-2, \\ p \geq 0,\, q \geq 0, \\ p \equiv n \pmod 2}} (p\Lambda_1 + q\Lambda_2) \otimes (V_{n-2q} + V_{n-2q-2} + \cdots + V_{n-2p-2q} \\ + V_{-(n-2p-2q)} + \cdots + V_{-(n-2q-2)} + V_{-(n-2q)})$$

(cf. [p.127; 9]). As stated before, the multiplicity of each component in this space is at most 2, and the component $(p\Lambda_1 + q\Lambda_2) \otimes V_k$ is multiplicity 2 if and only if $p + 2q \leq n - 2$, $p + q \geq n/2$ and $|k| \leq 2p + 2q - n$. In the following we decompose $\mathcal{LH}_n$ into two subspaces. We set

$$\mathcal{LH}_n^+ = \sum_{\substack{p+2q \leq n-2, \\ p \geq 0,\, q \geq 0, \\ p \equiv n \,(\mathrm{mod}\, 2)}} (p\Lambda_1 + q\Lambda_2) \otimes (V_{n-2q} + V_{n-2q-2} + \cdots + V_{n-2p-2q})$$

and

$$\mathcal{LH}_n^- = \sum_{\substack{p+2q \leq n-2, \\ p \geq 0,\, q \geq 0, \\ p \equiv n \,(\mathrm{mod}\, 2)}} (p\Lambda_1 + q\Lambda_2) \otimes (V_{-(n-2p-2q)} + \cdots + V_{-(n-2q-2)} + V_{-(n-2q)}).$$

Then, formally, we obtain a direct sum decomposition $\mathcal{LH}_n = \mathcal{LH}_n^+ \oplus \mathcal{LH}_n^-$, whose two components are both multiplicity free. But there remains a problem how to actually decompose reducible components of $\mathcal{LH}_n$ with multiplicity 2 into irreducible factors. (It is easy to see that the first and the second term (if exists) of $\mathcal{LH}_n^+$ have multiplicity 1, when considered in the total space $\mathcal{LH}_n$. Thus the above problem occurs for the third, fourth, $\cdots$ components in $\mathcal{LH}_n^+$.) In the following we will consider the problem to find a generator of each irreducible component of $\mathcal{LH}_n^+$. Generators of the remaining part $\mathcal{LH}_n^-$ can be obtained simply by changing the letters z and w in generators of $\mathcal{LH}_n^+$.

At first, for later use, we give formulas to calculate two derivatives

$$\sum_i \frac{\partial^2 f}{\partial z_i \partial w_i}, \qquad \sum_{i,j} \frac{\partial^2}{\partial z_i^2}\left(\frac{\partial^2 f}{\partial w_j^2}\right)$$

for the polynomial

$$f = (z^2)^s (z \cdot w)^t (w^2)^u (z \cdot \alpha)^\lambda (w \cdot \alpha)^\nu \{(z \cdot \alpha)(w \cdot \beta) - (z \cdot \beta)(w \cdot \alpha)\}^\xi$$

with degree $n = 2s + 2t + 2u + \lambda + \nu + 2\xi$. For simplicity we will express the above polynomial as

$$f = F[s, t, u, \lambda, \nu, \xi]$$

in the following. Remind that, in case $\alpha^2 = \alpha \cdot \beta = \beta^2 = 0$, the polynomial $f = F[s, t, u, \lambda, \nu, \xi]$ gives a generator of the $SO(d) \times SO(2)$-irreducible component

$$((\lambda + \nu)\Lambda_1 + \xi\Lambda_2) \otimes V_{2s-2u+\lambda-\nu}.$$

It gives a generator of a principal part if and only if $s = t = u = 0$.

The derivatives of f can be again expressed as a linear combination of $F[\bar{s}, \bar{t}, \bar{u}, \bar{\lambda}, \bar{\nu}, \bar{\xi}]$ for some $\bar{s}, \bar{t}, \bar{u}, \bar{\lambda}, \bar{\nu}, \bar{\xi}$ in the following way:

Proposition 5.1. *Assume $\alpha^2 = \alpha \cdot \beta = \beta^2 = 0$. Then we have the following formulas for $f = F[s, t, u, \lambda, \nu, \xi]$:*

$$\sum_i \frac{\partial^2 f}{\partial z_i \partial w_i} = 4su\, F[s-1, t+1, u-1, \lambda, \nu, \xi]$$
$$+ 2sv\, F[s-1, t, u, \lambda+1, \nu-1, \xi] + 2u\lambda\, F[s, t, u-1, \lambda-1, \nu+1, \xi]$$
$$+ t(d+2s+t+2u+\lambda+\nu+2\xi-1)\, F[s, t-1, u, \lambda, \nu, \xi],$$

$$\sum_{i,j} \frac{\partial^2}{\partial z_i^2}\left(\frac{\partial^2 f}{\partial w_j^2}\right)$$
$$= 4su(d+2s+2t+2\lambda+2\xi-2)(d+2t+2u+2\nu+2\xi-2)\, F[s-1, t, u-1, \lambda, \nu, \xi]$$
$$+ 4stv(d+2s+2t+2\lambda+2\xi-2)\, F[s-1, t-1, u, \lambda+1, \nu-1, \xi]$$
$$+ 4tu\lambda(d+2t+2u+2\nu+2\xi-2)\, F[s, t-1, u-1, \lambda-1, \nu+1, \xi]$$
$$+ 2t(t-1)[d(s+u+1) + 2\{s(s+t+\lambda+\xi-1) + u(t+u+\nu+\xi-1)$$
$$+ (\lambda+1)(\nu+1) + t+\xi-3\}]\, F[s, t-2, u, \lambda, \nu, \xi]$$
$$+ 2t(t-1)(t-2)\lambda\, F[s+1, t-3, u, \lambda-1, \nu+1, \xi]$$
$$+ 2t(t-1)(t-2)\nu\, F[s, t-3, u+1, \lambda+1, \nu-1, \xi]$$
$$+ t(t-1)(t-2)(t-3)\, F[s+1, t-4, u+1, \lambda, \nu, \xi].$$

Proof. As for the first derivative, without the assumption $\alpha^2 = \alpha \cdot \beta = \beta^2 = 0$, we have directly the formula

$$\sum_i \frac{\partial^2 f}{\partial z_i \partial w_i} = 4su\, F[s-1, t+1, u-1, \lambda, \nu, \xi]$$
$$+ 2sv\, F[s-1, t, u, \lambda+1, \nu-1, \xi] + 2u\lambda\, F[s, t, u-1, \lambda-1, \nu+1, \xi]$$
$$+ t(d+2s+t+2u+\lambda+\nu+2\xi-1)\, F[s, t-1, u, \lambda, \nu, \xi]$$
$$+ (\alpha)^2(\lambda \cdot \nu)\, F[s, t, u, \lambda-1, \nu-1, \xi]$$
$$- (\alpha)^2(\lambda \cdot \xi)(z \cdot \beta)\, F[s, t, u, \lambda-1, \nu, \xi-1]$$
$$+ (\alpha)^2(\nu \cdot \xi)(w \cdot \beta)\, F[s, t, u, \lambda, \nu-1, \xi-1]$$
$$- (\alpha)^2\xi(\xi-1)(z \cdot \beta)(w \cdot \beta)\, F[s, t, u, \lambda, \nu, \xi-2]$$
$$+ (\alpha \cdot \beta)\{(\lambda \cdot \xi) - (\nu \cdot \xi)\}\, F[s, t, u, \lambda, \nu, \xi-1]$$
$$+ (\alpha \cdot \beta)\xi(\xi-1)(z \cdot \beta)\, F[s, t, u, \lambda, \nu+1, \xi-2]$$
$$+ (\alpha \cdot \beta)\xi(\xi-1)(w \cdot \beta)\, F[s, t, u, \lambda+1, \nu, \xi-2]$$
$$- (\beta)^2\xi(\xi-1)\, F[s, t, u, \lambda+1, \nu+1, \xi-2].$$

Then, assuming $\alpha^2 = \alpha \cdot \beta = \beta^2 = 0$, many terms drop out and we obtain the desired formula. Note that the coefficient $t(d+2s+t+2u+\lambda+\nu+2\xi-1)$ in the last term is equal to $t(d+n-t-1)$.

Similarly, as for the second derivative, under the same assumption $\alpha^2 = \alpha \cdot \beta = \beta^2 = 0$, we can show the formula by calculation. But actually we must use computers, since tremendous calculations are required to obtain the final result.   q.e.d.

In the rest of this paper, we always assume $\alpha^2 = \alpha \cdot \beta = \beta^2 = 0$, unless otherwise stated.

From the above formulas, we can easily see that in case $s = t = u = 0$ the polynomial $f = F[0,0,0,\lambda,\nu,\xi]$ is harmonic. This means that the principal part $P_n \subset S_n$ is always harmonic, the fact which we already showed in [p.88; 10].

We can also easily see that the polynomials

$$F[s+1,0,0,p,0,q] = (z^2)^{s+1}(z \cdot \alpha)^p \{(z \cdot \alpha)(w \cdot \beta) - (z \cdot \beta)(w \cdot \alpha)\}^q$$
$$\in (p\Lambda_1 + q\Lambda_2) \otimes V_{n-2q},$$
$$F[0,0,u+1,0,p,q] = (w^2)^{u+1}(w \cdot \alpha)^p \{(z \cdot \alpha)(w \cdot \beta) - (z \cdot \beta)(w \cdot \alpha)\}^q$$
$$\in (p\Lambda_1 + q\Lambda_2) \otimes V_{-(n-2q)}$$

are also harmonic, since the values corresponding to t, u and ν are all zero, for example for the former case. These are the generators of the first and the last irreducible components of $\mathcal{LH}_n^+$ and $\mathcal{LH}_n^-$, respectively. For the former polynomial $F[s+1,0,0,p,0,q]$ we have $n = 2s + p + 2q + 2$, and the number of triples (s,p,q) satisfying this condition is given by

$$\begin{cases} \frac{1}{8}(n+1)(n-1) & (n \text{ is odd}), \\ \frac{1}{8}n(n+2) & (n \text{ is even}). \end{cases}$$

In case $n \geq 3$ the second term of $\mathcal{LH}_n^+$ actually appears and it is generated by the polynomial

$$(d + 2s + p + 2q)\,F[s+1,0,0,p-1,1,q] - 2(s+1)\,F[s,1,0,p,0,q]$$
$$\in (p\Lambda_1 + q\Lambda_2) \otimes V_{n-2q-2},$$

where $p \geq 1$, $s \geq 0$, $q \geq 0$ and $n = 2s + p + 2q + 2$.

This fact can be verified in the following way. We can easily see that $F[\overline{s},\overline{t},\overline{u},\lambda,\nu,\xi] \in (p\Lambda_1 + q\Lambda_2) \otimes V_{n-2q-2}$ if and only if

$$\begin{cases} \lambda + \nu = p, \\ \xi = q, \\ 2\overline{s} - 2\overline{u} + \lambda - \nu = n - 2q - 2, \\ n = 2\overline{s} + 2\overline{t} + 2\overline{u} + \lambda + \nu + 2\xi. \end{cases}$$

From these equalities we have

$$\overline{t} + 2\overline{u} + \nu = 1,$$

which implies $(\overline{t},\overline{u},\nu) = (0,0,1)$ or $(1,0,0)$. In case $(\overline{t},\overline{u},\nu) = (0,0,1)$ we have

$$(\overline{s},\overline{t},\overline{u},\lambda,\nu,\xi) = ((n-p-2q)/2, 0, 0, p-1, 1, q)$$

and in case $(\overline{t},\overline{u},\nu) = (1,0,0)$ we have

$$(\overline{s},\overline{t},\overline{u},\lambda,\nu,\xi) = ((n-p-2q-2)/2, 1, 0, p, 0, q).$$

Thus, by putting $s = (n-p-2q-2)/2$, we have $n = p + 2q + 2s + 2$ and the second term can be expressed as a linear combination of $F[s+1,0,0,p-1,1,q]$ and

$F[s, 1, 0, p, 0, q]$. Since this linear combination must be harmonic, we can determine its coefficients uniquely up to a non-zero constant by calculating their derivatives. This gives a generator of the second term of $\mathcal{LH}_n^+$, which we already listed above.

The number of triples (s, p, q) satisfying $p \geq 1$, $s \geq 0$, $q \geq 0$ and $n = 2s+p+2q+2$ is

$$\begin{cases} \frac{1}{8}(n+1)(n-1) & (n \text{ is odd}), \\ \frac{1}{8}n(n-2) & (n \text{ is even}). \end{cases}$$

The third term of $\mathcal{LH}_n^+$ appears in case $n \geq 4$, and in this case we have $p \geq 2$ (for details, see the next section). Its generator can be obtained in a similar way as above. But its explicit form becomes more complicated. First, we can easily show that it is expressed in the following linear combination of four polynomials

$$f = a_{00}^3 F[s+1, 0, 0, p-2, 2, q] + a_{01}^3 F[s, 0, 1, p, 0, q] + a_{10}^3 F[s, 1, 0, p-1, 1, q]$$
$$+ a_{20}^3 F[s-1, 2, 0, p, 0, q] \in (p\Lambda_1 + q\Lambda_2) \otimes V_{n-2q-4}$$

with $p \geq 2$. (For details, see the next section.) Then, applying the formulas in Proposition 5.1 to f, we see that f is harmonic if and only if

$$\begin{cases} 4(s+1) a_{00}^3 + 2p\, a_{01}^3 + (d + 2s + p + 2q) a_{10}^3 = 0, \\ 2s\, a_{01}^3 + s\, a_{10}^3 + (d + 2s + p + 2q - 1) a_{20}^3 = 0, \\ (d + 2q) a_{01}^3 + a_{10}^3 + a_{20}^3 = 0 \end{cases}$$

in case $s \geq 1$. The first two conditions follow from the second derivative of f, and the third one follows from the fourth derivative of f. By direct calculations it follows that the solution is uniquely determined up to a non-zero constant:

$$\begin{cases} a_{00}^3 = s(s+1)(q_d - 1) + (s+1)(p_d - 1)(q_d - 1) + \frac{1}{4}(p_d - 1)(p_d - 2)(q_d - 2), \\ a_{01}^3 = (s+1)(s + p_d - 1), \\ a_{10}^3 = -(s+1)\{2s(q_d - 1) + (p_d - 1)q_d\}, \\ a_{20}^3 = s(s+1)(q_d - 2), \end{cases}$$

where $q_d = d+2q$, $p_d = q_d+p = d+p+2q$, $p \geq 2$, $s \geq 1$, $q \geq 0$ and $n = 2s+p+2q+2$.

In case $s = 0$ the condition that f is harmonic reduces to a single equation

$$4 a_{00}^3 + 2p\, a_{01}^3 + (d + p + 2q) a_{10}^3 = 0.$$

For example, the fourth derivative of f automatically vanishes in this case.

The number of triples (s, p, q) satisfying the conditions $p \geq 2$, $s \geq 0$, $q \geq 0$ is

$$\begin{cases} \frac{1}{8}(n-1)(n-3) & (n \text{ is odd}), \\ \frac{1}{8}n(n-2) & (n \text{ is even}). \end{cases}$$

Here we consider the case $n = 5$. Then from the equality $n = 2s+p+2q+2$ and from the conditions $p \geq 2$, $s \geq 0$, $q \geq 0$, we have a unique triple $(s, p, q) = (0, 3, 0)$. We adopt the above formula of f, which we obtained under the condition $s \geq 1$. Of course it is also harmonic in the case $s = 0$. (Actually, its coefficients a_{ij}^3 satisfy redundant conditions in this case.) Thus the polynomial f gives a generator of a component $(3\Lambda_1) \otimes V_1$. It is explicitly given by

$$f = a_{00}^3 \, F[1,0,0,1,2,0] + a_{01}^3 \, F[0,0,1,3,0,0] + a_{10}^3 \, F[0,1,0,2,1,0]$$

with

$$\begin{cases} a_{00}^3 = (d+2)\{d-1+\tfrac{1}{4}(d+1)(d-2)\}, \\ a_{01}^3 = d+2, \\ a_{10}^3 = -d(d+2). \end{cases}$$

(Note that $p_d = d+3$, $q_d = d$, $a_{20}^3 = 0$ in this case.)

From the result in p.102 of [10] we know that the multiplicity of the space $(3\Lambda_1) \otimes V_1$ in $\mathcal{LH}_5$ is 2, and their generators are explicitly given by

$$\begin{aligned} F_1 &= (z \cdot \alpha)(w \cdot \alpha)\{(d+3)z^2(w \cdot \alpha) - 4(z \cdot w)(z \cdot \alpha)\} \\ &= (d+3)F[1,0,0,1,2,0] - 4F[0,1,0,2,1,0], \\ F_2 &= (z \cdot \alpha)\{3z^2(w \cdot \alpha)^2 - 2w^2(z \cdot \alpha)^2\} \\ &= 3F[1,0,0,1,2,0] - 2F[0,0,1,3,0,0] \end{aligned}$$

in the notation of this paper. We can easily see that

$$\frac{4}{d+2} f = d\, F_1 - 2\, F_2.$$

We consider that this polynomial f gives a generator of $(3\Lambda_1) \otimes V_1$ in $\mathcal{LH}_5^+$, though $s = 0$ does not satisfy the assumption $s \geq 1$. That is say, we extend the formula of the generator f outside the range $s \geq 1$.

Next, we consider the remaining generator of $(3\Lambda_1) \otimes V_1$ which is contained in $\mathcal{LH}_5^-$. We remind that the decompositions of the subspaces in $\mathcal{LH}_5^\pm$ corresponding to $p = 3$, $q = 0$ are given by

$$\begin{aligned} \mathcal{LH}_5^+ &\supset (3\Lambda_1) \otimes (V_5 + V_3 + V_1 + V_{-1}), \\ \mathcal{LH}_5^- &\supset (3\Lambda_1) \otimes (V_1 + V_{-1} + V_{-3} + V_{-5}). \end{aligned}$$

Thus, to obtain a generator of the component $(3\Lambda_1) \otimes V_1$ in $\mathcal{LH}_5^-$, we have only to find a generator of $(3\Lambda_1) \otimes V_{-1}$ in $\mathcal{LH}_5^+$, which is the fourth component of $\mathcal{LH}_5^+$ corresponding to $p = 3$, $q = 0$, and then exchange the letters z and w in this polynomial. We can obtain a generator of $(3\Lambda_1) \otimes V_{-1}$ in $\mathcal{LH}_5^+$ completely in the same way as above. It is explicitly given by

$$12\, F[0,0,1,2,1,0] + (d^2+5d-2)\, F[1,0,0,0,3,0] - 6(d+2)\, F[0,1,0,1,2,0].$$

Thus, by exchanging the letters, we obtain a generator

$$12\, F[1,0,0,1,2,0] + (d^2+5d-2)\, F[0,0,1,3,0,0] - 6(d+2)\, F[0,1,0,2,1,0],$$

which is equal to

$$\frac{3}{2}(d+2)F_1 - \frac{1}{2}(d^2+5d-2)F_2.$$

In the following we consider that the irreducible component $(3\Lambda_1) \otimes V_1$ in $\mathcal{LH}_5^-$ is generated by this polynomial. Two polynomials

$$d\, F_1 - 2\, F_2, \qquad 3(d+2)F_1 - (d^2 + 5d - 2)F_2$$

are linearly independent since $d \geq 4$, and generate the space $2\,(3\Lambda_1) \otimes V_1$ contained in $\mathcal{LH}_5$, where the coefficient 2 implies the multiplicity. These polynomials take a slightly complicated form, compared with F_1 and F_2 themselves. But their forms should certainly possess some reasonable meaning from the representation theoretic standpoint.

6. Some Conjectures on Lower Harmonic Polynomials

As we see in the previous section, an algorithm to obtain generators of lower harmonic irreducible components of $\mathcal{LH}_n^+$ is established, and generators are obtained explicitly up to the first three terms. But the results are complicated as we have seen, when compared with generators of the principal parts P_n stated in §4.

At present we do not yet obtain the final forms of generators of lower harmonic irreducible components of $\mathcal{LH}_n^+$ for general cases. In this section we give some results and conjectures concerning them. Since the multiplicity of this space is always 1, their generators are uniquely determined up to a non-zero constant, and should be explicitly investigated in the future studies.

In general, generators of lower harmonic components are expressed as a linear combination of polynomials of the form $F[s,t,u,\lambda,\nu,\xi]$. Hence, there exist two problems in order to obtain the generators: One is to determine their basis, i.e., which kind of $F[s,t,u,\lambda,\nu,\xi]$ appear in generators, and the other is to determine their coefficients. The former problem is relatively simple, and the latter one is a hard problem, not solved yet.

As stated before, the space $\mathcal{LH}_n^+$ is decomposed in the form

$$\mathcal{LH}_n^+ = \sum_{\substack{p+2q \leq n-2, \\ p \geq 0,\, q \geq 0, \\ p \equiv n \,(\text{mod } 2)}} (p\Lambda_1 + q\Lambda_2) \otimes (V_{n-2q} + V_{n-2q-2} + \cdots + V_{n-2p-2q}).$$

The m-th component is given by $(p\Lambda_1 + q\Lambda_2) \otimes V_{n-2q-2(m-1)}$ for $m = 1, 2, \cdots, p+1$. We fix integers n, p, q and m satisfying $p+2q \leq n-2$, $p \geq 0$, $q \geq 0$, $p \equiv n \,(\text{mod}\,2)$ and $1 \leq m \leq p+1$ in the following. Then the polynomial $F[\bar{s}, \bar{t}, \bar{u}, \lambda, \nu, \xi]$ is contained in $(p\Lambda_1 + q\Lambda_2) \otimes V_{n-2q-2(m-1)}$ if and only if

$$\begin{cases} \lambda + \nu = p, \\ \xi = q, \\ 2\bar{s} - 2\bar{u} + \lambda - \nu = n - 2q - 2(m-1), \end{cases}$$

and in addition we have $n = 2\bar{s} + 2\bar{t} + 2\bar{u} + \lambda + \nu + 2\xi$. We here put $s = (n-p-2q-2)/2$. Then, s is a fixed non-negative integer. Furthermore, we put $\bar{t} = i$, $\bar{u} = j$. Then from the above equalities we have

$$\begin{cases} \bar{s} = s - i - j + 1, \\ \lambda = p - \nu, \\ \xi = q, \end{cases}$$

and the triple (i, j, ν) satisfies $i + 2j + \nu = m - 1$. Non-negative integers i and j also satisfy the inequality $i + j \leq s + 1$. We can easily count the number of (i, j, ν) satisfying these conditions.

As a result, generators of the m-th irreducible component $(p\Lambda_1 + q\Lambda_2) \otimes V_{n-2q-2(m-1)}$ in $\mathcal{LH}_n^+$ can be expressed as a linear combination of polynomials

$$F[s - i - j + 1, i, j, p - \nu, \nu, q],$$

satisfying the conditions $i + 2j + \nu = m - 1$ and $i + j \leq s + 1$. As we explain in the conjecture, we may drop the latter condition $i + j \leq s + 1$ since the coefficients automatically vanish in case $i + j > s + 1$. We express a generator of $(p\Lambda_1 + q\Lambda_2) \otimes V_{n-2q-2(m-1)}$ in $\mathcal{LH}_n^+$ as

$$\sum_{i+2j \leq m-1} a_{ij}^m F[s - i - j + 1, i, j, p + i + 2j - m + 1, m - i - 2j - 1, q].$$

(Note that in this notation we have $n = 2s + p + 2q + 2$.) Actually, the coefficient a_{ij}^m depends also on d, n, p, q and s. But we omit them in a symbol, since they are fixed throughout our arguments. We remark that the m-th component appears in $\mathcal{LH}_n^+$ only in the case $n \geq m + 1$. In addition, the inequality $p \geq m - 1$ holds. We can easily see that the multiplicity of $(p\Lambda_1 + q\Lambda_2) \otimes V_{n-2q-2(m-1)}$ in $\mathcal{LH}_n$ is 1 in case $s \geq [(m-1)/2]$, and the coefficient a_{ij}^m is uniquely determined in this range, by applying Proposition 5.1.

Now we state several conjectures on the above coefficients a_{ij}^m. We remark that the coefficients a_{ij}^m are uniquely determined up to a non-zero constant in case $s \geq [(m-1)/2]$, and we fix this constant appropriately such that the coefficients take relatively simple forms, though actually they are never "simple". In this paper, we only treat the case $m = 2l + 1$ ($l \geq 0$), where we gathered a large amount of data by using computers. In the following, all statements are "Conjectures", unless otherwise stated. As before, we use the convenient notations

$$p_d = d + p + 2q, \qquad q_d = d + 2q.$$

First, we state a general conjecture:

$$a_{ij}^{2l+1} = (-1)^i \sum_{v=i+j}^{2l} b_{ij,v}^{2l+1} (s - v + 2)_v (p_d + v - 2)_{2l-v} f_{ij,v}^{l-j}(q_d),$$

where

$$\begin{cases} b_{ij,v}^{2l+1} = \dfrac{1}{2^{2l+j-v}} \dfrac{(2l)!}{(2l-v)!\,(v-i-j)!\,i!} \sum_{h=0}^{[j/2]} (-1)^h \binom{2l-v}{h} \binom{4l-i-j-v-2h}{j-2h}, \\ (s - v + 2)_v = (s - v + 2)(s - v + 3) \cdots (s - 1)s(s + 1), \\ (p_d + v - 2)_{2l-v} = (p_d + v - 2)(p_d + v - 1) \cdots (p_d + 2l - 4)(p_d + 2l - 3), \end{cases}$$

and $f_{ij,v}^{l-j}(q_d)$ is a monic polynomial of q_d with degree $l - j$. Here we use the notation

$$(A)_B = A(A+1)(A+2) \cdots (A + B - 1),$$

and we put $(A)_0 = 1$. Remark that i, j satisfy the inequality $i + 2j \leq m - 1 = 2l$, and in particular we have $i + j \leq 2l$. If $i + j \geq s + 2$, then the term $(s - v + 2)_v$ automatically vanishes, as we stated before. The symbol d appears only in two terms $(p_d + v - 2)_{2l-v}$ and $f_{ij,v}^{l-j}(q_d)$. The coefficient a_{ij}^{2l+1} is a polynomial of d with total degree $3l - (i + 2j)$.

Example. We put

$$\begin{cases} f_{ij,v}^0(q_d) = 1, \\ f_{00,0}^1(q_d) = q_d - 2, \quad f_{00,1}^1(q_d) = q_d - 1, \quad f_{00,2}^1(q_d) = q_d - 1, \\ f_{10,1}^1(q_d) = q_d, \quad f_{10,2}^1(q_d) = q_d - 1, \\ f_{20,2}^1(q_d) = q_d - 2. \end{cases}$$

In case $m = 1$, i.e., $l = 0$, we have $i = j = 0$ from the inequality $i + 2j \leq m - 1 = 2l$. Thus we have

$$a_{00}^1 = b_{00,0}^1 f_{00,0}^0(q_d) = 1,$$

and hence the first term of $\mathcal{LH}_n^+$ is

$$F[s+1, 0, 0, p, 0, q] = (z^2)^{s+1}(z \cdot \alpha)^p \{(z \cdot \alpha)(w \cdot \beta) - (z \cdot \beta)(w \cdot \alpha)\}^q,$$

as we stated before.

Next, assume $m = 3$, i.e., $l = 1$. In this case we have $(i, j) = (0, 0), (0, 1), (1, 0), (2, 0)$ from the inequality $i + 2j \leq 2$. Then, we have

$$a_{00}^3 = \sum_{v=0}^{2} b_{00,v}^3 (s - v + 2)_v (p_d + v - 2)_{2-v} f_{00,v}^{1-j}(q_d)$$

$$= \frac{1}{4}(p_d - 2)(p_d - 1) f_{00,0}^1(q_d) + (s+1)(p_d - 1) f_{00,1}^1(q_d) + s(s+1) f_{00,2}^1(q_d)$$

$$= \frac{1}{4}(p_d - 2)(p_d - 1)(q_d - 2) + (s+1)(p_d - 1)(q_d - 1) + s(s+1)(q_d - 1),$$

$$a_{01}^3 = \sum_{v=1}^{2} b_{01,v}^3 (s - v + 2)_v (p_d + v - 2)_{2-v} f_{01,v}^0(q_d)$$

$$= (s+1)(p_d - 1) + s(s+1),$$

$$a_{10}^3 = -\sum_{v=1}^{2} b_{10,v}^3 (s - v + 2)_v (p_d + v - 2)_{2-v} f_{10,v}^1(q_d)$$

$$= -(s+1)(p_d - 1) f_{10,1}^1(q_d) - 2s(s+1) f_{10,2}^1(q_d)$$

$$= -(s+1)(p_d - 1)q_d - 2s(s+1)(q_d - 1),$$

$$a_{20}^3 = b_{20,2}^3 (s)_2 f_{20,2}^1(q_d) = s(s+1)(q_d - 2).$$

These coefficients all just coincide with our previous results in §5.

Thus our remaining problem is to state a conjecture on the forms of monic polynomials $f_{ij,v}^{l-j}(q_d)$. But actually, their forms are quite complicated and mysterious, which we cannot imagine from the previous examples. At present, we only have partial conjectures concerning this problem.

In the following, we state conjectures for the cases where j takes a small value. We first consider the case a_{i0}^{2l+1}, i.e., the case $j = 0$. In this case the monic polynomial $f_{i0,v}^{l}(q_d)$ can be factored into a product of linear forms:

$$f_{i0,v}^{l}(q_d) = \prod_{a=1}^{l}(q_d + m_{i0,va}^{l}).$$

Thus we have only to list up the values $m_{i0,va}^{l}$. For this purpose we must divide the situation into two cases: $0 \leq i \leq l$ and $l \leq i \leq 2l$.

In case $l \leq i \leq 2l$, the parameter v moves in the range $i \leq v \leq 2l$, and the values $m_{i0,va}^{l}$ are given in the following table:

$v \backslash a$	1	2	$\cdots$	$i-l$	$i-l+1$	$i-l+2$	$i-l+3$	$\cdots$	$l-2$	$l-1$	l
i	$4l-2i-2$	$4l-2i$	$\cdots$	$2l-4$	$2i-2$	$2i$	$2i+2$	$\cdots$	$4l-8$	$4l-6$	$4l-4$
$i+1$	$4l-2i-2$	$4l-2i$	$\cdots$	$2l-4$	$2l-3$	$2i$	$2i+2$	$\cdots$	$4l-8$	$4l-6$	$4l-4$
$i+2$	$4l-2i-2$	$4l-2i$	$\cdots$	$2l-4$	$2l-3$	$2l-2$	$2i+2$	$\cdots$	$4l-8$	$4l-6$	$4l-4$
$i+3$	$4l-2i-2$	$4l-2i$	$\cdots$	$2l-4$	$2l-3$	$2l-2$	$2l-1$	$\cdots$	$4l-8$	$4l-6$	$4l-4$
$\vdots$		$\vdots$					$\vdots$				
$2l-3$	$4l-2i-2$	$4l-2i$	$\cdots$	$2l-4$	$2l-3$	$2l-2$	$2l-1$	$\cdots$	$4l-8$	$4l-6$	$4l-4$
$2l-2$	$4l-2i-2$	$4l-2i$	$\cdots$	$2l-4$	$2l-3$	$2l-2$	$2l-1$	$\cdots$	$4l-i-6$	$4l-6$	$4l-4$
$2l-1$	$4l-2i-2$	$4l-2i$	$\cdots$	$2l-4$	$2l-3$	$2l-2$	$2l-1$	$\cdots$	$4l-i-6$	$4l-i-5$	$4l-4$
$2l$	$4l-2i-2$	$4l-2i$	$\cdots$	$2l-4$	$2l-3$	$2l-2$	$2l-1$	$\cdots$	$4l-i-6$	$4l-i-5$	$4l-i-4$

In other words, for $i \leq v \leq 2l$, we have

$$f_{i0,v}^{l}(q_d) = (q_d + 4l - 2i - 2)(q_d + 4l - 2i)(q_d + 4l - 2i + 2) \cdots (q_d + 2l - 4)$$
$$\times (q_d + 2l - 3)(q_d + 2l - 2) \cdots (q_d + 2l + v - i - 4)$$
$$\times (q_d + 2v - 2)(q_d + 2v) \cdots (q_d + 4l - 6)(q_d + 4l - 4).$$

By using this table, we can easily verify

$$f_{10,1}^{1}(q_d) = q_d, \quad f_{10,2}^{1}(q_d) = q_d - 1, \quad f_{20,2}^{1}(q_d) = q_d - 2.$$

As another example, we consider the case $l = 4$, $i = 6$. Then we have

$$\begin{cases} f_{60,6}^{4}(q_d) = (q_d + 2)(q_d + 4)(q_d + 10)(q_d + 12), \\ f_{60,7}^{4}(q_d) = (q_d + 2)(q_d + 4)(q_d + 5)(q_d + 12), \\ f_{60,8}^{4}(q_d) = (q_d + 2)(q_d + 4)(q_d + 5)(q_d + 6), \end{cases}$$

from which we know the coefficient a_{60}^{9}:

$$a_{60}^{9} = \sum_{v=6}^{8} b_{60,v}^{9} (s - v + 2)_v (p_d + v - 2)_{8-v} f_{60,v}^{4}(q_d)$$
$$= 7(s-4)(s-3) \cdots s(s+1)(p_d + 4)(p_d + 5) f_{60,6}^{4}(q_d)$$
$$+ 28(s-5)(s-4) \cdots s(s+1)(p_d + 5) f_{60,7}^{4}(q_d)$$
$$+ 28(s-6)(s-5) \cdots s(s+1) f_{60,8}^{4}(q_d).$$

Next we consider the case $0 \leq i \leq l$. To state the result for general cases, we must first consider the case $i = 0$. The parameter v moves in the range $0 \leq v \leq 2l$. The table of $m_{00,va}^{l}$ is given by

Generators of Irreducible Components

$v \backslash a$	1	2	3	......	$l-2$	$l-1$	l
0	-2	0	2	......	$2l-8$	$2l-6$	$2l-4$
1	0	2	4	......	$2l-6$	$2l-4$	$2l-3$
2	2	4	6	......	$2l-4$	$2l-3$	$2l-2$
$\vdots$			$\vdots$		$\vdots$		
$l-4$	$2l-10$	$2l-8$	$2l-6$	......	$3l-10$	$3l-9$	$3l-8$
$l-3$	$2l-8$	$2l-6$	$2l-4$	......	$3l-9$	$3l-8$	$3l-7$
$l-2$	$2l-6$	$2l-4$	$2l-3$	......	$3l-8$	$3l-7$	$3l-6$
$l-1$	$2l-4$	$2l-3$	$2l-2$	......	$3l-7$	$3l-6$	$3l-5$
l	$2l-3$	$2l-2$	$2l-1$	......	$3l-6$	$3l-5$	$3l-4$
$l+1$	$2l-3$	$2l-1$	$2l$	......	$3l-5$	$3l-4$	$3l-3$
$l+2$	$2l-3$	$2l-1$	$2l+1$	......	$3l-4$	$3l-3$	$3l-2$
$\vdots$			$\vdots$		$\vdots$		
$2l-4$	$2l-3$	$2l-1$	$2l+1$	......	$4l-10$	$4l-9$	$4l-8$
$2l-3$	$2l-3$	$2l-1$	$2l+1$	......	$4l-9$	$4l-8$	$4l-7$
$2l-2$	$2l-3$	$2l-1$	$2l+1$	......	$4l-9$	$4l-7$	$4l-6$
$2l-1$	$2l-3$	$2l-1$	$2l+1$	......	$4l-9$	$4l-7$	$4l-5$
$2l$	$2l-3$	$2l-1$	$2l+1$	......	$4l-9$	$4l-7$	$4l-5$

Explicitly, we have for $0 \leq v \leq l-1$

$$f^l_{00,v}(q_d) = (q_d + 2v - 2)(q_d + 2v)(q_d + 2v + 2) \cdots (q_d + 2l - 6)$$
$$\times (q_d + 2l - 4)(q_d + 2l - 3) \cdots (q_d + 2l + v - 4),$$

and in case $l - 1 \leq v \leq 2l - 1$ we have

$$f^l_{00,v}(q_d) = (q_d + 2l - 3)(q_d + 2l - 1)(q_d + 2l + 1) \cdots (q_d + 2v - 3)$$
$$\times (q_d + 2v - 2)(q_d + 2v - 1) \cdots (q_d + 2l + v - 4).$$

For the remaining case $v = 2l$, we have

$$f^l_{00,2l}(q_d) = (q_d + 2l - 3)(q_d + 2l - 1)(q_d + 2l + 1) \cdots (q_d + 4l - 5).$$

Mysterious enough, in spite of these different appearances, we have a common expansion of $f^l_{00,v}(q_d)$:

$$f^l_{00,v}(q_d) = q_d^l + \frac{1}{2}\{2l^2 + 2(2v-3)l - v(v+1)\}q_d^{l-1}$$
$$+ \frac{1}{24}\{12l^4 + 8(6v-11)l^3 + 12(3v^2 - 17v + 15)l^2$$
$$- 4(6v^3 + 3v^2 - 51v + 26)l + 3v(v-2)(v+1)(v+7)\}q_d^{l-2}$$
$$+ \frac{1}{48}\{8l^6 + 8(6v-13)l^5 + 4(21v^2 - 115v + 122)l^4$$
$$+ 8(2v^3 - 61v^2 + 195v - 131)l^3$$
$$- 2(21v^4 - 42v^3 - 435v^2 + 1180v - 520)l^2$$
$$+ 2(6v^5 + 39v^4 - 164v^3 - 203v^2 + 762v - 192)l$$
$$- v(v-2)(v+1)(v^3 + 16v^2 + 31v - 144)\}q_d^{l-3} + \cdots.$$

The above table itself is already mysterious, which starts from the even sequence ($v = 0$) and ending at the odd sequence ($v = 2l$), namely numbers are shifted from even to odd step by step by adding the number $2l - 1$ after all. These phenomena can be more well understood by viewing the table consisting explicit numbers, not including the letter l. The following table is the the case of $l = 4$:

$v \backslash a$	1	2	3	4
0	−2	0	2	4
1	0	2	4	5
2	2	4	5	6
3	4	5	6	7
4	5	6	7	8
5	5	7	8	9
6	5	7	9	10
7	5	7	9	11
8	5	7	9	11

Under these preparations, we state conjectures on $m^l_{i0,va}$ for general i with $0 \leq i \leq l$:

$v \backslash a$	1	2	$\cdots$	$l-i-1$	$l-i$	$l-i+1$	$l-i+2$	$\cdots\cdots$	$l-1$	l
i	$2i-2$	$2i$	$\cdots$	$2l-6$	$2l-4$	$4l-2i-2$	$4l-2i$	$\cdots\cdots$	$4l-6$	$4l-4$
$i+1$						$4l-2i-2$	$4l-2i$	$\cdots\cdots$	$4l-6$	$4l-4$
$\vdots$										
$2l-i$						$4l-2i-2$	$4l-2i$	$\cdots\cdots$	$4l-6$	$4l-4$
$2l-i+1$			(A)			$4l-2i-3$	$4l-2i$	$\cdots\cdots$	$4l-6$	$4l-4$
$2l-i+2$						$4l-2i-3$	$4l-2i-2$	$\cdots\cdots$	$4l-6$	$4l-4$
$\vdots$										
$2l-2$						$4l-2i-3$	$4l-2i-2$	$\cdots\cdots$	$4l-6$	$4l-4$
$2l-1$						$4l-2i-3$	$4l-2i-2$	$\cdots\cdots$	$4l-i-5$	$4l-4$
$2l$	$2l-3$	$2l-1$	$\cdots$	$4l-2i-7$	$4l-2i-5$	$4l-2i-3$	$4l-2i-2$	$\cdots\cdots$	$4l-i-5$	$4l-i-4$

The left-half part (A) is filled with the numbers taken from the table corresponding to $i = 0$. It is filled with the first $l - i$ columns and the bottom $2l - i + 1$ rows of the table $m^l_{00,va}$ which we presented above. This situation can be well understood by comparing the following tables, corresponding to the case $l = 4$, $i = 4$ and the above, corresponding to $l = 4$, $i = 0$:

$v \backslash a$	1	2	3	4
2	2	4	10	12
3	4	5	10	12
4	5	6	10	12
5	5	7	10	12
6	5	7	10	12
7	5	7	9	12
8	5	7	9	10

We thus present two tables of $m^l_{i0,va}$ corresponding to the cases $l \leq i \leq 2l$ and $0 \leq i \leq l$, which give the polynomial $f^l_{i0,v}(q_d)$ in the coefficient $a^{2l+1}_{i0,v}$. Note that for the boundary case $i = l$, both tables are applicable.

Next we state conjectures for the case $j = 1$. In this case i moves in the range $0 \leq i \leq 2l-2$, and we must divide the conjectures into three cases $i = 0$, $1 \leq i \leq l-2$

Generators of Irreducible Components

and $l-1 \leq i \leq 2l-2$. In any case the monic polynomial $f_{i1,v}^{l-1}(q_d)$ also can be expressed as a product of linear forms:

$$f_{i1,v}^{l-1}(q_d) = \prod_{a=1}^{l-1}(q_d + m_{i1,va}^{l-1}).$$

We first treat the case $l - 1 \leq i \leq 2l - 2$. The result is given in the following table of $m_{i1,va}^{l-1}$:

$v \backslash a$	1	2	$\cdots$	$i-l+1$	$i-l+2$	$i-l+3$	$i-l+4$	$\cdots$	$l-3$	$l-2$	$l-1$
$i+1$	$4l-2i-4$	$4l-2i-2$	$\cdots$	$2l-4$	$2i$	$2i+2$	$2i+4$	$\cdots$	$4l-10$	$4l-8$	$4l-6$
$i+2$	$4l-2i-4$	$4l-2i-2$	$\cdots$	$2l-4$	c_{i+2}	$2i+2$	$2i+4$	$\cdots$	$4l-10$	$4l-8$	$4l-6$
$i+3$	$4l-2i-4$	$4l-2i-2$	$\cdots$	$2l-4$	$2l-3$	c_{i+3}	$2i+4$	$\cdots$	$4l-10$	$4l-8$	$4l-6$
$i+4$	$4l-2i-4$	$4l-2i-2$	$\cdots$	$2l-4$	$2l-3$	$2l-2$	c_{i+4}	$\cdots$	$4l-10$	$4l-8$	$4l-6$
$\vdots$		$\vdots$				$\vdots$					
$2l-4$	$4l-2i-4$	$4l-2i-2$	$\cdots$	$2l-4$	$2l-3$	$2l-2$	$2l-1$	$\cdots$	$4l-10$	$4l-8$	$4l-6$
$2l-3$	$4l-2i-4$	$4l-2i-2$	$\cdots$	$2l-4$	$2l-3$	$2l-2$	$2l-1$	$\cdots$	c_{2l-3}	$4l-8$	$4l-6$
$2l-2$	$4l-2i-4$	$4l-2i-2$	$\cdots$	$2l-4$	$2l-3$	$2l-2$	$2l-1$	$\cdots$	$4l-i-8$	c_{2l-2}	$4l-6$
$2l-1$	$4l-2i-4$	$4l-2i-2$	$\cdots$	$2l-4$	$2l-3$	$2l-2$	$2l-1$	$\cdots$	$4l-i-8$	$4l-i-7$	c_{2l-1}
$2l$	$4l-2i-4$	$4l-2i-2$	$\cdots$	$2l-4$	$2l-3$	$2l-2$	$2l-1$	$\cdots$	$4l-i-8$	$4l-i-7$	$4l-i-6$

We emphasize that in case $i \leq 2l - 3$ there appears a curious strip $\{c_v\}$ in the right-half part of the table, where c_v is given by

$$c_v = \frac{8l - 4i - 4}{4l - i - v - 1} l - 4$$

for $i + 2 \leq v \leq 2l - 1$. For example in the case $l = 5$ and $i = 5$ we have

$v \backslash a$	1	2	3	4
6	6	10	12	14
7	6	$\frac{52}{7}$	12	14
8	6	7	$\frac{56}{6}$	14
9	6	7	8	$\frac{60}{5}$
10	6	7	8	9

Next we consider the case $1 \leq i \leq l - 2$. In this case we have the following table of $m_{i1,va}^{l-1}$:

$v \backslash a$	1	2	$\cdots$	$l-i-2$	$l-i-1$	$l-i$	$i-l+1$	$\cdots$	$l-3$	$l-2$	$l-1$
$i+1$	$2i$	$2i+2$	$\cdots$	$2l-6$	$4l-2i-4$	$4l-2i-2$	$4l-2i$	$\cdots$	$4l-8$	$4l-6$	d_{i+1}
$i+2$					$4l-2i-4$	$4l-2i-2$	$4l-2i$	$\cdots$	$4l-8$	$4l-6$	d_{i+2}
$\vdots$		$\vdots$			$\vdots$		$\vdots$				$\vdots$
$2l-i-2$					$4l-2i-4$	$4l-2i-2$	$4l-2i$	$\cdots$	$4l-8$	$4l-6$	d_{2l-i-2}
$2l-i-1$					$4l-2i-4$	$4l-2i-2$	$4l-2i$	$\cdots$	$4l-8$	$4l-6$	$4l-2i-7$
$2l-i$					$4l-2i-7$	$4l-2i-2$	$4l-2i$	$\cdots$	$4l-8$	$4l-6$	d_{2l-i}
$2l-i+1$		(B)			$4l-2i-7$	$4l-2i-5$	$4l-2i$	$\cdots$	$4l-8$	$4l-6$	d_{2l-i+1}
$2l-i+2$					$4l-2i-7$	$4l-2i-5$	$4l-2i-4$	$\cdots$	$4l-8$	$4l-6$	d_{2l-i+2}
$\vdots$		$\vdots$			$\vdots$		$\vdots$				$\vdots$
$2l-3$					$4l-3i-7$	$4l-2i-5$	$4l-2i-4$	$\cdots$	$4l-8$	$4l-6$	d_{2l-3}
$2l-2$					$4l-2i-7$	$4l-2i-5$	$4l-2i-4$	$\cdots$	$4l-i-8$	$4l-6$	d_{2l-2}
$2l-1$					$4l-2i-7$	$4l-2i-5$	$4l-2i-4$	$\cdots$	$4l-i-8$	$4l-i-7$	d_{2l-1}
$2l$	$2l-3$	$2l-1$	$\cdots$	$4l-2i-9$	$4l-2i-7$	$4l-2i-5$	$4l-2i-4$	$\cdots$	$4l-i-8$	$4l-i-7$	$4l-i-6$

The left-half part (B) is taken from the table of $m_{00,va}^l$ in a similar way as in (A). In this case it is filled with the first $l-i-2$ columns and the bottom $2l-i$ rows. The numbers d_v at the right most column are given by

$$d_v = \begin{cases} \dfrac{4(2l-i-1)}{4l-i-v-1}l - 4 & (v \neq 2l-i-1,\ 2l), \\ 4l-2i-7 & (v = 2l-i-1), \\ 4l-i-6 & (v = 2l) \end{cases}$$

for $i+1 \leq v \leq 2l$. Substituting $v = i+1$ into the above, we easily have $d_{i+1} = 2l-4$. Remaining d_v's except $v = i+1,\ 2l-i-1,\ 2l$ are fractions in general. As an explicit example, we have the following table for the case $l=7$, $i=3$:

$v \backslash a$	1	2	3	4	5	6
4	6	8	18	20	22	$\frac{200}{20}$
5	8	10	18	20	22	$\frac{204}{19}$
6	10	11	18	20	22	$\frac{208}{18}$
7	11	12	18	20	22	$\frac{212}{17}$
8	11	13	18	20	22	$\frac{216}{16}$
9	11	13	18	20	22	$\frac{220}{15}$
10	11	13	18	20	22	15
11	11	13	15	20	22	$\frac{228}{13}$
12	11	13	15	17	22	$\frac{232}{12}$
13	11	13	15	17	18	$\frac{236}{11}$
14	11	13	15	17	18	19

Next, we consider the case $i=0$, i.e., the monic polynomial $f_{01,v}^{l-1}(q_d)$. In this case we have the following table:

$v \backslash a$	1	2	$\cdots$	$l-2$	$l-1$
1	0	2	$\cdots$	$2l-6$	e_1
2					e_2
$\vdots$		(C)	$\vdots$		$\vdots$
$2l-2$					e_{2l-2}
$2l-1$					e_{2l-1}
$2l$	$2l-3$	$2l-1$	$\cdots$	$4l-9$	e_{2l}

The left-half part (C) is taken from the table of $m_{01,va}^l$, corresponding to the first $l-2$ columns and the bottom $2l$ rows. The numbers e_v at the right column are given by

$$e_v = \begin{cases} \dfrac{4(2l-1)}{4l-v-1}l - 4 & (v \neq 2l-1,\ 2l), \\ 4l-7 & (v = 2l-1,\ 2l) \end{cases}$$

for $1 \leq v \leq 2l$. Note that in case $v=1$ we have $e_1 = 2l-4$. Remaining $d_2 \sim d_{2l-2}$ are in general fractions. As an explicit example, we have the following table for the case $l=4$, $i=0$, $j=1$:

$v \backslash a$	1	2	3
1	0	2	$\frac{56}{14}$
2	2	4	$\frac{60}{13}$
3	4	5	$\frac{64}{12}$
4	5	6	$\frac{68}{11}$
5	5	7	$\frac{72}{10}$
6	5	7	$\frac{76}{9}$
7	5	7	9
8	5	7	9

Next we consider the coefficient a_{i2}^{2l+1} (the case $j = 2$). In this case i moves in the range $0 \leq i \leq 2l - 4$. Here we state conjectures only in the case $l - 2 \leq i \leq 2l - 4$. In contrast to the previous cases, the monic polynomials $f_{i2,v}^{l-2}(q_d)$ are not in general factored into the products of linear forms, namely in some times, contain quadratic terms as follows:

$v \backslash a$	1	2	$\cdots$	$i-l+2$	$i-l+3$	$l-i+4$	$l-i+5$	$\cdots\cdots$	$l-4$	$l-3$	$l-2$
$i+2$	$4l-2i-6$	$4l-2i-4$	$\cdots$	$2l-4$	$2i+2$	$2i+4$	$2i+6$	$\cdots\cdots$	$4l-12$	$4l-10$	$4l-8$
$i+3$					h_{i+3}	$2i+4$	$2i+6$	$\cdots\cdots$	$4l-12$	$4l-10$	$4l-8$
$i+4$					g_{i+4}	h_{i+4}	$2i+6$	$\cdots\cdots$	$4l-12$	$4l-10$	$4l-8$
$i+5$					$2l-3$	g_{i+5}	h_{i+5}	$\cdots\cdots$	$4l-12$	$4l-10$	$4l-8$
$i+6$					$2l-3$	$2l-2$	g_{i+6}	$\cdots\cdots$	$4l-12$	$4l-10$	$4l-8$
$i+7$					$2l-3$	$2l-2$	$2l-1$	$\cdots\cdots$	$4l-12$	$4l-10$	$4l-8$
$\vdots$		$\vdots$						$\vdots$			
$2l-5$					$2l-3$	$2l-2$	$2l-1$	$\cdots\cdots$	$4l-12$	$4l-10$	$4l-8$
$2l-4$					$2l-3$	$2l-2$	$2l-1$	$\cdots\cdots$	h_{2l-4}	$4l-10$	$4l-8$
$2l-3$					$2l-3$	$2l-2$	$2l-1$	$\cdots\cdots$	g_{2l-3}	h_{2l-3}	$4l-8$
$2l-2$					$2l-3$	$2l-2$	$2l-1$	$\cdots\cdots$	$4l-i-10$	g_{2l-2}	h_{2l-2}
$2l-1$					$2l-3$	$2l-2$	$2l-1$	$\cdots\cdots$	$4l-i-10$	$4l-i-9$	g_{2l-1}
$2l$	$4l-2i-6$	$4l-2i-4$	$\cdots$	$2l-4$	$2l-3$	$2l-2$	$2l-1$	$\cdots\cdots$	$4l-i-10$	$4l-i-9$	$4l-i-8$

Here we have

$$\begin{cases} h_{i+3} = \dfrac{2(2l-i-2)}{2l-i-3}l - \dfrac{1}{2l-i-3} - 5, \\ g_{2l-1} = \dfrac{4(2l-i-2)}{2l-i}l - 4. \end{cases}$$

Remaining g_v, h_v for $v = i+4 \sim 2l-2$ are determined up to order as follows:

$$(q_d + g_v)(q_d + h_v)$$
$$= q_d^2 + (g_v + h_v)q_d + g_v h_v$$
$$= \frac{A(q_d + 4l - 6)(q_d + 4l - 4) + B(q_d + 4l - 6)(q_d - 4) + C(q_d - 2)(q_d - 4)}{A + B + C},$$

where

$$A = \binom{2l-i-2}{2}, \quad B = \binom{2l-i-3}{1}\binom{2l-v}{1}, \quad C = \binom{2l-v}{2}.$$

We substitute $v = i + 3$ into this quadratic polynomial, though $i + 3$ is out of the range of v. Then it can be factored in the form

$$(q_d + 2l - 4)(q_d + h_{i+3}),$$

and the number h_{i+3} naturally appears. Similarly, we substitute $v = 2l - 1$ into this polynomial. Then it is factored in the form

$$(q_d + g_{2l-1})(q_d + 4l - 6).$$

Again, the number g_{2l-1} appears. The denominator $A+B+C$ has another expression

$$A + B + C = \sum_{h=0}^{1}(-1)^h \binom{2l-v}{h}\binom{4l - i - 2 - v - 2h}{2 - 2h},$$

which constitutes a part of the coefficient $b_{i2,v}^{2l+1}$. (Note that we are considering the case $j = 2$.)

As an explicit example, we give a table for the case $l = 8$, $i = 8$, $j = 2$:

$v \backslash a$	1	2	3	4	5	6
10	10	12	18	20	22	24
11	10	12	14	20	22	24
12	10	12	g_{12}	h_{12}	22	24
13	10	12	13	g_{13}	h_{13}	24
14	10	12	13	14	g_{14}	h_{14}
15	10	12	13	14	15	20
16	10	12	13	14	15	16

The values $g_{12} \sim h_{14}$ are determined by

$$(q_d + g_{12})(q_d + h_{12}) = q_d^2 + \frac{1214}{41} q_d + \frac{8888}{41},$$
$$(q_d + g_{13})(q_d + h_{13}) = q_d^2 + 34\, q_d + \frac{3128}{11},$$
$$(q_d + g_{14})(q_d + h_{14}) = q_d^2 + \frac{512}{13} q_d + \frac{4944}{13}.$$

We can unify these polynomials as

$$(q_d + g_v)(q_d + h_v) = q_d^2 - \frac{2(3v^2 + 17v - 1850)}{v^2 - 41v + 430} q_d + \frac{8(v + 10)(v + 89)}{v^2 - 41v + 430}$$

for $v = 12 \sim 14$.

Generally, we conjecture that polynomials of q_d with degree j sometimes appear in the coefficient a_{ij}^{2l+1}.

7. Reproducing Kernels of Irreducible Subspaces of $\mathcal{LH}_n$ for $n \leq 5$

In this section we give the reproducing kernels of the irreducible subspaces of $\mathcal{LH}_n$ on some orbits for $n \leq 5$ in the multiplicity free cases.

Here we give tables of the generators of irreducible components of $\mathcal{LH}_n$ for $n \leq 5$. In the following we assume that $\alpha, \beta \in \mathbf{C}^d$, $\alpha^2 = \alpha \cdot \beta = \beta^2 = 0$. The coefficient of $(p\Lambda_1 + q\Lambda_2) \otimes V_k$ implies its multiplicity. In the following we identify $f \in \mathcal{H}_n$ and $f \circ \Psi^{-1} \in \mathcal{H}_n(\mathbf{C}^{2d})$.

$\mathcal{LH}_2$: components
$\quad (0) \otimes V_2 : z^2$,
$\quad (0) \otimes V_{-2} : w^2$.

$\mathcal{LH}_3$: components
$\quad (\Lambda_1) \otimes V_3 : z^2(z \cdot \alpha)$,
$\quad (\Lambda_1) \otimes V_1 : (d+1)z^2(w \cdot \alpha) - 2(z \cdot w)(z \cdot \alpha)$,
$\quad (\Lambda_1) \otimes V_{-1} : (d+1)w^2(z \cdot \alpha) - 2(z \cdot w)(w \cdot \alpha)$,
$\quad (\Lambda_1) \otimes V_{-3} : w^2(w \cdot \alpha)$.

$\mathcal{LH}_4$: components
$\quad (2\Lambda_1) \otimes V_4 : z^2(z \cdot \alpha)^2$,
$\quad (2\Lambda_1) \otimes V_2 : (z \cdot \alpha)\{(d+2)z^2(w \cdot \alpha) - 2(z \cdot w)(z \cdot \alpha)\}$,
$\quad 2\,(2\Lambda_1) \otimes V_0 : (w \cdot \alpha)\{(d+2)z^2(w \cdot \alpha) - 4(z \cdot w)(z \cdot \alpha)\}$,
$\qquad\qquad\qquad\quad (z \cdot \alpha)\{(d+2)w^2(z \cdot \alpha) - 4(z \cdot w)(w \cdot \alpha)\}$,
$\quad (2\Lambda_1) \otimes V_{-2} : (w \cdot \alpha)\{(d+2)w^2(z \cdot \alpha) - 2(z \cdot w)(w \cdot \alpha)\}$,
$\quad (2\Lambda_1) \otimes V_{-4} : w^2(w \cdot \alpha)^2$,
$\quad (\Lambda_2) \otimes V_2 : z^2\{(z \cdot \alpha)(w \cdot \beta) - (z \cdot \beta)(w \cdot \alpha)\}$,
$\quad (\Lambda_2) \otimes V_{-2} : w^2\{(z \cdot \alpha)(w \cdot \beta) - (z \cdot \beta)(w \cdot \alpha)\}$,
$\quad (0) \otimes V_4 : (z^2)^2$,
$\quad (0) \otimes V_{-4} : (w^2)^2$.

$\mathcal{LH}_5$: components
$\quad (3\Lambda_1) \otimes V_5 : z^2(z \cdot \alpha)^3$,
$\quad (3\Lambda_1) \otimes V_3 : (z \cdot \alpha)^2\{(d+3)z^2(w \cdot \alpha) - 2(z \cdot w)(z \cdot \alpha)\}$,
$\quad 2\,(3\Lambda_1) \otimes V_1 : (z \cdot \alpha)(w \cdot \alpha)\{(d+3)z^2(w \cdot \alpha) - 4(z \cdot w)(z \cdot \alpha)\}$,
$\qquad\qquad\qquad\quad (z \cdot \alpha)\{3z^2(w \cdot \alpha)^2 - 2w^2(z \cdot \alpha)^2\}$,
$\quad 2\,(3\Lambda_1) \otimes V_{-1} : (z \cdot \alpha)(w \cdot \alpha)\{(d+3)w^2(z \cdot \alpha) - 4(z \cdot w)(w \cdot \alpha)\}$,
$\qquad\qquad\qquad\quad (w \cdot \alpha)\{2z^2(w \cdot \alpha)^2 - 3w^2(z \cdot \alpha)^2\}$,
$\quad (3\Lambda_1) \otimes V_{-3} : (w \cdot \alpha)^2\{(d+3)w^2(z \cdot \alpha) - 2(z \cdot w)(w \cdot \alpha)\}$,
$\quad (3\Lambda_1) \otimes V_{-5} : w^2(w \cdot \alpha)^3$,
$\quad (\Lambda_1 + \Lambda_2) \otimes V_3 : z^2(z \cdot \alpha)\{(z \cdot \alpha)(w \cdot \beta) - (z \cdot \beta)(w \cdot \alpha)\}$,
$\quad (\Lambda_1 + \Lambda_2) \otimes V_1 : \{(z \cdot \alpha)(w \cdot \beta) - (z \cdot \beta)(w \cdot \alpha)\}\{(d+3)z^2(w \cdot \alpha) - 2(z \cdot w)(z \cdot \alpha)\}$,
$\quad (\Lambda_1 + \Lambda_2) \otimes V_{-1} : \{(z \cdot \alpha)(w \cdot \beta) - (z \cdot \beta)(w \cdot \alpha)\}\{(d+3)w^2(z \cdot \alpha) - 2(z \cdot w)(w \cdot \alpha)\}$,
$\quad (\Lambda_1 + \Lambda_2) \otimes V_{-3} : w^2(w \cdot \alpha)\{(z \cdot \alpha)(w \cdot \beta) - (z \cdot \beta)(w \cdot \alpha)\}$,
$\quad (\Lambda_1) \otimes V_5 : (z^2)^2(z \cdot \alpha)$,
$\quad (\Lambda_1) \otimes V_3 : z^2\{(d+3)z^2(w \cdot \alpha) - 4(z \cdot w)(z \cdot \alpha)\}$,
$\quad (\Lambda_1) \otimes V_{-3} : w^2\{(d+3)w^2(z \cdot \alpha) - 4(z \cdot w)(w \cdot \alpha)\}$,
$\quad (\Lambda_1) \otimes V_{-5} : (w^2)^2(w \cdot \alpha)$.

Remark that the dimension of the $K_{\mathbf{R}}$-irreducible component $(r\Lambda_1 + s\Lambda_2) \otimes V_k$ can be calculated by the formula

$$\frac{1}{(d-2)!(d-4)!}(r+1)(2s+d-4)(r+2s+d-3)$$
$$\times (2r+2s+d-2) \cdot \prod_{l=1}^{d-5}(s+l) \cdot \prod_{l=2}^{d-4}(r+s+l).$$

In the following we denote by dh the Haar measure on $SO(d)$, and we put $e_j = {}^t(0\cdots 0\overset{j}{1} 0\cdots 0)$. For $\widetilde{X} = \begin{pmatrix} 0 & X \\ {}^t X & 0 \end{pmatrix} \in \mathfrak{p}$ and $X = (x\ y)$ and $g = \operatorname{Ad}\begin{pmatrix} A & 0 \\ 0 & R(\theta) \end{pmatrix} \in K_{\mathbf{R}}$ ($A \in SO(d)$), where $R(\theta) = \begin{pmatrix} \cos\theta & -\sin\theta \\ \sin\theta & \cos\theta \end{pmatrix}$, we have

$$\Psi(g\widetilde{X}) = \begin{pmatrix} e^{-i\theta}Az \\ e^{i\theta}Aw \end{pmatrix}$$

and it is valid that for $f \in S(\mathfrak{p})$

$$\int_{K_{\mathbf{R}}} f(g\widetilde{X}_0)dg = \frac{1}{2\pi}\int_0^{2\pi}\int_{SO(d)} f \circ \Psi^{-1}\left(\begin{pmatrix} e^{-i\theta}hz_0 \\ e^{i\theta}hw_0 \end{pmatrix}\right) dh d\theta,$$

where $\widetilde{X}_0 = \Psi^{-1}\left(\begin{pmatrix} z_0 \\ w_0 \end{pmatrix}\right) \in \mathfrak{p}$. We put

$$\widetilde{Z}_0 = \Psi^{-1}\left(\begin{pmatrix} e_1 \\ e_1 \end{pmatrix}\right), \quad \widetilde{Z}_1 = \Psi^{-1}\left(\begin{pmatrix} e_1 \\ e_2 \end{pmatrix}\right),$$
$$\widetilde{Z}_2 = \Psi^{-1}\left(\begin{pmatrix} e_1 \\ e_2+ie_3 \end{pmatrix}\right), \quad \widetilde{Z}_3 = \Psi^{-1}\left(\begin{pmatrix} e_2+ie_3 \\ e_1 \end{pmatrix}\right).$$

For $f \in \mathcal{H}_n$ we denote by $\langle f \rangle$ the subspace generated by the set $\{f(gX)\,;\, g \in K_{\mathbf{R}}\}$. Let $\widetilde{X} = \Psi^{-1}\left(\begin{pmatrix} z \\ w \end{pmatrix}\right)$, $\widetilde{X}' = \Psi^{-1}\left(\begin{pmatrix} z' \\ w' \end{pmatrix}\right) \in \mathfrak{p}$. From the formulas of spherical harmonics we have the following reproducing formulas on irreducible subspaces of $\mathcal{LH}_n$ ($n = 1 \sim 5$). We have the following proposition easily.

Proposition 7.1. *Suppose $\widetilde{X}_0 \in \mathfrak{p}\backslash\{0\}$, $f \in \mathcal{H}_n$ and V is the irreducible subspace of $\mathcal{H}_n$. Let $K(\widetilde{X}, \widetilde{Y})$ be the function on $\mathfrak{p} \times \mathfrak{p}$ which satisfies the following conditions:*

$$K(\ , g\widetilde{X}_0) \in V \qquad (g \in K_{\mathbf{R}}), \tag{7.1}$$
$$K(\widetilde{X}, \widetilde{X}') = \overline{K(\widetilde{X}', \widetilde{X})} \qquad (\widetilde{X}, \widetilde{X}' \in \mathfrak{p}), \tag{7.2}$$
$$K(\widetilde{X}, \widetilde{X}') = K(g\widetilde{X}, g\widetilde{X}') \qquad (g \in K_{\mathbf{R}}), \tag{7.3}$$
$$\int_{K_{\mathbf{R}}} f(g\widetilde{X}_0)K(\widetilde{X}, g\widetilde{X}_0)dg = \begin{cases} f(\widetilde{X}) & (f \in V), \\ 0 & (f \notin V). \end{cases} \tag{7.4}$$

We put for $\widetilde{X}, \widetilde{Y} \in \mathfrak{p}$

$$H(\widetilde{X},\widetilde{Y}) = \int_{K_{\mathbf{R}}} K(\widetilde{X}, g\widetilde{X}_0) K(g\widetilde{X}_0, \widetilde{Y}) dg.$$

Then $H(\widetilde{X},\widetilde{Y})$ is the reproducing kernel in V on the orbit $K_{\mathbf{R}}\widetilde{X}_0$, i.e. for any $f \in \mathcal{H}_n$

$$\begin{aligned}
&H(\ ,Y) \in V & (Y \in \mathfrak{p}), \\
&H(\widetilde{X},\widetilde{X}') = \overline{H(\widetilde{X}',\widetilde{X})} & (\widetilde{X},\widetilde{X}' \in \mathfrak{p}), \\
&H(\widetilde{X},\widetilde{X}') = H(g\widetilde{X}, g\widetilde{X}') & (g \in K_{\mathbf{R}}), \\
&\int_{K_{\mathbf{R}}} f(g\widetilde{X}_0) H(\widetilde{X}, g\widetilde{X}_0) dg = \begin{cases} f(\widetilde{X}) & (f \in V), \\ 0 & (f \notin V). \end{cases}
\end{aligned}$$

Furthermore we have for any $g \in K_{\mathbf{R}}$

$$K(\widetilde{X}, g\widetilde{X}_0) = H(\widetilde{X}, g\widetilde{X}_0).$$

Example 7.1.

(1) We put
$$\mathcal{LH}_{2,1}^{+} = \langle z^2 \rangle,$$
and
$$\mathcal{LH}_{2,1}^{-} = \langle w^2 \rangle,$$
respectively. We define
$$\begin{aligned}
K_{2,1}^{+}(\widetilde{X},\widetilde{X}') &= z^2 \overline{z}'^2, \\
K_{2,1}^{-}(\widetilde{X},\widetilde{X}') &= w^2 \overline{w}'^2.
\end{aligned}$$

Then we can see that $K_{2,1}^{+}$ and $K_{2,1}^{-}$ satisfies (7.1)–(7.4) for $\widetilde{X}_0 = \widetilde{Z}_0$. From Proposition 7.1 the reproducing kernel in $H_{2,1}^{\pm}$ on the orbit $K_{\mathbf{R}}\widetilde{Z}_0$ is

$$H_{2,1}^{\pm}(\widetilde{X},\widetilde{Y}) = \int_{K_{\mathbf{R}}} K_{2,1}^{\pm}(\widetilde{X}, g\widetilde{Z}_0) K_{2,1}^{\pm}(g\widetilde{Z}_0, \widetilde{Y}) dg.$$

Example 7.2.

(1) We put
$$\mathcal{LH}_{3,1}^{+} = \langle z^2 (z \cdot \alpha) \rangle,$$
and
$$\mathcal{LH}_{3,1}^{-} = \langle w^2 (w \cdot \alpha) \rangle,$$
respectively. We define
$$\begin{aligned}
K_{3,1}^{+}(\widetilde{X},\widetilde{X}') &= dz^2 \overline{z}'^2 (z \cdot \overline{z}'), \\
K_{3,1}^{-}(\widetilde{X},\widetilde{X}') &= dw^2 \overline{w}'^2 (w \cdot \overline{w}').
\end{aligned}$$

Then we can see that $K_{3,1}^+$ and $K_{3,1}^-$ satisfies (7.1)–(7.4) for $\widetilde{X}_0 = \widetilde{Z}_0$. From Proposition 7.1 the reproducing kernel in $\mathcal{LH}_{3,1}^\pm$ on the orbit $K_{\mathbf{R}}\widetilde{Z}_0$ is

$$H_{3,1}^\pm(\widetilde{X}, \widetilde{Y}) = \int_{K_{\mathbf{R}}} K_{3,1}^\pm(\widetilde{X}, g\widetilde{Z}_0) K_{3,1}^\pm(g\widetilde{Z}_0, \widetilde{Y}) dg.$$

(2) We put
$$\mathcal{LH}_{3,2}^+ = \langle (d+1)z^2(w \cdot \alpha) - 2(z \cdot w)(z \cdot \alpha) \rangle,$$

and
$$\mathcal{LH}_{3,2}^- = \langle (d+1)w^2(z \cdot \alpha) - 2(w \cdot z)(w \cdot \alpha) \rangle,$$

respectively. We define

$$K_{3,2}^+(\widetilde{X}, \widetilde{X}') = C_{3,2}\{(d+1)z^2\,\overline{z}'^2(w \cdot \overline{w}') - 2(z \cdot w)(z \cdot \overline{z}')(\overline{z}' \cdot \overline{w}')\},$$
$$K_{3,2}^-(\widetilde{X}, \widetilde{X}') = C_{3,2}\{(d+1)w^2\,\overline{w}'^2(z \cdot \overline{z}') - 2(w \cdot z)(w \cdot \overline{w}')(\overline{w}' \cdot \overline{z}')\},$$

where $C_{3,2} = (d-1)/d$. Then we can see that $K_{3,2}^+$ and $K_{3,2}^-$ satisfies (7.1)–(7.4) for $\widetilde{X}_0 = \widetilde{Z}_0$. From Proposition 7.1 the reproducing kernel in $\mathcal{LH}_{3,2}^\pm$ on the orbit $K_{\mathbf{R}}\widetilde{Z}_0$ is

$$H_{3,2}^\pm(\widetilde{X}, \widetilde{Y}) = \int_{K_{\mathbf{R}}} K_{3,2}^\pm(\widetilde{X}, g\widetilde{Z}_0) K_{3,2}^\pm(g\widetilde{Z}_0, \widetilde{Y}) dg.$$

Example 7.3.
(1) We put
$$\mathcal{LH}_{4,1}^+ = \langle z^2(z \cdot \alpha)^2 \rangle,$$

and
$$\mathcal{LH}_{4,1}^- = \langle w^2(w \cdot \alpha)^2 \rangle,$$

respectively. We define

$$K_{4,1}^+(\widetilde{X}, \widetilde{X}') = C_{4,1}\{-(z^2)^2(\overline{z}'^2)^2 + dz^2(\overline{z}'^2)(z \cdot \overline{z}')^2\},$$
$$K_{4,1}^-(\widetilde{X}, \widetilde{X}') = C_{4,1}\{-(w^2)^2(\overline{w}'^2)^2 + dw^2(\overline{w}'^2)(w \cdot \overline{w}')^2\},$$

where $C_{4,1} = (d+2)/2$. Then we can see that $K_{4,1}^+$ and $K_{4,1}^-$ satisfies (7.1)–(7.4) for $\widetilde{X}_0 = \widetilde{Z}_0$. From Proposition 7.1 the reproducing kernel in $\mathcal{LH}_{4,1}^\pm$ on the orbit $K_{\mathbf{R}}\widetilde{Z}_0$ is

$$H_{4,1}^\pm(\widetilde{X}, \widetilde{Y}) = \int_{K_{\mathbf{R}}} K_{4,1}^\pm(\widetilde{X}, g\widetilde{Z}_0) K_{4,1}^\pm(g\widetilde{Z}_0, \widetilde{Y}) dg.$$

(2) We put
$$\mathcal{LH}_{4,2}^+ = \langle (z \cdot \alpha)\{(d+2)z^2(w \cdot \alpha) - 2(z \cdot w)(z \cdot \alpha)\} \rangle,$$

and
$$\mathcal{LH}_{4,2}^- = \langle (w \cdot \alpha)\{(d+2)w^2(z \cdot \alpha) - 2(z \cdot w)(w \cdot \alpha)\} \rangle,$$

respectively. We define

$$K_{4,2}^+(\widetilde{X}, \widetilde{X}') = C_{4,2}\{-(z \cdot w)z^2(\overline{z}' \cdot \overline{w}')\overline{z}'^2 + (d+2)(z \cdot \overline{z}')(w \cdot \overline{w}')z^2\overline{z}'^2$$
$$- 2(z \cdot \overline{z}')^2(z \cdot w)(\overline{z}' \cdot \overline{w}')\},$$

$$K_{4,2}^-(\widetilde{X}, \widetilde{X}') = C_{4,2}\{-(z \cdot w)w^2(\overline{z}' \cdot \overline{w}')\overline{w}'^2 + (d+2)(w \cdot \overline{w}')(z \cdot \overline{z}')w^2\overline{w}'^2$$
$$- 2(w \cdot \overline{w}')^2(z \cdot w)(\overline{z}' \cdot \overline{w}')\},$$

where $C_{4,2} = (d+2)/2$. Then we can see that $K_{4,2}^+$ and $K_{4,2}^-$ satisfies (7.1)–(7.4) for $\widetilde{X}_0 = \widetilde{Z}_0$. From Proposition 7.1 the reproducing kernel in $\mathcal{LH}_{4,2}^\pm$ on the orbit $K_{\mathbf{R}}\widetilde{Z}_0$ is

$$H_{4,2}^\pm(\widetilde{X}, \widetilde{Y}) = \int_{K_{\mathbf{R}}} K_{4,2}^\pm(\widetilde{X}, g\widetilde{Z}_0) K_{4,2}^\pm(g\widetilde{Z}_0, \widetilde{Y}) dg.$$

(3) We put
$$\mathcal{LH}_{4,4}^+ = \langle z^2\{(z \cdot \alpha)(w \cdot \beta) - (z \cdot \beta)(w \cdot \alpha)\}\rangle,$$

and
$$\mathcal{LH}_{4,4}^- = \langle w^2\{(z \cdot \alpha)(w \cdot \beta) - (z \cdot \beta)(w \cdot \alpha)\}\rangle,$$

respectively. We define

$$K_{4,4}^+(\widetilde{X}, \widetilde{X}') = C_{4,4} z^2 \overline{z}'^2 \{(z \cdot \overline{z}')(w \cdot \overline{w}') - (z \cdot \overline{w}')(\overline{z}' \cdot w)\},$$
$$K_{4,4}^-(\widetilde{X}, \widetilde{X}') = C_{4,4} w^2 \overline{w}'^2 \{(w \cdot \overline{w}')(z \cdot \overline{z}') - (w \cdot \overline{z}')(\overline{w}' \cdot z)\},$$

where $C_{4,4} = d(d-1)/2$. Then we can see that $K_{4,4}^+$ and $K_{4,4}^-$ satisfies (7.1)–(7.4) for $\widetilde{X}_0 = \widetilde{Z}_1$. From Proposition 7.1 the reproducing kernel in $\mathcal{LH}_{4,4}^\pm$ on the orbit $K_{\mathbf{R}}\widetilde{Z}_1$ is

$$H_{4,4}^\pm(\widetilde{X}, \widetilde{Y}) = \int_{K_{\mathbf{R}}} K_{4,4}^\pm(\widetilde{X}, g\widetilde{Z}_1) K_{4,4}^\pm(g\widetilde{Z}_1, \widetilde{Y}) dg.$$

(4) We put
$$\mathcal{LH}_{4,5}^+ = \langle (z^2)^2 \rangle,$$

and
$$\mathcal{LH}_{4,5}^- = \langle (w^2)^2 \rangle,$$

respectively. We define

$$K_{4,5}^+(\widetilde{X}, \widetilde{X}') = (z^2)^2(\overline{z}'^2)^2,$$
$$K_{4,5}^-(\widetilde{X}, \widetilde{X}') = (w^2)^2(\overline{w}'^2)^2.$$

Then we can see that $K_{4,5}^+$ and $K_{4,5}^-$ satisfies (7.1)–(7.4) for $\widetilde{X}_0 = \widetilde{Z}_0$. From Proposition 7.1 the reproducing kernel in $\mathcal{LH}_{4,5}^\pm$ on the orbit $K_{\mathbf{R}}\widetilde{Z}_0$ is

$$H_{4,5}^\pm(\widetilde{X}, \widetilde{Y}) = \int_{K_{\mathbf{R}}} K_{4,5}^\pm(\widetilde{X}, g\widetilde{Z}_0) K_{4,5}^\pm(g\widetilde{Z}_0, \widetilde{Y}) dg.$$

(5) We put
$$\mathcal{LH}^+_{4,3} = \langle (w\cdot\alpha)\{(d+2)z^2(w\cdot\alpha) - 4(z\cdot w)(z\cdot\alpha)\}\rangle,$$
and
$$\mathcal{LH}^-_{4,3} = \langle (z\cdot\alpha)\{(d+2)w^2(z\cdot\alpha) - 4(z\cdot w)(w\cdot\alpha)\}\rangle,$$
respectively. (Remark that we here adopt the definition of $\mathcal{LH}^{\pm}_{4,3}$ that was different from the one given in §5. The above generators are taken from our previous paper [p.102; 10].) Then we have $\mathcal{LH}^+_{4,3} \cong \mathcal{LH}^-_{4,3}$. We define
$$K^+_{4,3}(\widetilde{X},\widetilde{X}') = C_{4,3}\{(d+2)z^2\overline{z}'^2(w\cdot\overline{w}')^2 - 4\overline{z}'^2(z\cdot w)(z\cdot\overline{w}')(w\cdot\overline{w}')$$
$$- 4z^2(\overline{z}'\cdot w)(\overline{z}'\cdot\overline{w}')(w\cdot\overline{w}')\},$$
$$K^-_{4,3}(\widetilde{X},\widetilde{X}') = C_{4,3}\{(d+2)w^2\overline{w}'^2(z\cdot\overline{z}')^2 - 4\overline{w}'^2(w\cdot z)(w\cdot\overline{z}')(z\cdot\overline{z}')$$
$$- 4w^2(\overline{w}'\cdot z)(\overline{w}'\cdot\overline{z}')(z\cdot\overline{z}')\},$$
where $C_{4,3} = (d-1)/8$. We can see that $K^+_{4,3}$ satisfies (7.1)–(7.4) for $\widetilde{X}_0 = \widetilde{Z}_2$ and $K^-_{4,3}$ satisfies (7.1)–(7.4) for $\widetilde{X}_0 = \widetilde{Z}_3$, respectively.

From Proposition 7.1 the reproducing kernels in $\mathcal{LH}^+_{4,3}$ and $\mathcal{LH}^-_{4,3}$ on the orbits $K_{\mathbf{R}}\widetilde{Z}_2$ and $K_{\mathbf{R}}\widetilde{Z}_3$ are
$$H^+_{4,3}(\widetilde{X},\widetilde{Y}) = \int_{K_{\mathbf{R}}} K^+_{4,3}(\widetilde{X},g\widetilde{Z}_2)K^+_{4,3}(g\widetilde{Z}_2,\widetilde{Y})dg,$$
$$H^-_{4,3}(\widetilde{X},\widetilde{Y}) = \int_{K_{\mathbf{R}}} K^-_{4,3}(\widetilde{X},g\widetilde{Z}_3)K^-_{4,3}(g\widetilde{Z}_3,\widetilde{Y})dg,$$
respectively. Remark that $\mathcal{LH}^+_{4,3}|_{K_{\mathbf{R}}\widetilde{Z}_3} = \mathcal{LH}^-_{4,3}|_{K_{\mathbf{R}}\widetilde{Z}_2} = \{0\}$.

Example 7.4.
(1) We put
$$\mathcal{LH}^+_{5,1} = \langle z^2(z\cdot\alpha)^3\rangle,$$
and
$$\mathcal{LH}^-_{5,1} = \langle w^2(w\cdot\alpha)^3\rangle,$$
respectively. We define
$$K^+_{5,1}(\widetilde{X},\widetilde{X}') = C_{5,1}\{(d+2)z^2\overline{z}'^2(z\cdot\overline{z}')^3 - 3(z^2)^2(\overline{z}'^2)^2(z\cdot\overline{z}')\},$$
$$K^-_{5,1}(\widetilde{X},\widetilde{X}') = C_{5,1}\{(d+2)w^2\overline{w}'^2(w\cdot\overline{w}')^3 - 3(w^2)^2(\overline{w}'^2)^2(w\cdot\overline{w}')\},$$
where $C_{5,1} = d(d+4)/6$. Then we can see that $K^+_{5,1}$ and $K^-_{5,1}$ satisfies (7.1)–(7.4) for $\widetilde{X}_0 = \widetilde{Z}_0$. From Proposition 7.1 the reproducing kernel in $\mathcal{LH}^{\pm}_{5,1}$ on the orbit $K_{\mathbf{R}}\widetilde{Z}_0$ is
$$H^{\pm}_{5,1}(\widetilde{X},\widetilde{Y}) = \int_{K_{\mathbf{R}}} K^{\pm}_{5,1}(\widetilde{X},g\widetilde{Z}_0)K^{\pm}_{5,1}(g\widetilde{Z}_0,\widetilde{Y})dg.$$

(2) We put
$$\mathcal{LH}^+_{5,2} = \langle (z\cdot\alpha)^2\{(d+3)z^2(w\cdot\alpha) - 2(z\cdot w)(z\cdot\alpha)\}\rangle,$$

Generators of Irreducible Components

and
$$\mathcal{LH}_{5,2}^- = \langle (w \cdot \alpha)^2 \{(d+3)w^2(z \cdot \alpha) - 2(z \cdot w)(w \cdot \alpha)\} \rangle,$$
respectively. We define
$$K_{5,2}^+(\widetilde{X}, \widetilde{X}') = C_{5,2}\{(d+2)(d+3)z^2 \overline{z}'^2(z \cdot \overline{z}')^2(w \cdot \overline{w}') - (d+3)(z^2)^2(\overline{z}'^2)^2(w \cdot \overline{w}')$$
$$- 2dz^2 \overline{z}'^2 (z \cdot w)(z \cdot \overline{z}')(\overline{z}' \cdot \overline{w}') - 2(d+2)(z \cdot w)(z \cdot \overline{z}')^3(\overline{z}' \cdot \overline{w}')\},$$
$$K_{5,2}^-(\widetilde{X}, \widetilde{X}') = C_{5,2}\{(d+2)(d+3)w^2 \overline{w}'^2(w \cdot \overline{w}')^2(z \cdot \overline{z}') - (d+3)(w^2)^2(\overline{w}'^2)^2(z \cdot \overline{z}')$$
$$- 2dw^2 \overline{w}'^2 (z \cdot w)(w \cdot \overline{w}')(\overline{w}' \cdot \overline{z}') - 2(d+2)(z \cdot w)(w \cdot \overline{w}')^3(\overline{w}' \cdot \overline{z}')\},$$

where $C_{5,2} = d(d+4)/(6(d+1))$. Then we can see that $K_{5,2}^+$ and $K_{5,2}^-$ satisfies (7.1)–(7.4) for $\widetilde{X}_0 = \widetilde{Z}_0$. From Proposition 7.1 the reproducing kernel in $\mathcal{LH}_{5,2}^\pm$ on the orbit $K_\mathbf{R}\widetilde{Z}_0$ is
$$H_{5,2}^\pm(\widetilde{X}, \widetilde{Y}) = \int_{K_\mathbf{R}} K_{5,2}^\pm(\widetilde{X}, g\widetilde{Z}_0) K_{5,2}^\pm(g\widetilde{Z}_0, \widetilde{Y}) dg.$$

(3) We put
$$\mathcal{LH}_{5,3}^+ = \langle z^2\{(d+3)z^2(w \cdot \alpha) - 4(z \cdot w)(z \cdot \alpha)\} \rangle,$$
and
$$\mathcal{LH}_{5,3}^- = \langle w^2\{(d+3)w^2(z \cdot \alpha) - 4(z \cdot w)(w \cdot \alpha)\} \rangle,$$
respectively. We define
$$K_{5,3}^+(\widetilde{X}, \widetilde{X}')$$
$$= C_{5,3}\{(d+3)(z^2)^2(\overline{z}'^2)^2(w \cdot \overline{w}') - 4z^2 \overline{z}'^2(z \cdot w)(z \cdot \overline{z}')(\overline{z}' \cdot \overline{w}')\},$$
$$K_{5,3}^-(\widetilde{X}, \widetilde{X}')$$
$$= C_{5,3}\{(d+3)(w^2)^2(\overline{w}'^2)^2(z \cdot \overline{z}') - 4w^2 \overline{w}'^2(z \cdot w)(w \cdot \overline{w}')(\overline{z}' \cdot \overline{w}')\},$$

where $C_{5,3} = d/(d-1)$. Then we can see that $K_{5,3}^+$ and $K_{5,3}^-$ satisfies (7.1)–(7.4) for $\widetilde{X}_0 = \widetilde{Z}_0$. From Proposition 7.1 the reproducing kernel in $\mathcal{LH}_{5,3}^\pm$ on the orbit $K_\mathbf{R}\widetilde{Z}_0$ is
$$H_{5,3}^\pm(\widetilde{X}, \widetilde{Y}) = \int_{K_\mathbf{R}} K_{5,3}^\pm(\widetilde{X}, g\widetilde{Z}_0) K_{5,3}^\pm(g\widetilde{Z}_0, \widetilde{Y}) dg.$$

(4) We put
$$\mathcal{LH}_{5,4}^+ = \langle (z^2)^2(z \cdot \alpha) \rangle,$$
and
$$\mathcal{LH}_{5,4}^- = \langle (w^2)^2(w \cdot \alpha) \rangle,$$
respectively. We define
$$K_{5,4}^+(\widetilde{X}, \widetilde{X}') = d(z^2)^2(\overline{z}'^2)^2(z \cdot \overline{z}'),$$
$$K_{5,4}^-(\widetilde{X}, \widetilde{X}') = d(w^2)^2(\overline{w}'^2)^2(w \cdot \overline{w}').$$

Then we can see that $K_{5,4}^+$ and $K_{5,4}^-$ satisfies (7.1)–(7.4) for $\widetilde{X}_0 = \widetilde{Z}_0$. From Proposition 7.1 the reproducing kernel in $\mathcal{LH}_{5,4}^\pm$ on the orbit $K_{\mathbf{R}}\widetilde{Z}_0$ is

$$H_{5,4}^\pm(\widetilde{X},\widetilde{Y}) = \int_{K_{\mathbf{R}}} K_{5,4}^\pm(\widetilde{X}, g\widetilde{Z}_0) K_{5,4}^\pm(g\widetilde{Z}_0, \widetilde{Y}) dg.$$

References

[1] C. DeConcini, D. Eisenbud, C. Procesi, Young diagrams and determinantal varieties, *Inv. Math.*, **56** (1980), 129–165.
[2] S. Helgason, *Groups and Geometric Analysis*, Academic Press Inc., Orlando, 1984.
[3] K. Koike and I. Terada, Young-diagrammatic methods for the representation theory of the classical groups of type B_n, C_n, D_n, *J. Algebra*, **107** (1987), 466–511.
[4] B. Kostant and S. Rallis, Orbits and representations associated with symmetric spaces, *Amer. J. Math.*, **93** (1971), 753–809.
[5] M. Takeuchi, *Modern Spherical Functions*, Translations of Mathematical Monographs vol.**135**, Amer. Math. Soc., 1994.
[6] R. Wada, Explicit formulas for the reproducing kernels of the space of harmonic polynomials in the case of classical real rank 1, *Scientiae Mathematicae Japonicae*, **65** (2007), 384–406.
[7] R. Wada and Y. Agaoka, The reproducing kernels of the space of harmonic polynomials in the case of real rank 1, in *Microlocal Analysis and Complex Fourier Analysis* (Ed. T. Kawai, K. Fujita), 297–316, World Scientific, New Jersey (2002).
[8] R. Wada and Y. Agaoka, Some properties of harmonic polynomials in the case of $\mathfrak{so}(p,2)$, in *Legal Informatics, Economic Science and Mathematical Research* (Ed. M. Kitahara, C. Czerkawski), 81–88, Kyushu University Press, (2014).
[9] R. Wada and Y. Agaoka, On some properties of harmonic polynomials in the case of $\mathfrak{so}(p,2)$: Irreducible decomposition and integral formulas, in *New Solutions in Legal Informatics, Economic Sciences and Mathematics* (Ed. M. Kitahara, K. Okamura), 123–142, Kyushu University Press, (2015).
[10] R. Wada and Y. Agaoka, Explicit irreducible decomposition of harmonic polynomials in the case of $\mathfrak{so}(p,2)$, in *Contemporary Works in Economic Sciences* (Ed. M. Kitahara, H. Teramoto), 83–109, Kyushu University Press, (2016).

Chapter 6

The solvable models of noncompact real Grassmannians

Akira Kubo[*]
[*]*Faculty of Economic Sciences, Hiroshima Shudo University,
1-1 Ozuka-Higashi 1-chome, Asaminami-Ku, Hiroshima, Japan 731-3195.*

Abstract
Any Riemannian symmetric space of noncompact type is isometric to the solvable part of the Iwasawa decomposition of its isometry groups with a left-invariant Riemannian metric. The solvable Lie group, or the corresponding metric solvable Lie algebra is called the solvable model of the symmetric space. In this paper, we construct the solvable models of noncompact real Grassmannians explicitly.

Key Words:
Symmetric spaces of noncompact type, The solvable model, Noncompact real Grassmannians

1. Introduction

Homogeneous submanifolds in Riemannian symmetric spaces of noncompact type have been studied actively, and in the studies the solvable parts of the Iwasawa decompositions of the isometry groups have played important roles. Let G/K be a Riemannian symmetric space of noncompact type, and denote by $G = KAN$ the Iwasawa decomposition. Then, we focus on the solvable Lie group $S := AN$. Note that S acts on G/K simply-transitively, and can be isometric to G/K via a certain left-invariant metric $\langle,\rangle$. We call $(S, \langle,\rangle)$, or the corresponding metric solvable Lie algebra $(\mathfrak{s}, \langle,\rangle)$, *the solvable model* of the symmetric space.

Lie subgroups of S provide many examples of interesting homogeneous foliations and submanifolds. For example, it is known that

- the action of the nilpotent part N induces so-called the horocycle foliations,

- Lie hypersurfaces, which are defined as orbits of cohomogeneity one action without singular orbits, are given by codimension one subgroups of AN, up to isometry ([4]),

- hyperpolar homogeneous foliations on Riemannian symmetric spaces are induced certain subgroup of S, up to isometry ([3]),

- the actions of the solvable parts of parabolic subgroups of G, all of whose orbits are also isometrically congruent to each other, provide homogeneous minimal submanifolds in G/K ([11, 12]).

Note that, for a subgroup S' of S, the orbit $S'.o$ through the origin $o \in G/K$ can be identified with S' equipped with induced left-invariant metric, and hence the corresponding metric Lie subalgebra $\mathfrak{s}'$. Therefore, in order to study the geometry of such orbits, it is a key step to determine the Lie-algebraic structures of the solvable models $(\mathfrak{s}, \langle, \rangle)$.

We here need to emphasize that, for each symmetric space G/K, the structure of the solvable model can be described in terms of the root systems, and for some symmetric spaces their explicit descriptions have been known. For example, the solvable models of real hyperbolic spaces $\mathbb{R}H^n$ are well-known, and for the cases of other hyperbolic spaces, their solvable models are given as Damek-Ricci spaces (see [1]). Note that the symmetric spaces above are of rank one. In particular, the geometry of homogeneous submanifolds in complex hyperbolic spaces $\mathbb{C}H^n$ have been studied actively via the solvable models. Refer to [2, 6, 8, 10], and a survey [7]. Recently, we have described the solvable mode of noncompact real two-plane Grassmannians $G_2^*(\mathbb{R}^{n+2})$, which are of rank two, and studied Lie hypersurfaces in $G_2^*(\mathbb{R}^{n+2})$ ([5]). However, for other cases than the above their explicit descriptions are not given in the literature, as far as we know.

In this article, we give explicit descriptions of the solvable models of noncompact real r-plane Grassmannians $G_r^*(\mathbb{R}^{r+n})$ for $n \geq r > 2$. Note that the symmetric space is of rank r.

Definition 1.1. Let $c > 0$. We call $(\mathfrak{s}(c), \langle, \rangle)$ the *solvable model* of the noncompact real Grassmannian $G_r^*(\mathbb{R}^{r+n})$ if

(1) $\mathfrak{s}(c) := \mathrm{span}\{A_i \mid 1 \leq i \leq r\} \oplus \mathrm{span}\{X_{i,j} \mid 1 \leq i < j \leq r\} \oplus \mathrm{span}\{Y_i^k \mid 1 \leq i \leq r, 1 \leq k \leq n-r\} \oplus \mathrm{span}\{Z_{i,j} \mid 1 \leq i < j \leq r\}$ is an rn-dimensional Lie algebra whose bracket relations are defined by

- $[A_i, X_{i,j}] = (c/\sqrt{2})X_{i,j}$, $[A_j, X_{i,j}] = -(c/\sqrt{2})X_{i,j}$,
- $[A_i, Y_i^k] = (c/\sqrt{2})Y_i^k$,
- $[A_i, Z_{i,j}] = [A_j, Z_{i,j}] = (c/\sqrt{2})Z_{i,j}$,
- $[X_{i,j}, X_{j,k}] = cX_{i,k}$,
- $[X_{i,j}, Y_j^k] = cY_i^k$,
- $[X_{i,j}, Z_{j,k}] = cZ_{i,k}$, $[X_{i,j}, Z_{k,j}] = -cZ_{i,k}$ if $i < k$, $[X_{i,j}, Z_{k,j}] = cZ_{k,i}$ if $k < i$,
- $[Y_i^k, Y_j^k] = -cZ_{i,j}$,
- and other relations vanish,

(2) $\langle, \rangle$ is an inner product on $\mathfrak{s}(c)$ which makes the above basis orthonormal,

Let $S(c)$ be the simply-connected Lie group with Lie algebra $\mathfrak{s}(c)$, and denote by the same symbol $\langle, \rangle$ the induced left-invariant metric on $S(c)$.

The main theorem in this article is the following.

Theorem 1.2. *The Lie group* $(S(c), \langle, \rangle)$ *is isomorphic to* $G_r^*(\mathbb{R}^{r+n})$ *with minimal sectional curvature* $-c^2$.

We remark that the above is a natural generalization of the result given in [5].

2. Preliminaries

In this section, we recall some fundamental notions of symmetric spaces of noncompact type. Refer to [9].

Let $M = G/K$ be an irreducible Riemannian symmetric space of noncompact type, where G is the identity component of the isometry group, and K is the isotropy subgroup of G at some point o, called the *origin*. Denote by $\mathfrak{g}$ and $\mathfrak{k}$ the Lie algebras of G and K, respectively, and by θ the corresponding Cartan involution. Then, one can obtain $\mathfrak{g} = \mathfrak{k} \oplus \mathfrak{p}$, the Cartan decomposition of $\mathfrak{g}$. where $\mathfrak{p}$ denotes the (-1)-eigenspace of θ. Note that we identify $\mathfrak{p} \cong T_o(G/K)$ as usual. Denote by B the Killing form of $\mathfrak{g}$. We define a positive definite inner product on $\mathfrak{g}$ by $\langle X, Y \rangle_\mathfrak{g} := -B(\theta X, Y)$.

Let us fix $\mathfrak{a}$ as a maximal abelian subspace of $\mathfrak{p}$, and denote by $\mathfrak{a}^*$ the dual space of $\mathfrak{a}$. Then we define

$$\mathfrak{g}_\lambda := \{X \in \mathfrak{g} \mid \mathrm{ad}(H)X = \lambda(H)X \ (\forall H \in \mathfrak{a})\} \tag{1}$$

for each $\lambda \in \mathfrak{a}^*$. Note that $[\mathfrak{g}_\lambda, \mathfrak{g}_\mu] \subset \mathfrak{g}_{\lambda+\mu}$ holds for $\lambda, \mu \in \mathfrak{a}^*$. We call $\lambda \in \mathfrak{a}^*$ a *(restricted) root* with respect to $\mathfrak{a}$ if $\lambda \neq 0$ and $\mathfrak{g}_\lambda \neq 0$. Denote by Σ the set of restricted roots. Let Λ be a set of simple roots of Σ, and then denote by Σ^+ the set of positive roots associated with Λ. Put

$$\mathfrak{n} := \bigoplus_{\lambda \in \Sigma^+} \mathfrak{g}_\lambda. \tag{2}$$

Then, one can obtain $\mathfrak{g} = \mathfrak{k} \oplus \mathfrak{a} \oplus \mathfrak{n}$, the Iwasawa decomposition of $\mathfrak{g}$. Note that $\mathfrak{a} \oplus \mathfrak{n}$ is a solvable Lie subalgebra, which is called the *solvable part* of the Iwasawa decomposition of $\mathfrak{g}$.

Let S be the connected Lie subgroup of G whose Lie algebra is $\mathfrak{a} \oplus \mathfrak{n}$. Note that S is simply-connected and acts simply transitively on $M = G/K$. Thus, we obtain an isomorphism

$$\Phi : S \to G/K = M : g \mapsto [g] = g.o, \tag{3}$$

where o denotes the origin. Under the identification of $\mathfrak{p} \cong T_o M$, the differential of Φ at the identity e is given by

$$(d\Phi)_e : \mathfrak{a} \oplus \mathfrak{n} \to \mathfrak{p} : X \mapsto X_\mathfrak{p} = (1/2)(X - \theta X), \tag{4}$$

where $\mathfrak{p}$-subscript means the orthogonal projection.

Proposition 2.1 ([12, Proposition 4.4]). *Define a left-invariant metric on S by*

$$\begin{aligned} \langle X, Y \rangle &:= \langle (d\Phi)_e X, (d\Phi)_e Y \rangle_\mathfrak{g} \\ &= \langle X_\mathfrak{a}, Y_\mathfrak{a} \rangle_\mathfrak{g} + (1/2)\langle X_\mathfrak{n}, Y_\mathfrak{n} \rangle_\mathfrak{g}, \quad (X, Y \in \mathfrak{a} \oplus \mathfrak{n}) \end{aligned} \tag{5}$$

where $\mathfrak{a}$- and $\mathfrak{n}$-subscripts mean the orthogonal projections respectively. Then, $(S, \langle, \rangle)$ is isomorphic to the symmetric space $M = G/K$.

Finally, we recall root vectors, and study the minimal sectional curvature of $M = G/K$.

Definition 2.2. For any $\alpha \in \mathfrak{a}^*$, we define $H_\alpha \in \mathfrak{a}$ by

$$\langle H_\alpha, H \rangle = \alpha(H) \quad (\forall H \in \mathfrak{a}). \tag{6}$$

If α is a root, moreover, we call H_α the *root vector* with respect to α.

The following is easy to check.

Lemma 2.3. *Choose* $\{H^i\}$ *as an orthogonal basis of* $\mathfrak{a}$, *and denote by* $\varepsilon_i \in \mathfrak{a}^*$ *the dual basis of* $\{H^i\}$, *namely* $\varepsilon_i(H^j) = \delta_{ij}$. *Then, if* $\alpha = \sum c_i \varepsilon_i \in \mathfrak{a}^*$, *one has*

$$H_\alpha = \sum (c_i / \langle H^i, H^i \rangle) H^i. \tag{7}$$

Denote by $\tilde{\alpha}$ the highest root. According to [9], the minimal sectional curvature of a symmetric space of noncompact type can be calculated by the root vector $H_{\tilde{\alpha}}$.

Theorem 2.4 ([9, Theorem 11.1, Ch. VII]). *The minimal sectional curvature of* $M = G/K$ *is equal to* $-\langle H_{\tilde{\alpha}}, H_{\tilde{\alpha}} \rangle$, *where* $\tilde{\alpha}$ *is the highest root.*

3. The Structure of Noncompact Real Grassmannian Manifolds

In this section, we consider the noncompact real r-plane Grassmannian manifold

$$G_r^*(\mathbb{R}^{r+n}) = \mathrm{SO}_0(r,n)/(\mathrm{SO}(r) \times \mathrm{SO}(n)) \quad (n \geq r \geq 2), \tag{8}$$

and give matrix expressions for root spaces of $\mathfrak{so}(r,n)$. We omit the case of $(r,n) = (2,2)$, since the symmetric space $G_2^*(\mathbb{R}^4)$ is not irreducible.

First of all, we recall the Cartan decomposition of $\mathfrak{so}(r,n)$. Denote by $\mathfrak{g}$ and $\mathfrak{k}$ the Lie algebras of $\mathrm{SO}(r,n)$ and $\mathrm{S}(\mathrm{O}(r) \times \mathrm{O}(n))$, respectively.

Here and hereafter, we denote by $E_{i,j}$ (or E_{ij}) the usual matrix unit, and put

$$I_{r,n} := -E_{1,1} - \cdots - E_{r,r} + E_{r+1,r+1} + \cdots + E_{r+n,r+n}. \tag{9}$$

Then one can show that

$$\mathfrak{g} = \{X \in \mathfrak{sl}(r+n, \mathbb{R}) \mid {}^t X I_{r,n} + I_{r,n} X = 0\},$$

$$\mathfrak{k} = \left\{ \begin{pmatrix} X & \\ \hline & Y \end{pmatrix} \,\middle|\, X \in \mathfrak{so}(r), Y \in \mathfrak{so}(n) \right\},$$

and that the Cartan involution θ is given by

$$\theta : \mathfrak{g} \to \mathfrak{g} : X \mapsto I_{r,n} X I_{r,n}. \tag{10}$$

And also, we obtain

$$\mathfrak{p} = \left\{ \begin{pmatrix} & v \\ \hline {}^t v & \end{pmatrix} \,\middle|\, v \in M_{r,n}(\mathbb{R}) \right\}, \tag{11}$$

which yields the Cartan decomposition $\mathfrak{g} = \mathfrak{k} \oplus \mathfrak{p}$.

We next recall the restricted root system, and the root space decomposition of $\mathfrak{g}$. Let us put $H^i := E_{i,i+r} + E_{i+r,i}$, and

$$\mathfrak{a} := \mathrm{span}\{H^1, \ldots, H^r\} \subset \mathfrak{p}, \tag{12}$$

which is a maximal abelian subspace in $\mathfrak{p}$. Define $\varepsilon_i \in \mathfrak{a}^*$ ($i \in \{1, \ldots, r\}$) by

$$\varepsilon_i : \mathfrak{a} \to \mathbb{R} : \sum a_i H^i \mapsto a_i. \tag{13}$$

Then, one can see that
$$\Lambda := \{\pm\varepsilon_i, \pm(\varepsilon_i \pm \varepsilon_j)\} \subset \mathfrak{a}^* \tag{14}$$
is a restricted root system Σ of type B_r. We can choose as simple roots
$$\begin{aligned} \alpha_i &:= \varepsilon_i - \varepsilon_{i+1}, \quad (i \in \{1, \ldots, r-1\}) \\ \alpha_r &:= \varepsilon_r. \end{aligned} \tag{15}$$

Then, the set of positive root is
$$\Sigma^+ = \{\varepsilon_i \mid 1 \le i \le r\} \cup \{\varepsilon_i \pm \varepsilon_j \mid 1 \le i < j \le r\}, \tag{16}$$
and the highest root is $\alpha_1 + \cdots + \alpha_{r-1} + 2\alpha_r = \varepsilon_1 + \varepsilon_r$.

We now give an explicit matrix expression for each root space. For convenience, we put
$$U_{i,j} := E_{i,j} - E_{j,i}, \quad V_{i,j} := E_{i,j} + E_{j,i} \in M_{r,r}(\mathbb{R}) \tag{17}$$
for $1 \le i < j \le r$.

Lemma 3.1. *We have the following:*

$$\mathfrak{g}_{\varepsilon_i} = \left\{ \left(\begin{array}{c|c|c} & & y \\ \hline & & y \\ \hline {}^t y & -{}^t y & \end{array} \right) \,\middle|\, y = \sum y_m E_{i,m} \in M_{r,n-r}(\mathbb{R}) \right\},$$

$$\mathfrak{g}_{\varepsilon_i - \varepsilon_j} = \operatorname{span} \left\{ \left(\begin{array}{c|c|c} U_{i,j} & V_{i,j} & \\ \hline V_{i,j} & U_{i,j} & \\ \hline & & \end{array} \right) \right\},$$

$$\mathfrak{g}_{\varepsilon_i + \varepsilon_j} = \operatorname{span} \left\{ \left(\begin{array}{c|c|c} -U_{i,j} & U_{i,j} & \\ \hline -U_{i,j} & U_{i,j} & \\ \hline & & \end{array} \right) \right\},$$

where every size of the block decompositions is $(r, r, n-r)$. In particular, $\dim \mathfrak{g}_{\varepsilon_i} = n - r$, and $\dim \mathfrak{g}_{\varepsilon_i \pm \varepsilon_j} = 1$.

Proof. First of all, we check each inclusion ($\supset$) by direct calculations. Hereafter, we use $A := \sum \varepsilon_k E_{k,k} \in M_{r,r}(\mathbb{R})$, and
$$H := \left(\begin{array}{c|c|c} & A & \\ \hline A & & \\ \hline & & \end{array} \right) \in \mathfrak{a}. \tag{18}$$

We check the first assertion. Let us take $y_i = \sum y_m E_{i,m} \in M_{r,n-r}(\mathbb{R})$, and
$$Y_i := \left(\begin{array}{c|c|c} & & y_i \\ \hline & & y_i \\ \hline {}^t y_i & -{}^t y_i & \end{array} \right). \tag{19}$$

One can easily see that
$$A y_i = \left(\sum \varepsilon_k E_{k,k} \right) \left(\sum y_m E_{i,m} \right) = \varepsilon_i \left(\sum y_m E_{i,m} \right) = \varepsilon_i y_i. \tag{20}$$

Hence, we obtain
$$[H, Y_i] = \left(\begin{array}{c|c|c} & & Ay_i \\ \hline & & Ay_i \\ \hline {}^t(Ay_i) & -{}^t(Ay_i) & \end{array} \right) = \varepsilon_i Y_i, \tag{21}$$

which means $Y_i \in \mathfrak{g}_{\varepsilon_i}$.

We check the second assertion. Let us take

$$X_{i,j} := \begin{pmatrix} U_{i,j} & V_{i,j} \\ \hline V_{i,j} & U_{i,j} \\ \hline & \end{pmatrix} \qquad (22)$$

One can easily see that

$$\begin{aligned} AU_{i,j} &= \left(\sum \varepsilon_k E_{k,k}\right)(E_{i,j} - E_{j,i}) = \varepsilon_i E_{i,j} - \varepsilon_j E_{j,i}, \\ U_{i,j} A &= (E_{i,j} - E_{j,i})\left(\sum \varepsilon_k E_{k,k}\right) = \varepsilon_j E_{i,j} - \varepsilon_i E_{j,i}, \end{aligned} \qquad (23)$$

and hence that $[A, U_{i,j}] = (\varepsilon_i - \varepsilon_j)V_{i,j}$. Similarly, one obtain that $[A, V_{i,j}] = (\varepsilon_i - \varepsilon_j)U_{i,j}$. Therefore, we obtain

$$[H, X_{i,j}] = \begin{pmatrix} [A, V_{i,j}] & [A, U_{i,j}] \\ \hline [A, U_{i,j}] & [A, V_{i,j}] \\ \hline & \end{pmatrix} = (\varepsilon_i - \varepsilon_j)X_{i,j}, \qquad (24)$$

which means $X_{i,j} \in \mathfrak{g}_{\varepsilon_i - \varepsilon_j}$.

We check the final assertion. Let us take

$$Z_{i,j} := \begin{pmatrix} -U_{i,j} & U_{i,j} \\ \hline -U_{i,j} & U_{i,j} \\ \hline & \end{pmatrix} \qquad (25)$$

From the argument above, one has that $AU_{i,j} + U_{i,j}A = (\varepsilon_i + \varepsilon_j)U_{i,j}$. Therefore, we obtain

$$[H, Z_{i,j}] = \begin{pmatrix} -(AU_{i,j} + U_{i,j}A) & AU_{i,j} + U_{i,j}A \\ \hline -(AU_{i,j} + U_{i,j}A) & AU_{i,j} + U_{i,j}A \\ \hline & \end{pmatrix} = (\varepsilon_i + \varepsilon_j)Z_{i,j}, \qquad (26)$$

which means $Z_{i,j} \in \mathfrak{g}_{\varepsilon_i + \varepsilon_j}$.

Note that
$$\begin{aligned} \dim \mathfrak{n} &= \dim \mathfrak{p} - \dim \mathfrak{a} \\ &= rn - r \\ &= r(n-r) + r(r-1)/2 + r(r-1)/2. \end{aligned} \qquad (27)$$

By the dimension reason, it follows that each equality holds. $\square$

Finally, we recall the metric $\langle , \rangle_\mathfrak{g}$ on $\mathfrak{g}$, and calculate the minimal sectional curvature of $G_r^*(\mathbb{R}^{r+n})$.

Recall that $\mathfrak{g} = \mathfrak{so}(r,n)$ is a simple Lie algebra. According to the Schur lemma, one knows that any invariant bilinear form on $\mathfrak{g}$ is a scalar multiple of the Killing form B. Thus there exists $c = c(r,n) > 0$ such that $B(X,Y) = (1/c^2)\operatorname{tr}(XY)$. Therefore, we obtain that

$$\langle X, Y \rangle_\mathfrak{g} = (1/c^2)\operatorname{tr}({}^t XY) \qquad (28)$$

for any $X, Y \in \mathfrak{g}$.

Proposition 3.2. *With respect to the metric above, the minimal sectional curvature of $G_r^*(\mathbb{R}^{r+n})$ is equal to $-c^2$.*

Proof. Recall that the highest root $\tilde{\alpha}$ is given by $\alpha_1 + \cdots + \alpha_{r-1} + 2\alpha_r = \varepsilon_1 + \varepsilon_r$. It then follows from Lemma 2.3 that $H_{\tilde{\alpha}} = (c^2/2)H^1 + H^r$. Therefore, from Theorem 2.4, one can see that the minimal sectional curvature of $G_r^*(\mathbb{R}^{r+n})$ is given by

$$\begin{aligned}-\langle H_{\tilde{\alpha}}, H_{\tilde{\alpha}}\rangle &= -(c^2/2)^2 \langle H^1 + H^r, H^1 + H^r\rangle \\ &= -(c^2/2)^2 \cdot (2/c^2) \cdot 2 \\ &= -c^2,\end{aligned} \qquad (29)$$

which completes the proof. □

4. Proof of the Main Theorem

In this section, we prove Theorem 1.2.

Recall that, in general, a symmetric space M is isometric to the solvable Lie group AN via the metric given by

$$\langle X, Y\rangle = \langle X_{\mathfrak{a}}, Y_{\mathfrak{a}}\rangle_{\mathfrak{g}} + (1/2)\langle X_{\mathfrak{n}}, Y_{\mathfrak{n}}\rangle_{\mathfrak{g}}. \quad (X, Y \in \mathfrak{a} \oplus \mathfrak{n}). \qquad (30)$$

Therefore, we have only to obtain an orthonormal basis of $(\mathfrak{a} \oplus \mathfrak{n}, \langle,\rangle)$ satisfying the bracket relations mentioned in Definition 1.1.

As previous sections, we denote by $\mathfrak{a} \oplus \mathfrak{n}$ the solvable part of the Iwasawa decomposition of $\mathfrak{g} = \mathfrak{so}(r, n)$.

Now we define an canonical basis on $\mathfrak{a} \oplus \mathfrak{n}$ as follows:

$$\begin{aligned}X_{i,j} &:= (c/2)\begin{pmatrix} U_{i,j} & V_{i,j} & \\ V_{i,j} & U_{i,j} & \\ & & \end{pmatrix} \in \mathfrak{g}_{\varepsilon_i - \varepsilon_j}, \\ Z_{i,j} &:= (c/2)\begin{pmatrix} -U_{i,j} & U_{i,j} & \\ -U_{i,j} & U_{i,j} & \\ & & \end{pmatrix} \in \mathfrak{g}_{\varepsilon_i + \varepsilon_j},\end{aligned} \qquad (31)$$

for $1 \leq i < j \leq r$, and

$$\begin{aligned}A_i &:= (c/\sqrt{2})H^i \in \mathfrak{a}, \\ Y_i^k &:= (c/\sqrt{2})\begin{pmatrix} & & E_{ik} \\ & & E_{ik} \\ {}^tE_{ik} & -{}^tE_{ik} & \end{pmatrix} \in \mathfrak{g}_{\varepsilon_i},\end{aligned} \qquad (32)$$

for $i \in \{1, \ldots, r\}$ and $k \in \{1, \ldots, n-r\}$, where $E_{ik} \in M_{r,n-r}(\mathbb{R})$. Since one knows that $\dim(\mathfrak{a} \oplus \mathfrak{n}) = rn$, it is clear that

$$\begin{aligned}\{A_i, \mid 1 \leq i \leq r\} &\cup \{X_{i,j}, Z_{i,j} \mid 1 \leq i < j \leq r\} \\ &\cup \{Y_i^k \mid 1 \leq i \leq r, 1 \leq k \leq n-r\}\end{aligned} \qquad (33)$$

is a basis of $\mathfrak{a} \oplus \mathfrak{n}$. For our goal, we check the orthonormality and the bracket relations.

Lemma 4.1. *The metric $\langle,\rangle$ on $\mathfrak{a} \oplus \mathfrak{n}$ makes the above basis orthonormal.*

Proof. Recall that the metric on $\mathfrak{a} \oplus \mathfrak{n}$ is given by

$$\langle X, Y\rangle = (1/c^2)\operatorname{tr}({}^tX_{\mathfrak{a}}Y_{\mathfrak{a}}) + (1/(2c^2))\operatorname{tr}({}^tX_{\mathfrak{n}}Y_{\mathfrak{n}}) \qquad (34)$$

for $X, Y \in \mathfrak{a} \oplus \mathfrak{n}$. Thus, one can check the orthonormality of the basis directly. □

Proposition 4.2. *The basis above satisfies that*

(1) $[A_i, X_{i,j}] = (c/\sqrt{2})X_{i,j}$, $[A_j, X_{i,j}] = -(c/\sqrt{2})X_{i,j}$, $[A_i, Y_i^k] = (c/\sqrt{2})Y_i^k$, $[A_i, Z_{i,j}] = (c/\sqrt{2})Z_{i,j}$, $[A_j, Z_{i,j}] = (c/\sqrt{2})Z_{i,j}$

(2) $[X_{i,j}, X_{j,k}] = cX_{i,k}$, for $i < j < k$,

(3) $[X_{i,j}, Y_j^k] = cY_i^k$, for $i < j$,

(4) $[X_{i,j}, Z_{k,l}] = \begin{cases} cZ_{i,l}, & \text{for } i < j = k < l, \\ -cZ_{i,k}, & \text{for } i < k < j = l, \\ cZ_{k,i}, & \text{for } k < i < j = l, \end{cases}$

(5) $[Y_i^k, Y_j^k] = -cZ_{i,j}$, for $i < j$,

and other relations vanish.

Proof. Recall that $X_{i,j} \in \mathfrak{g}_{\varepsilon_i - \varepsilon_j}$, $Y_i^k \in \mathfrak{g}_{\varepsilon_i}$, and $Z_{i,j} \in \mathfrak{g}_{\varepsilon_i + \varepsilon_j}$. From the definition of root spaces and $\varepsilon_i(H^j) = \delta_{ij}$, therefore, the assertion (1) follows readily.

We next prove (2). Take $i, j, k \in \{1, \ldots, r\}$ satisfying $i < j < k$. From direct calculations, one obtains that, for $\varepsilon, \varepsilon' \in \{\pm 1\}$,

$$\begin{aligned}(E_{ij} + \varepsilon E_{ji})(E_{jk} + \varepsilon' E_{kj}) \\ = E_{ij}E_{jk} + \varepsilon' E_{ij}E_{kj} + \varepsilon E_{ji}E_{jk} + \varepsilon\varepsilon' E_{ji}E_{kj} \\ = E_{ik},\end{aligned} \tag{35}$$

which yields that

$$U_{i,j}U_{j,k} = U_{i,j}V_{j,k} = V_{i,j}U_{j,k} = V_{i,j}V_{j,k} = E_{ik}. \tag{36}$$

And also, for $\varepsilon, \varepsilon' \in \{\pm 1\}$,

$$\begin{aligned}(E_{jk} + \varepsilon E_{kj})(E_{ij} + \varepsilon' E_{ji}) \\ = E_{jk}E_{ij} + \varepsilon' E_{jk}E_{ji} + \varepsilon E_{kj}E_{ij} + \varepsilon\varepsilon' E_{kj}E_{ji} \\ = \varepsilon\varepsilon' E_{ki},\end{aligned} \tag{37}$$

which yields that

$$U_{j,k}U_{i,j} = V_{j,k}V_{i,j} = E_{ki}, \quad U_{j,k}V_{i,j} = U_{j,k}V_{i,j} = -E_{ki}. \tag{38}$$

Therefore, it follows that

$$\begin{aligned}[X_{i,j}, X_{j,k}] \\ &= \frac{c}{2} \cdot \frac{c}{2} \cdot \left[\left(\begin{array}{c|c} U_{i,j} & V_{i,j} \\ \hline V_{i,j} & U_{i,j} \end{array}\right), \left(\begin{array}{c|c} U_{j,k} & V_{j,k} \\ \hline V_{j,k} & U_{j,k} \end{array}\right) \right] \\ &= \frac{c}{2} \cdot \frac{c}{2} \cdot \left(\begin{array}{c|c} 2E_{ik} + 2E_{ik} & 2E_{ik} - 2E_{ik} \\ \hline 2E_{ik} - 2E_{ik} & 2E_{ik} + 2E_{ik} \end{array}\right) \\ &= \frac{c}{2} \cdot \frac{c}{2} \cdot 2 \left(\begin{array}{c|c} U_{i,k} & V_{i,k} \\ \hline V_{i,k} & U_{i,k} \end{array}\right) \\ &= cX_{i,k}.\end{aligned} \tag{39}$$

We prove (3). Take $i, j \in \{1, \ldots, r\}$ satisfying $i < j$, and $k \in \{1, \ldots, n-r\}$. From direct calculations, one obtains that,

$$(U_{i,j} + V_{i,j})E_{jk} = 2E_{ij}E_{jk} = 2E_{ik},$$
$$-{}^tE_{jk}(U_{i,j} - V_{i,j}) = 2E_{kj}E_{ji} = 2\,{}^tE_{ik}. \tag{40}$$

Therefore, it follows that

$$[X_{i,j}, Y_j^k]$$
$$= \frac{c}{2} \cdot \frac{c}{\sqrt{2}} \cdot \left[\left(\begin{array}{cc|c} U_{i,j} & V_{i,j} & \\ V_{i,j} & U_{i,j} & \\ \hline & & \end{array} \right), \left(\begin{array}{cc|c} & & E_{jk} \\ & & E_{jk} \\ \hline {}^tE_{jk} & -{}^tE_{jk} & \end{array} \right) \right]$$
$$= \frac{c}{2} \cdot \frac{c}{\sqrt{2}} \cdot \left(\begin{array}{cc|c} & & 2E_{ik} \\ & & 2E_{ik} \\ \hline 2\,{}^tE_{ik} & -2\,{}^tE_{ik} & \end{array} \right) \tag{41}$$
$$= cY_i^l.$$

We prove (4). Take $i, j, k, l \in \{1, \ldots, r\}$ satisfying $i < j$, $k < l$ and $j \in \{k, l\}$. From direct calculations, one obtains that,

$$E' := (U_{i,j} + V_{i,j})U_{k,l} = 2E_{ij}(E_{kl} - E_{lk}) = \begin{cases} 2E_{il}, & \text{if } j = k, \\ -2E_{ik}, & \text{if } j = l, \end{cases} \tag{42}$$

and

$$U_{k,l}(V_{i,j} - U_{i,j}) = -{}^tE' = \begin{cases} -2E_{li}, & \text{if } j = k, \\ 2E_{ki}, & \text{if } j = l. \end{cases} \tag{43}$$

Altogether, one has

$$E' - {}^tE' = \begin{cases} 2(E_{il} - E_{li}) = 2U_{i,l}, & \text{if } i < j = k < l, \\ 2(-E_{ik} + E_{ki}) = -2U_{i,k}, & \text{if } i < k < j = l, \\ 2(-E_{ik} + E_{ki}) = 2U_{k,i}, & \text{if } k < i < j = l. \end{cases} \tag{44}$$

Therefore, it follows that

$$[X_{i,j}, Z_{k,l}]$$
$$= \frac{c}{2} \cdot \frac{c}{2} \cdot \left[\left(\begin{array}{cc|c} U_{i,j} & V_{i,j} & \\ V_{i,j} & U_{i,j} & \\ \hline & & \end{array} \right), \left(\begin{array}{cc|c} -U_{k,l} & U_{k,l} & \\ -U_{k,l} & U_{k,l} & \\ \hline & & \end{array} \right) \right]$$
$$= \frac{c}{2} \cdot \frac{c}{2} \cdot \left(\begin{array}{cc|c} -(E' - {}^tE') & E' - {}^tE' & \\ -(E' - {}^tE') & E' - {}^tE' & \\ \hline & & \end{array} \right) \tag{45}$$
$$= \begin{cases} cZ_{i,l}, & \text{if } i < j = k < l, \\ -cZ_{i,k}, & \text{if } i < k < j = l, \\ cZ_{k,i}, & \text{if } k < i < j = l. \end{cases}$$

We now prove (5) and $[Y_i^k, Y_j^l] = 0$ if $k \neq l$. Take $i, j \in \{1, \ldots, r\}$ satisfying $i < j$, and $k, l \in \{1, \ldots, n-r\}$. From direct calculations, one obtains that,

$$E'' := E_{ik}\,{}^tE_{jl} - E_{jl}\,{}^tE_{ik} = \begin{cases} U_{i,j}, & \text{if } k = j, \\ 0, & \text{if } k \neq j. \end{cases} \tag{46}$$

Therefore, it follows that

$$
\begin{aligned}
[Y_i^k, Y_j^l] &= \frac{c}{\sqrt{2}} \cdot \frac{c}{\sqrt{2}} \cdot \left[\left(\begin{array}{c|c} & E_{ik} \\ \hline {}^tE_{ik} & -{}^tE_{ik} \\ \hline & E_{ik} \end{array} \right), \left(\begin{array}{c|c} & E_{jl} \\ \hline {}^tE_{jl} & -{}^tE_{jl} \\ \hline & E_{jl} \end{array} \right) \right] \\
&= c \cdot \frac{c}{2} \cdot \left(\begin{array}{c|c} E'' & -E'' \\ \hline E'' & -E'' \end{array} \right) \\
&= \begin{cases} -cZ_{i,j}, & \text{if } k = l, \\ 0, & \text{if } k \neq l. \end{cases}
\end{aligned}
\tag{47}
$$

Finally, it follows from the property of root systems that other bracket relations vanish. Thus we complete the proof. □

Altogether, we conclude the proof of Theorem 1.2.

References

[1] J. Berndt, Homogeneous hypersurfaces in hyperbolic spaces. *Math. Z.* **229** (1998), no. 4, 589–600.

[2] J. Berndt, J. C. Díaz-Ramos, Homogeneous polar foliations of complex hyperbolic spaces. *Comm. Anal. Geom.* **20** (2012), no. 3, 435–454.

[3] J. Berndt, J. C. Díaz-Ramos, H. Tamaru, Hyperpolar homogeneous foliations on symmetric spaces of noncompact type. *J. Differential Geom.* **86** (2010), no. 2, 191–235.

[4] J. Berndt, H. Tamaru, Homogeneous codimension one foliations on noncompact symmetric spaces. *J. Differential Geom.* **63** (2003), no. 1, 1–40.

[5] J. T. Cho, T. Hashinaga, A. Kubo, Y. Taketomi, H. Tamaru, Realizations of some contact metric manifolds as Ricci soliton real hypersurfaces. (preprint)

[6] T. Hamada, Y. Hoshikawa, H. Tamaru, Curvatures properties of Lie hypersurfaces in the complex hyperbolic space. *J. Geom.* **103** (2012), no. 2, 247–261.

[7] T. Hashinaga, A. Kubo, H. Tamaru, Some topics of homogeneous submanifolds in complex hyperbolic spaces. *Differential geometry of submanifolds and its related topics*, 230–244, World Sci. Publ., Hackensack, NJ, 2014.

[8] T. Hashinaga, A. Kubo, H. Tamaru, Homogeneous Ricci soliton hypersurfaces in the complex hyperbolic spaces. *Tohoku Math. J. (2)* **68** (2016), no. 3, 559–568.

[9] S. Helgason, Differential geometry, Lie groups, and symmetric spaces. Graduate Studies in Mathematics, **34**. *American Mathematical Society, Providence, RI*, 2001.

[10] A. Kubo, Geometry of homogeneous polar foliations of complex hyperbolic spaces. *Hiroshima Math. J.* **45** (2015), no. 1, 109–123.

[11] A. Kubo, H. Tamaru, A sufficient condition for congruency of orbits of Lie groups and some applications. *Geom. Dedicata* **167** (2013), 233–238.

[12] H. Tamaru, Parabolic subgroups of semisimple Lie groups and Einstein solvmanifolds. *Math. Ann.* **351** (2011), no. 1, 51–66.

Contributors

Munenori KITAHARA, *Professor, Hiroshima Shudo University*

Munenori Kitahara (LL.M) is Professor of legal informatics (Rechtsinformatik) at the Faculty of Economic Sciences and the Graduate School of Economic Sciences in Hiroshima Shudo University, Japan. He lectures "Research on Information Society," "Legal Informatics," and "Personal Data Protection Management System." He was a guest professor at the Legal Informatics Institute of Hannover University in Germany (1999-2000).

He was a research member of legal expert systems (Legal Expert System Les-2, Lecture Note in Computer Science, No.264, Springer Verlag 1987). He is also a member of IVR. He presented several papers: "The Impact of the Computer on the Interpretation of Law (ARSP Beiheft 39, 1991), "Personal Data Processing and Business Ethics"(IVR 22nd World Congress, Granada, Spain 2005), "Ethics of Cyberspace: Information Ethics and Information Moral" (IVR 23rd World Congress, Krakow, Poland 2007), "The Right to Data Protection in Digital Society" (IVR 24th World Congress, Beijin, China 2009), "The Fusion of Law and Information Technology" and "Law and Technology Security Standard" (IVR 25th World Congress, Frankfurt am Main, Germany 2011), "The Information Society Law in Japan" (The 3rd International Seminar on Information Law 2010, Ionian University, Corfu, Greece). "The Information Society Law : The Fusion of Law and Information Technology" (The 5th International Conference on Information Law and Ethics 2012, Ionian University, Corfu). "Law and Technology: The Fusion of Law and Information Technology" and "Law and Technology: Legal Justice through Deploying Information Technology in Law" (IVR 26th World Congress, Belo Horizonte, Brazil 2013). He also published a paper titled "Legal Justice through the Fusion of Law and Information Technology" (*Legal Informatics, Economic Science and Mathematical Research*, Kyushu Univ. Press 2014). "Law and Technology: Regulations Compliance through Deploying Information Technology"(IVR 27th World Congress, Washington D.C. 2015).

One of his latest researches is "Systematizing and Networking Information Society Law." The legal system consists of twelve legal groups and some fifty acts which have been related to information, information devices and information networks. He also proposes networking the legal system, and the fusion of law and information technology. He is researching on realizing a legal justice through using information technology. Another is "propertization of personal information based on the ownership."

Hiroaki TERAMOTO, *Professor, Hiroshima Shudo University*

He received his Master degree in Economics from Hitotsubashi University in 1972. Since 1989, he has been teaching Hiroshima Shudo University as a professor. His main teaching experiences include Modern Economics (1975~1997), Consumption Economics (1997~) at Hiroshima Shudo University. His special fields of study are consumer behavior and entrepreneur behavior. His major publications are as follows; "Productivity in Consumption — The Application of Household Production Function Approach—", Hitotsubashi Ronsou, 1986, Vol.95, No.5, pp.661-676; "Intergenerational Transfer of Income and Wealth", Keizai Kagaku Kenkyu, 1998, Vol.2, No.1, pp.91-112; "External Effects of Consumption and Economic Development", Keizai Kagaku Kenkyu, 2007, Vol.10, No.2, pp.39-56; "The Economic Analysis of Altruistic Consumer Behavior", in S. Hiraki and N. Chang (eds.), The New Viewpoints and New Solutions of Economic Sciences in the Information Society, Kyushu Univ. Press, 2011, pp.13-25; "Health and Consumer Behavior", in M. Kitahara and H. Teramoto (eds.), Contemporary Works in Economic Sciences, Kyushu Univ. Press, 2016, pp.35-45.

Chris CZERKAWSKI, *Professor, Hiroshima Shudo University*

Professor of International Finance, Graduate School of Economic Sciences, Hiroshima Shudo University. Published in the area of International Capital Markets, Foreign Exchange Economics, Corporate Finance in journals in Japan, Australia and the USA.

Osamu KURIHARA, *Professor, Hiroshima Kokusai Gakuin University*

Osamu Kurihara was educated at Meiji Gakuin University, Hiroshima University and Hiroshima Shudo University, where he completed his PhD. He joined Hiroshima Kokusai Gakuin University as a Professor in 2006. He lectures Macroeconomics and International Economics in the University.

His research interests are Balance of Payments, Exchange rates and capital flows, currently and historically. He has been a director in Japan Academy for International Trade and Business from 2009.

Hiroshi HASEGAWA, *Professor, Hiroshima Shudo University*

He received his Master degree in Agricultural & Resource Economics from University of Hawaii in 1989, following under-graduate years in Tokyo University of Agriculture (1974-79) and Michigan State University (1977-78). He also obtained in 1996 nationally authorized license of Registered Professional Engineer in Rural Environment, based on his 21-year career including FAO associate expert (1983-85), JICA program officer (1989-1990) as well as international environmental consultant (1990-2002). In addition to teaching experience in Utsunomiya University (Environmental Economics, 2002-2005), he has been lecturing in Hiroshima Shudo University as a professor since 2002 (mainly on Environmental Impact Assessment, Economic Evaluation of Environment, and Environment & Politics/Administration). His special fields of study are environmental assessment and cost-benefit analysis of environmental projects. His major publications are as follows; Japanese version of "Economic Valuation Techniques for the Environment – A Case Study Workbook –" edited by J. A. Dixon, Tsukiji Shokan, 1993; "Economic Assessment of Environmental Impacts", Tokyo Shuppan, 1998; "Economic Evaluation Methods and Case Studies for Environment of Agriculture/Forestry Projects in Developing Countries", JICA, 2005; and

"Economic Values of Forest Ecological Functions in Sabah, Malaysia – Cost Benefit Analysis Comparison between Forest Certification System and Oil Palm Plantation –", Ningen Kankyogaku Kenkyu, 2012, Vol. 10, pp.105-121.

Setsuko SAKAI, *Professor, Hiroshima Shudo University*

Setsuko Sakai graduated from the Faculty of Education, Fukui University, 1979. She finished her doctoral course of Informatics and Mathematical Science at Osaka University in 1984. She became a lecturer at the College of Business Administration and Information Science, Koshien University, in 1986, and then an associate professor of the Faculty of Education, Fukui University, in 1990. Since 1998, she has been with the Faculty of Commercial Sciences of Hiroshima Shudo University, where she is a professor in the Department of Business Administration. She is currently working on game theory, decision making, fuzzy mathematical programming, optimization of fuzzy control by genetic algorithms and CAI. She is a member of the Operations Research Society of Japan, Japan Society for Fuzzy Theory and Intelligent Informatics, and the Japan Society for Production Management. She holds a D.Eng.degree. She has published papers such as "Tuning fuzzy control rules by α constrained method which solves constrained nonlinear optimization problems"(1999) and "Reducing the Number of Function Evaluations in Differential Evolution by Estimated Comparison Method using an Approximation Model with Low Accuracy"(2008) in The Transactions of the Institute of Electronics, Information and Communication Engineers, "Fast and Stable Constrained Optimization by the Constrained Differential Evolution", in Pacific Journal of Optimization (2009) and so on. She has also published papers in such journals as IEEE Transactions on Evolutionary Computation, Journal of Optimization Theory and its Applications, Transactions of the Japanese Society for Artificial Intelligence etc.

Tetsuyuki TAKAHAMA, *Professor, Hiroshima City University*

Tetsuyuki Takahama graduated from the Department of Electrical Engineering II, Kyoto University, in 1982. He finished his doctoral course in 1987. He became an assistant professor, and then a lecturer, at Fukui University in 1994. Since 1998, he has been with the Faculty of Information Science of Hiroshima City University, where he is an associate professor in the Department of Intelligent Systems. He is currently working on nonlinear optimization methods, learning of fuzzy control rules, machine learning, inference, CAI, and natural language processing. He is a member of the Information Processing Society of Japan, the Japan Society for Artificial Intelligence, the Japanese Society of Information and Systems in Education, the Association for Natural Language Processing and IEEE. He holds a D.Eng.degree. He has published papers such as "Structural Optimization by Genetic Algorithm with Degeneration (GAd)", in The Transactions of the Institute of Electronics, Information and Communication Engineers (2003). "Constrained Optimization by Applying the α Constrained Method to the Nonlinear Simplex Method with Mutations", in IEEE Transactions on Evolutionary Computation (2005), "Efficient Constrained Optimization by the Constrained Differential

Evolution Using an Approximation Model with Low Accuracy", in Transactions of the Japanese Society for Artificial Intelligence (2009) and so on. He has also published papers in such journals as Information Processing Society of Japan Journal, International Journal of Innovative Computing, Information and Control Journal of Japan Society for Fuzzy Theory and Systems etc.

Ryoko WADA, *Professor, Hiroshima Shudo University*

Ryoko Wada is a Professor at the Faculty and Graduate School of Economic Sciences of Hiroshima Shudo University. She received the Doctor Degree of Science from Sophia University, Japan, in 1988. Her major research areas are harmonic analysis on homogeneous spaces. Especially she is engaged in topics on integral representations of harmonic polynomials. She also presented at a paper titled "Fantappié Transformations of Analytic Functionals on the Truncated Complex Sphere", M.Kitahara/K.Morioka (eds.), Social Systems Solutions by Legal Informatics, Economic Sciences and Computer Sciences, Kyushu Univ. Press (2010).

Yoshio AGAOKA, *Professor, Hiroshima University*

Yoshio Agaoka is a Professor at the Graduate School of Science of Hiroshima University. He graduated from Kyoto University (Faculty of Science) in 1977, and entered the Graduate School of Science, received the Doctor Degree of Science from Kyoto University in 1985. His major research areas are Differential Geometry, Representation Theory and Discrete Geometry. Especially he is engaged in topics on local isometric imbeddings of Riemannian symmetric spaces, decomposition formula of plethysms and classification of tilings of the two-dimensional sphere, etc. Recently, he is mainly engaged in the subject on elementary geometry from the viewpoint of classical invariant theory.

Akira KUBO, *Assistant Professor, Hiroshima Shudo University*

Akira Kubo is an assistant professor at the Faculty of Economic Science in Hiroshima Shudo University, and he has lectured on "Mathematical Economics" and "Basic Calculus" since 2015. He received his Ph.D. in Mathematics from Hiroshima University in 2014. His major research areas are submanifold theory in symmetric spaces. Especially he has been studying homogeneous submanifolds in Riemannian symmetric spaces of noncompact type. His major papers are as follows; Kubo, A., Tamaru, H.: A sufficient condition for congruency of orbits of Lie groups and some applications, Geom. Dedicata **167** (2013), no.1, 233--238; Kubo, A.: Geometry of homogeneous polar foliations of complex hyperbolic spaces, Hiroshima Math. J. **45** (2015), no.1, 109--123; Hashinaga, T., Kubo, A., Tamaru, H.: Homogeneous Ricci soliton hypersurfaces in the complex hyperbolic spaces, Tohoku Math. J., to appear.

Series of Monographs of Contemporary Social Systems Solutions
Produced by
the Faculty of Economic Sciences, Hiroshima Shudo University

190 × 265 mm   5,000 yen (tax not included)

Volume 1   Social Systems Solutions by Legal Informatics, Economic Sciences and Computer Sciences

Edited by Munenori Kitahara and Kazunori Morioka   160 pages   ISBN 978-4-7985-0011-9

Preface
Chapter 1   The Concept of Personal Data Protection in Information Society   ⋯ *Munenori Kitahara*
Chapter 2   On the Evaluation System of Public Sector   ⋯ *Kazunori Morioka*
Chapter 3   Effects of Property Right Restriction: An Analysis Using a Product Differentiation Model   ⋯ *Koshiro Ota*
Chapter 4   Tax Coordination between Asymmetric Regions in a Repeated Game Setting   ⋯ *Chikara Yamaguchi*
Chapter 5   The Household Production and Comsumer Behavior   ⋯ *Hiroaki Teramoto*
Chapter 6   Modeling a Sequencing Problem for a Mixed-model Assembly Line   ⋯ *Shusaku Hiraki, Hugejile and Zhuqi Xu*
Chapter 7   Long-run Superneutrality of Money in Japanese Economy   ⋯ *Md. Jahanur Rahman*
Chapter 8   A Parametric Study on Estimated Comparison in Differential Evolution with Rough Approximation Model   ⋯ *Setsuko Sakai and Tetsuyuki Takahama*
Chapter 9   Fantappié Transformations of Analytic Functionals on the Truncated Complex Sphere   ⋯ *Ryoko Wada*

Volume 2   The New Viewpoints and New Solutions of Economic Sciences in the Information Society

Edited by Shusaku Hiraki and Nan Zhang   160 pages   ISBN 978-4-7985-0055-3

Preface
Chapter 1   Economic Evaluation of the Recovery Process from a Great Disaster in Japan: The Case of Hanshin-Awaji Earthquake   ⋯ *Toshihisa Toyoda*
Chapter 2   The Economic Analysis of Altruistic Consumer Behavior   ⋯ *Hiroaki Teramoto*
Chapter 3   External Debt Default and Renegotiation Economics   ⋯ *Chris Czerkawski*
Chapter 4   Statistical Observations on the External Flow of Funds between China and the U.S.   ⋯ *Nan Zhang*
Chapter 5   Trade Flows in ASEAN plus Alpha   ⋯ *Sithanonxay Suvannaphakdy and Toshihisa Toyoda*
Chapter 6   Inventory Policies Under Time-varying Demand   ⋯ *Michinori Sakaguchi*
Chapter 7   RIDE: Differential Evolution with a Rotation-Invariant Crossover Operation for Nonlinear Optimization   ⋯ *Setsuko Sakai and Tetsuyuki Takahama*
Chapter 8   The Network of Information Society Law   ⋯ *Munenori Kitahara*
Chapter 9   The Function of the Copyright Mechanism: The Coordination of Interests of an Inventor and an Improver   ⋯ *Koshiro Ota*

Volume 3 Social Systems Solutions Applied by Economic Sciences and Mathematical Solutions
Edited by Minenori Kitahara and Chris Czerkawski 156 pages ISBN 978-4-7985-0078-2

Preface

Chapter 1 The Collaboration of Law and InformationTechnology ··· *Munenori Kitahara*

Chapter 2 The Australian Broadband Policy: Theory and Reality ··· *Koshiro Ota*

Chapter 3 Evaluating the Impact of Mining Foreign Capital Inflows on the Lao Economy
··· *Phouphet Kyophilavong and Toshihisa Toyoda*

Chapter 4 Empirical Study of the Impact of the Thai Economy on the Lao Electricity Export
··· *Thongphet Lamphayphan, Chris Czerkawski and Toshihisa Toyoda*

Chapter 5 Calculating CO_2 Emissions for Coastal Shipping of Finished Cars by Pure Car Carriers in Japan ··· *Min Zhang, Shusaku Hiraki and Yoshiaki Ishihara*

Chapter 6 A Statistical Model for Global-Flow-of-Funds Analysis ··· *Nan Zhang*

Chapter 7 The Reproducing Kernels of the Space of Harmonic Polynomials ··· *Ryoko Wada*

Chapter 8 A Comparative Study on Neighborhood Structures for Speciation in Species-Based Differential Evolution ··· *Setsuko Sakai and Tetsuyuki Takahama*

Volume 4 Social Systems Solutions through Economic Sciences
Edited by Munenori Kitahara and Chris Czerkawski 156 pages ISBN 978-4-7985-0097-3

Preface

Chapter 1 Law and Technology: Privacy Protection through Technology ··· *Munenori Kitahara*

Chapter 2 The Signaling Role of Promotions in Japan ··· *Kazuaki Okamura*
—A Pseud-Panel Data Analysis

Chapter 3 The Chinese Spring Festival Model's Design and Application
··· *Gang Shi and Nan Zhang*

Chapter 4 Money and Real Output in Laos: An Econometric Analysis
··· *Inthiphone Xaiyavong and Chris Czerkawski*

Chapter 5 Literature Review on Ship Scheduling and Routing
··· *Min Zhang, Shusaku Hiraki and Yoshiaki Ishihara*

Chapter 6 Optimal Ordering Policies in a Multi-item Inventory Model
··· *Michinori Sakaguchi and Masanori Kodama*

Chapter 7 A Comparative Study on Graph-Based Speciation Methods for Species-Based Differential Evolution ··· *Setsuko Sakai and Tetsuyuki Takahama*

Chapter 8 Sino-Japanese Compounds ··· *Paul Jensen*

Volume 5 Legal Informatics, Economic Science and Mathematical Research
Edited by Munenori Kitahara and Chris Czerkawski 104 pages ISBN 978-4-7985-0125-3

Preface

Chapter 1 Legal Justice through the Fusion of Law and Information Technology
···*Munenori Kitahara*

Chapter 2   The Role of International Transportation in Trade and the Environment
⋯*Takeshi Ogawa*

Chapter 3   A Comparative Study on Estimation Methods of Landscape Modality for Evolutionary
Algorithms   ⋯*Setsuko Sakai and Tetsuyuki Takahama*

Chapter 4   Some Properties of Harmonic Polynomials in the Case of $\mathfrak{so}\,(p, 2)$
⋯*Ryoko Wada and Yoshio Agaoka*

Volume 6   New Solutions in Legal Informatics, Economic Sciences and Mathematics

Edited by Munenori Kitahara and Kazuaki Okamura   160 pages   ISBN 978-4-7985-0152-9

Preface

Chapter 1   Legality and Compliance through Deploying Information Technology
⋯*Munenori Kitahara*

Chapter 2   Three-Good Ricardian Model with Joint Production: A Schematic Reconsideration
⋯*Takeshi Ogawa*

Chapter 3   An Application of Cellular Automata to the Oligopolistic Market   ⋯*Kouhei Iyori*

Chapter 4   Development of a Multi-Country Multi-Sectoral Model in International Dollars
⋯*Takashi Yano and Hiroyuki Kosaka*

Chapter 5   Stochastic Inventory Model with Time-Varying Demand
⋯*Michinori Sakaguchi and Masanori Kodama*

Chapter 6   A Study on Adaptive Parameter Control for Interactive Differential Evolution
Using Pairwise Comparison   ⋯*Setsuko Sakai and Tetsuyuki Takahama*

Chapter 7   On Some Properties of Harmonic Polynomials in the Case of $\mathfrak{so}\,(p, 2)$:
Irreducible Decomposition and Integral Formulas   ⋯*Ryoko Wada and Yoshio Agaoka*

Volume 7   Contemporary Works in Economic Sciences:
Legal Informatics, Economics, OR and Mathematics

Edited by Munenori Kitahara and Hiroaki Teramoto   130 pages   ISBN 978-4-7985-0179-6

Preface

Chapter 1   Audit and Compliance through Proactive Engineering Method   ⋯*Munenori Kitahara*

Chapter 2   Some Notes on Macroeconomic Policies: Abenomics in Japan
⋯*Chris Czerkawski and Osamu Kurihara*

Chapter 3   Health and Consumer Behavior   ⋯*Hiroaki Teramoto*

Chapter 4   Measuring Global Flow of Funds:
Theoretical Framework, Data Sources and Approaches   ⋯*Nan Zhang*

Chapter 5   A Comparative Study on Detecting Ridge Structure for Population-Based
Optimization Algorithms   ⋯*Setsuko Sakai and Tetsuyuki Takahama*

Chapter 6   Explicit Irreducible Decomposition of Harmonic Polynomials
in the Case of $\mathfrak{so}\,(p, 2)$ ⋯*Ryoko Wada and Yoshio Agaoka*